# Freelance Counselling and Psychotherapy

There are far more qualified counsellors and therapists than there are salaried posts, so many recently qualified practitioners face the challenges of working freelance. They often face a difficult period of adjustment as they seek to find work, in competition with colleagues and fellow ex-students.

*Freelance Counselling and Psychotherapy* is an excellent guide on surviving and flourishing in a highly challenging field. Written by practitioners with extensive experience of the practical and emotional aspects of working independently, it covers the range of issues and choices which confront newly qualified practitioners, for example:

- Regulation, registration and accreditation
- Supervision
- Financial issues in freelance therapy
- The dynamics of competition and collaboration

Several contributors write about their experiences as they struggled to establish themselves, faced with these choices and challenges.

As freelance working continues to grow, more practitioners are needing reliable knowledge and informed understanding of the demands of working independently. This highly readable book provides an 'insider's' view of the field, and will be essential reading for trainers, established practitioners and newly qualified therapists alike.

**Jean Clark** has worked professionally as a counsellor since 1971, when she set up the first Student Counselling Service at Leicester Polytechnic. She is a Fellow of the British Association for Counselling and Psychotherapy, and a UKRC Registered Independent Counsellor and since 1982 has worked as a freelance counsellor, supervisor and trainer.

**Contributors**: Tania Barnett, Benita Cowen, Joe Daggers, Colin Feltham, Ian Horton, Leebert Hughes, Charlotte Johnson, Jacky Moss, Gabrielle Syme, Keith Tudor, Gerry Virgo, Sue Wheeler, Nigel White, Mike Worrall

# Freelance Counselling and Psychotherapy

## Competition and collaboration

Edited by Jean Clark

BRUNNER-ROUTLEDGE
Taylor & Francis Group

First published 2002 by Brunner-Routledge
27 Church Road, Hove, East Sussex, BN3 2FA

Simultaneously published in the USA and Canada
by Taylor & Francis Inc
29 West 35th Street, New York, NY 10001

*Brunner-Routledge is an imprint of the Taylor & Francis Group*

© 2002 Selection and editorial matter Jean Clark; individual chapters,
the contributors

Typeset in Times by Mayhew Typesetting, Rhayader, Powys
Printed and bound in the UK by Biddles Ltd, Guildford and King's Lynn
Cover design by Jim Wilkie.
Cover illustration by Jean Lamb

*British Library Cataloguing in Publication Data*
A catalogue record for this book is available from the British Library

*Library of Congress Cataloging-in-Publication Data*

Freelance counselling and psychotherapy : competition and
collaboration / edited by Jean Clark.
        p.  cm.
    Includes bibliographical references and index.
    ISBN 0-415-23724-6 – ISBN 0-415-23725-4 (pbk)
    1. Psychology–Vocational guidance.  2. Counseling–Vocational
guidance.  3. Self-employed.  I. Clark, Jean, 1926–

    BF76 .F74 2002
    361'.06–dc21

                                            2001043183

ISBN 0-415-23724-6 (hbk)
ISBN 0-415-23725-4 (pbk)

No one told me
it would lead to this

David Whyte
*Fire in the Earth*

# Contents

*Contributors*                                                          ix

*Foreword*                                                              xi

*Acknowledgements*                                                      xiii
BRIAN THORNE

Introduction                                                           1
JEAN CLARK

**PART I**
**Some facts and tensions**                                            7

1   The development and growth of freelance counselling               9
    GABRIELLE SYME

2   The internal dynamics of freelance                                20
    JEAN CLARK

**PART II**
**Setting up as freelance**                                            35

3   Starting in private practice                                       37
    COLIN FELTHAM

4   Regulation, registration and accreditation: some issues           49
    IAN HORTON

5   Sorting out supervision                                            64
    SUE WHEELER

6  The unspoken relationship: financial dynamics in
   freelance therapy                                          80
   KEITH TUDOR AND MIKE WORRALL


**PART III**
**The dynamics of survival**                                 91

7  The loneliness and freedoms of change                     93
   JEAN CLARK

8  A therapist in the family                                 105
   TANIA BARNETT

9  Personal and professional development                     115
   JEAN CLARK


**PART IV**
**Survival in practice**                                     133

10  The early years                                          135
    JOE DAGGERS, JACKY MOSS, LEEBERT HUGHES AND GERRY VIRGO

11  Counselling in primary care                              150
    BENITA COWEN AND NIGEL WHITE

12  Working with Employee Assistance Programmes               164
    CHARLOTTE JOHNSON

13  Working from home: a psychotherapist with long-term
    clients                                                  182
    GABRIELLE SYME

    *Postscript*                                             195
    JEAN CLARK

    *Recommended reading*                                    197
    *Index*                                                  198

# Contributors

**Tania Barnett** has worked as a part-time freelance individual and group counsellor for eight years in education, social services and a primary care counselling agency, and as a tutor in communication, counselling and management skills in higher education at the University of East Anglia.

**Jean Clark** is a BACP Fellow. In 1971 she set up a Student Counselling Service at Leicester Polytechnic, and was Senior Counsellor until 1981. Since then, while working freelance, she initiated the Norfolk trauma counselling network, supervised a hospice bereavement service and is a trustee for a voluntary counselling agency.

**Benita Cowen** is a freelance counsellor, psychotherapist, trainer and supervisor. Her particular interest is in the political psychology of primary care counselling. She is actively involved nationally in offering consultation and advice on the development of counselling to health authorities, primary care groups and counsellors.

**Joe Daggers** is a person-centred freelance counsellor who has been working in private practice for three years. Before turning to counselling, he worked for 20 years as a music librarian in public libraries. As well as counselling, he also tutors privately in English and history.

**Colin Feltham** is Senior Lecturer in Counselling at Sheffield Hallam University, co-editor of the *British Journal of Guidance and Counselling* and has been a practising counsellor and supervisor for 20 years in a variety of settings.

**Ian Horton** is Principal Lecturer in Counselling and Psychotherapy in the Department of Psychology at the University of London. He is a Fellow of BACP, Chair of the UKRC Executive and a BACP Accredited and UKRC Registered Independent Counsellor.

**Leebert Hughes** is a freelance counsellor and lecturer, working in primary care and private practice. He lectures at Salford University and teaches counselling for the Manchester Adult Education Service. He specialises in relationship and bereavement counselling.

**Charlotte Johnson** is a BACP Senior Registered Counsellor. She has experience of working with EAPs as a telephone affiliate, a face-to-face affiliate and an on-site counsellor. She works freelance in primary care and private practice, and as a supervisor and trainer.

**Jacky Moss**: after 22 years of teaching and many happy years offering art and drama to students with behavioural problems, she retrained as a person-centred counsellor. She now works as a freelance practitioner alongside her job as an addiction counsellor and group facilitator in two drug rehabilitation units.

**Gabrielle Syme** has worked as a freelance counsellor, psychotherapist, trainer and supervisor for over 20 years and for three years was Chair of BAC. Her particular interests are standards and ethics, developing good practice and bereavement, which are reflected in her three books.

**Keith Tudor** is a qualified, experienced and registered psychotherapist, a supervisor and trainer. He is a Director of Temenos in Sheffield and the author of a number of articles and papers in the field of counselling and psychotherapy.

**Gerry Virgo** added enthusiasm for the person-centred approach to a varied career in science and education, and now works as a youth counselling service coordinator and freelance practitioner.

**Sue Wheeler** is a Senior Lecturer in Counselling at the University of Birmingham. She leads a supervision training programme and other con-tinuing development courses for experienced counsellors. She has recently been awarded a doctorate for her published work investigating the profes-sionalisation of counselling.

**Nigel White** is a counsellor offering brief therapy at a university and in primary care in Leeds. He uses various models (solution-focused therapy, narrative therapy, cognitive analytic therapy and person-centred). He has worked in primary care for 10 years.

**Mike Worrall** is a qualified, experienced and accredited counsellor, a supervisor and trainer. He is a tutor and trainer at Temenos in Sheffield and the author of a number of articles and papers in the field of counselling and psychotherapy.

# Foreword

When Jean Clark phoned me in the summer of 1998 wearing her hat as a representative of the local branch of Psychotherapists and Counsellors for Social Responsibility, I did not envisage that we were about to embark on a fascinating and at some times somewhat unnerving adventure. The issue at stake was the nature of the challenge facing counsellors and psychotherapists who, either through choice or necessity, were plying their trade in the market-place as freelance practitioners. The conference that grew out of our discussions and took place at the University of East Anglia in the early summer of 1999 constituted in many ways an emergence from the closet of those therapists who can all too often live lonely and isolated lives with professional and financial anxieties seldom far away.

This book, with contributions from many of those who were active participants at the conference, takes the exploration much further and brings into broad daylight the concerns that not only impinge upon freelance practitioners and their clients but also serve to illuminate the increasingly influential and yet still precarious position of counselling and psychotherapy in our society and culture. The freelance practitioner must face squarely the professional and ethical questions that arise from offering paid assistance to those in mental and emotional distress. He or she must make personal decisions, for example, about the adequacy of his or her training and supervision and about the level of fee to be charged. What is more—especially for those working as 'affiliates' for Employee Assistance Programmes—there are inevitable dilemmas raised by the provision of short-term counselling for employees who have often been damaged by the very organisations that are footing the bill. The freelance practitioner who wishes to proceed in good faith and in full awareness cannot dodge such issues although the temptation to do so may be enormous in the light of the proliferation of trained therapists entering the field and the paucity of salaried posts. The realisation that one is in competition with colleagues or erstwhile fellow trainees for the privilege of responding to the suffering of others is not conducive to the preservation of an easy conscience or a quiet mind.

As Jean Clark aptly comments in her Introduction, the path of the freelance practitioner should not be entered upon by the faint-hearted. It is important, however, that the opportunities and challenges as well as the pitfalls of freelance work are examined and evaluated so that those who do enter upon this path are informed and equipped for the task. To engage in such work blindly and without effective preparation is a recipe for disaster and can lead to untold misery for therapists and clients alike. It is also likely to provide a field day for the legal profession in our increasingly litigious society.

I commend this book to a wide readership. It makes sombre but challenging reading for those who are considering a career in counselling and psychotherapy as well as those who are already in training. It also has much to say to trainers themselves. It will alert them to their responsibilities as they seek to equip trainees for a competitive and tough world where to collaborate with colleagues can seem like professional suicide rather than an ethical imperative. Not least, the book offers much to those who are already seasoned freelance practitioners but who wish to reflect upon their experience and to improve the quality of the service they offer. We live in a culture where the entrepreneurial spirit is admired and encouraged. Counsellors and psychotherapists must learn how to harness this spirit without losing the compassion and the deep respect for the individual that lie at the heart of their profession. We have reached the point where the majority of counsellors and psychotherapists now work either partly or entirely as freelance practitioners. It may well be that their capacity to maintain their integrity and enhance their effectiveness will determine whether in the years ahead counsellors and psychotherapists are seen as compliant servants of a dysfunctional society or respected and credible agents of change. It is not, after all, irrelevant that when Jean Clark first phoned me she did so as a representative of Psychotherapists and Counsellors for Social Responsibility.

Brian Thorne
Emeritus Professor of Counselling, University of East Anglia, Norwich; Fellow, British Association for Counselling and Psychotherapy; Co-founder, Norwich Centre for Personal and Professional Development

# Acknowledgements

This is a multi-authored book. My thanks to the established writers who contributed and also to the group of counsellors who had not written for publication before, but were willing to reflect and write out of their experiences on different aspects of counselling and freelance working and who have brought a freshness and immediacy to the book.

I wish to express my gratitude to the many colleagues who have given me their support; those who have given me permission to quote from personal communications, the many who have shared their experiences of working freelance with me, and those who have generously given me editorial advice and assistance, in particular Susan Cooper and Richard House. And to Kate Hawes at Brunner-Routledge for having faith in me.

Thanks are due also to Many Rivers Press, Langley, Washington, USA, for their kind permission to quote lines from David Whyte's poem 'No One Told Me', from *Fire in the Earth*, copyright 1997.

# Introduction

*Jean Clark*

Competition and collaboration are words that seldom appear in the counselling literature, yet for those who are unable or unwilling to find secure salaried posts as counsellors or psychotherapists, these words name the everyday experience of working independently. This book explores the tensions that are inherent in freelance work, and how these may be acknowledged and held in creative ways; when they are denied, then we are involved in various kinds of collusion and these too are discussed by some of the contributors.

I have deliberately used the word *freelance* in the title of this book, rather than *private* or *independent practitioner*. The word is defined as 'a person who sells his or her services to various employers, not employed by one only' (*Oxford English Dictionary*); it originally implied one who literally carried their lance, as a mercenary soldier in battle. The majority of counsellors, including myself, work freelance; that is to say, they are not in receipt of a regular salary, and are working independently in different settings. Throughout the book the terms 'counsellor' and 'psychotherapist' are used interchangeably.

In order to earn an adequate income, most counsellors will need to develop a portfolio of work—which may include some private clients, work for an agency such as a GP practice or an employee assistance programme, some sessional teaching, training or consultancy; and it might also include care work or other paid activity that will generate some regular income. As one colleague said, 'I have always had four or five jobs.' Some will also choose to undertake voluntary counselling in an agency in order to gain sufficient hours of supervised practice to be able to apply for accreditation, or to widen the range of their experience.

The book looks at some of the realities, the costs and challenges of freelance working, and issues that need consideration, perhaps even before applying for a training course, and certainly during training. As the subtitle suggests, to work freelance is to experience the tension between being in competition with colleagues, and yet sometimes working collaboratively with and seeking support from those same colleagues. It will not tell you how to succeed or how to survive, but it does raise many important questions and it is written by practitioners all of whom have had experience of working freelance, so that they know the satisfactions and problems, and the emotional pitfalls.

It will be relevant for counselling and psychotherapy trainees, and for those exploring the possibility of training with a view to a career change, for the recently qualified, and for the independent practitioner who may be feeling isolated. It also raises issues that trainers may wish to explore further in seminars for students, most of whom are unlikely initially to obtain a salaried post.

The impetus for the book came from the energy and feedback generated by a conference initiated by the Norwich branch of Psychotherapists and Counsellors for Social Responsibility (PCSR) and convened by the Centre for Counselling Studies, University of East Anglia, in May 1999. It was advertised as a conference to explore 'Collaboration Competition Collusion: The Challenges, Dynamics and Politics of Freelance Counselling and Psychotherapy', and was attended by 78 people including experienced, recently qualified and trainee counsellors and psychotherapists from different parts of the country.

The conference programme acknowledged that 'increasing numbers of people are qualifying as counsellors and psychotherapists, yet in most areas there are few full-time salaried posts. Most practitioners work freelance, with all the challenges and stresses that this involves. Agencies, including universities, continue to meet demands for training courses. It seems timely to explore some of the implications, both personal and professional' (conference publicity leaflet 1999).

The conference was offered as a space to reflect upon some of the implications of working freelance, alongside colleagues whom we may see as being more—or less—successful and asked 'Dare we look at the shadow and speak of our fears, envies, loneliness, as well as our satisfactions, strengths and coping strategies? How do individuals hold the tension of collaboration and competition and remain open?' It was also suggested that when these issues are not addressed, unhealthy collusions may occur. The response from participants showed an energy and a willingness to discuss issues that had not been explored so openly before. It seemed timely to consider writing a book that would acknowledge both the stresses and the freedoms and satisfactions of the work, and which might offer some companionship to those who decide to give up the security of a regular salaried post and seek to work freelance.

As the different contributors to the book make clear, the challenges are different for each person but they do include starting and maintaining a practice; fluctuations in income; finding support; coping with ill health; keeping up with new approaches and ongoing requirements for personal and professional development; accreditation; working alongside colleagues with different theoretical orientations; facing competition with those we know and respect; dealing with internal anxieties; feelings of envy, threat and inadequacy; balancing the public persona and the private person.

Then there are political issues; relationships between freelance therapists and NHS Mental Health services; building trust between statutory services and the freelance sector; who charges what and who pays; voluntary counselling services as practice grounds for trainees and newly trained counsellors seeking accreditation; the impact of Employee Assistance Programmes (EAPs); who pays for necessary long-term therapy? Does our mainly freelance status make us an invisible profession?

All these are a measure of the complexity faced by those who may have spent some time considering whether to undertake a training course in counselling or psychotherapy, and then gone through a selection procedure, followed by a time of waiting for the chosen course to commence; then a period of between one (full-time) and four (part-time) years in training (see Chapter 1). During this period, professional goalposts are changing, more newly qualified therapists are coming into the 'market-place', and the work opportunities are not what may have been envisaged when the journey began.

I have come to see this book as a kind of map. Each chapter describes part of the terrain through which a newly qualified practitioner will travel. Each person's route will be different. Maps are not there to say 'this is the road you will travel', but rather they indicate the territory, showing paths going in different directions or none, where there are obstacles, resting places offering refreshment. It is up to each of us to decide which path to take. But the goal is the same: to find and be found by those in emotional distress, to create a safe space where it is possible to work together over time, to contract together how this will be financed, and to observe certain ethical boundaries.

I am very grateful to those who have joined in this enterprise. Some are experienced writers, while for others it is the first time they have contributed to a published book. All have written out of their wide experience as practitioners. The book will not describe how to become a successful practitioner, but it does address some of the many issues that are faced by those working in the field, who are experiencing the inevitable tension between an inherent competition with colleagues and the ways in which colleagues may collaborate to develop new ideas, discuss issues and give and receive support. Although the subtitle of the book is 'competition and collaboration', the contributors were asked also to keep in mind the dimension of collusion that can exist in freelance working.

## Part I: Some facts and tensions

The opening chapter by Gabrielle Syme gives a historical overview of the development of counselling and psychotherapy in the UK, and gives some realistic costs for training, supervision and therapy. She raises the contro-versial question of when people might be considered to be adequately trained and experienced to be able to work safely with private clients.

Chapter 2 explores some of the internal dynamics of freelance work and the emotions evoked and endured by those who by choice or necessity seek to work independently. Jean Clark suggests that it is better not to collude with the denial of the reality of competition, so that we may eventually reach a point of healthy cooperative competition and ethical networking.

## Part II: Setting up as freelance

In Chapter 3 Colin Feltham explores, from his own experience, some of the issues that need to be taken into account before attempting to set up as freelance, though he points out that these are not a recipe for 'how to start in private practice'. He includes the need for some business acumen and entrepreneurial skills as well as psychological issues including loneliness, lack of certainty and security and challenge from peers inherent in freelance practice.

Ian Horton, in Chapter 4, seeks to clarify issues about regulation, regis-tration and accreditation of counsellors and psychotherapists. He gives an overview of some of the issues and points out that intending practitioners need to keep themselves up to date with current developments.

Sue Wheeler in her chapter 'Sorting out supervision' states very clearly her view that 'freelance work is not for the untrained novice'. She suggests that the three words collaboration, competition and collusion all have relevance for the supervisory relationship; therapist and supervisor may collaborate in some settings; they may be in competition with each other for clients; and as she says, 'collusion is possible in any supervisory relationship and warrants close scrutiny'.

In Chapter 6 Keith Tudor and Mike Worrall tackle the theme of an 'unspoken relationship'—the financial dynamics in freelance therapy. There can be personal, professional and psychological difficulties about dealing with money—how much to charge, how to negotiate, keeping accounts and the ethics of charging for therapy.

## Part III: The dynamics of survival

To undertake a training course is to embark on a process of change, of gaining new and sometimes disturbing insights and awareness, from which there is no going back. Then comes a further period of uncertainty when the course with its comradeship and support is over. Chapter 7 offers maps of these transitions with their loneliness and freedoms, which are also relevant to the work with clients.

A seldom-explored theme is that of the therapist in relation to their family. Tania Barnett, a married counsellor with two children, and herself the daughter of two psychotherapists, explores her own family relationships, as daughter, wife and mother, in Chapter 8. Searching the literature, she has found 'a visible lack of value given to the connection between "family dynamics" and being a freelance therapist', and yet the decision to become a therapist inevitably impacts on family relationships.

While personal and professional development have always been seen as part of the training experience and subsequent development as a therapist, it is now a requirement of the various accrediting bodies that Continuing Professional Development (CPD) be demonstrated on a regular basis. Chapter 9 offers the practitioner an overview of CPD activities and suggests how they may be used creatively to develop reflective practice and self-nurture.

## Part IV: Survival in practice

This section of the book is written directly out of the personal and professional experience of seven counsellors, each with their different story. It looks at the theme of survival, from the early days post-qualification through to the choices that have been made to work in different contexts, together with reflection upon the demands, stresses and satisfactions they have found.

In Chapter 10 four counsellors reflect upon the choices they made in their search for work after qualifying and describe the early years of working freelance. They have taken very different routes. Joe Daggers writes of his experience, together with two colleagues from the training course, in setting up a counselling partnership, with its challenges and struggles. Jacky Moss took a different route, which she describes as a journey 'from there to here'. She continued to work as a volunteer counsellor gaining more experience working with a variety of clients, until through contacts in the local counselling community she began to be offered some paid work. Two years on, she is earning her living as a freelance. Leebert Hughes was a qualified engineer who became interested in counselling through voluntary work. After qualifying as a counsellor, he found it harder than he had anticipated to find paid work. He reflects upon his experience as a black counsellor, who has from time to time faced prejudice. Gerry Virgo writes of her early decision 'not to give up the day job' and for several years after qualifying continued salaried work in a major public institution while working as a volunteer counsellor in an agency. Eventually she took the risk of giving up her full-time post and took a part-time salaried administrative role in a counselling agency.

In Chapter 11 Benita Cowen and Nigel White reflect upon their experiences of working in primary care, over a period during which the NHS has gone through many changes. They explore the stresses involved in surgery counselling working alongside a team who have a medical model. It is as if two different cultures meet, and cannot always find a common language.

Charlotte Johnson writes about EAPs from her own wide experience. Chapter 12 outlines many issues, including the level of training and experience required by most EAPS, the terms on which the counsellor is contracted to work, and the ways in which areas of responsibility and confidentiality are different from the client/counsellor contract in private practice.

In Chapter 13 Gabrielle Syme explores in some detail the implications of working from home and with long-term clients in a psychodynamic context, including questions of privacy, personal safety and the necessity for thorough supervision when a psychotherapist is working with the client over a period of years.

I want to thank all those who have contributed to the writing of this book. It contains a rich mix of perspectives and I hope it will inform, challenge and encourage those who read it. It may even discourage some people who had thought of counselling as a second career. It is not a path for the faint-hearted!

# Part I

# Some facts and tensions

There has been an immense growth in the practice of freelance counselling and psychotherapy since the early 1980s and 568 training courses were listed in the BAC Training Directory (2000). For those who are considering the possibility of training for work, which can be viewed as personally satisfying, flexible and free from the demands of bureaucratic institutions, it can be important to be aware of the broad context, and some of the issues that are involved in working freelance—practical and emotional as well as professional.

For those who are in the process of training there are likely to be a number of unspoken concerns and anxieties, and it can be healthy if these are acknowledged, explored and discussed while there is still the support of a training group. To work freelance, whether by choice or necessity, is at times lonely, and it can be hard to know how to deal with the confusions and challenges of competition while still finding support from colleagues, and to gain a realistic view of the practical and emotional challenges ahead.

# Chapter 1

# The development and growth of freelance counselling

*Gabrielle Syme*

## Introduction

All the psychological or talking therapies owe their origins to Freud, psychoanalysis and Vienna in the 1880s. In 1886 Freud went into private practice in Vienna as a neurologist and over the next 10 years developed a method of treating hysterical patients, which he called psychoanalysis. Many of his original analysands moved away from Vienna and also had profound disagreements with Freud. These disagreements led to new theories and methods of working, which have become the basis of the different theories of psychotherapy and counselling. These many theories can be fitted under three main headings: psychodynamic, person centred and behavioural. The first two can be clearly linked to Freud and his followers; psychodynamic owes its origins to Freud, Jung and Adler and person centred to Adler and Rank.

Coincidentally working in private practice as a psychological therapist also links back to Freud. At the time that he was working medicine was rarely free, so inevitably he and his followers were all private practitioners. In the UK medicine became free at the point of need in 1948, so from then on there was the possibility of some psychological therapists being salaried and all having some choice about whether to seek a salaried job or to work in private practice or voluntarily, or become freelance and mix the three.

Psychoanalysis developed very differently in Britain from the USA. In the latter almost all psychoanalysts are medically qualified, whereas in the UK most psychoanalysts, psychotherapists and counsellors are lay. A possible reason for this acceptance of a lay training in the UK is that Ernest Jones, one of Freud's analysands, brought psychoanalysis to Britain in 1913, subsequently founding the British Psychoanalytic Society in 1924. Although medically qualified himself he was very loyal to Freud and did not break away from him. He wrote the first biography of Freud (Jones, 1953). Freud vigorously supported the lay analyst, analysing a number of lay people, his daughter Anna being one. He did not consider a medical education essential for an analyst; what was needed was a 'special training necessary for the practice of analysis' (Freud, 1927). Another reason for the preponderance of lay people in the psychological therapies in Britain may also be that Freud and his daughter Anna escaped to London in 1938. Freud died in 1939 but his daughter, a distinguished and influential lay psychoanalyst in her own right, remained in the UK for the rest of her life.

Another difference in the USA is that counselling is a graduate entry profession, with psychology being an essential part of the undergraduate degree. In the UK psychotherapy is a graduate entry profession whereas counselling is not. Nonetheless in a survey of its members conducted in 1997 the British Association for Counselling (BAC) found that 61% were graduates and another 28% had diplomas, a number of which were of degree standard and indeed would be degrees nowadays. Neither counsellors nor psychotherapists need a psychology degree, though psychotherapists must have a degree in a human or social science. A degree in psychology is not common among members of BACP, maybe because counsellors with a psychology degree have the option of joining the British Psychological Society and becoming a Chartered Counselling Psychologist. There is one other significant difference between counselling in North America and the UK. This is that counselling in Great Britain has become focused on emotional and social development whereas in North America it is commonly in a school setting and is mainly directed towards vocational guidance and social action.

This prejudice against lay analysts and therapists in the USA may well be behind the development of a separate discipline of counselling and its focus on vocational work and social action. The actual word 'counseling' was first used in 1908 by a radical social activist called Frank Parsons (1854–1908). He set up a Vocational Bureau in the North End of Boston where there were many immigrants, with a 'counseling center' where 'interviews, testing, information and outreach' were offered (Bond, 2000). This tradition of counselling being very closely linked with social action has continued to this day in the USA. It seems that the word 'counseling' coined by Parsons was taken up by Carl Rogers to describe his work when as a psychologist and therefore 'lay' he was not permitted by the psychiatric profession in the USA to call himself a psychotherapist (Thorne, 1984). Another reason for Rogers choosing the word 'counseling' may have been that his background was an initial training as a Christian minister and pastoral care and counselling were being practised by some ministers.

## The start of counselling in the UK

Counselling first appeared in the UK in the voluntary sector. In 1948 David Mace, the general secretary of the National Marriage Guidance Council (NMGC, nowadays known as Relate), wrote a book entitled *Marriage Counselling: The First Full Account of the Remedial Work of the MGC*. The

NMGC had been set up 10 years earlier to offer some pre-marriage education. From this Mace had become aware that something akin to a Child Guidance Clinic, where doctors, clergy and other professionals were available for consultation, was also necessary for people with marriage problems. In 1946 counsellors started to be selected using interview techniques developed by the War Office Selection Boards. These counsellors were trained to ascertain in a single session the client's main source of difficulty and then make a referral to professionals such as psychiatrists, GPs, ministers of religion or family-planning advisers. In a sense they were first aid workers backed by consultants. Gradually counsellors wanted to be the main source of help and not merely to act as a referral agency. This indeed happened during the 1950s; marriage guidance counselling changed so that well-trained volunteer counsellors worked with their clients regularly over a period of time and maintained a relationship for a number of weeks (Tyndall, 1993). This has become the 'way' counsellors work.

At the same time counselling training was being given to some youth workers and clergy and the first university counselling courses were being set up specifically to offer counselling as part of in-service training for teachers. This proliferation of counselling during the 1950s and 1960s started to cause concern because counselling was being offered in some settings without the necessary safeguards and constraints. Under the auspices of the National Council of Social Service a new association was formed in 1970, named the Standing Conference for the Advancement of Counselling (SCAC), membership being drawn from the voluntary sector, such as the Albany Trust, NMGC and the Pregnancy Advisory Service, from a number of groupings of counsellors, such as the Association for Student Counselling (ASC, founded in 1970) and the Association for Pastoral Care and Counselling (APCC, founded in 1972) and from the youth workers (National Association of Young People's Counselling and Advisory Services). Of particular interest is that SCAC did not have any individual members initially despite the fact that there was already a small number of private practitioners and some people were asking for individual membership. In 1977 SCAC was disbanded and the British Association for Counselling (BAC) formed. It had 1400 individual members in the first year and also organisational members from the start. This association exists to the present day, although it was renamed the British Association for Counselling and Psychotherapy (BACP) in 2000. It is the biggest association of counsellors in the UK and in terms of membership as a percentage of the population it is the biggest counselling association in the world. Many of the interest groupings based round work setting or client groups, which were instrumental in the founding of BAC, still exist within BACP as divisions, though a number have changed their name. ASC has changed its name to the Association for University and College Counsellors (AUCC), and APCC has changed its name to the Association for Pastoral and Spiritual Care and Counselling (APSCC). The other divisions are Faculty of Healthcare Counsellors and Psychotherapists (FHCP) formerly known as Counselling in Medical Settings (CMS), Counselling in Education (CIE), Association for Counselling at Work (ACW), Race and Cultural Education in Counselling (RACE) and Therapists in Private Practice (TIPP) formerly, Personal, Relationship and Groupwork.

## The growth of private practice

It was probably inevitable that as people became trained by voluntary organisations as counsellors they would start to use a skill learned in one setting in another and thus become freelance. Marriage guidance counsellors wanted to be paid for their skills and so started working privately as well; pastoral counsellors were asked for help by people who were neither their church members nor Christians; some university counsellors eked out a low salary with a small amount of private work. Perhaps all were also doing a small amount of private work partly because of the pressure from friends and acquaintances asking for counselling, which was not freely available, and partly as a form of insurance in case they became redundant. This was particularly necessary as counselling has grown during a period when there have been two economic recessions.

In my research conducted partly by letter, partly by scouring the BAC archives and partly by word of mouth, I found the first person to offer counselling in his own free time and using his own premises but charging no fee did so in 1956. The first person to charge a fee did so in 1960. The first real indication of the existence of a number of freelance counsellors is from the first referral directory published by BAC in 1979/80. In this directory there are 127 names registered. The membership of BAC at that time was 1858 (Syme, 1994).

It is important to attach a caveat to all the numbers given for freelance counsellors; all they can do is indicate trends. There are a number of reasons for both overestimates and underestimates:

1   Counsellors, psychotherapists and psychoanalysts have registered in the directories.
2   Some people registered their names at least twice because of working in two places.
3   The first BAC directory only included names of BAC members; later ones were more catholic and accepted entries from anyone who would pay the entry fee.
4   There are a number of other directories, such as the Association of Sex and Marital Therapists.
5   Some people registered 'just in case they ever needed to work privately' but they never did so.

6   Until 1990 entrants into the directory did not have to belong to a professional body and thus anyone could register simply on their own assertion that they were a counsellor, psychotherapist or psychoanalyst.
7   Not all people in the private sector choose to pay to have their name in a directory.
8   An increase in numbers in a directory could simply be related to better publicity of the directory.

Despite these provisos there is no doubt that the number of freelance counsellors has increased dramatically. By 1990 there were 1270 names in BAC's Counselling and Psychotherapy Resources Directory, a 10-fold increase from the first referral directory in 1979/80, and in the United Kingdom Counselling and Psychotherapy Directory published by BAC in 2000 there are 2755 individual entries, over double the number in 1990. Over this same time span BAC grew in membership from 7218 in 1990/91 (a fourfold increase from 1979/80) to approximately 16,300 at the beginning of 2000. In this 10-year span the increase in membership of BAC and the number of entries in the directory have roughly paralleled one another.

This large increase in the number of entrants to the BAC published register and therefore presumably in private or freelance counsellors overall is partly a reflection of the number of training courses, but also a result of the current economic climate, which encourages both individualism and entre-preneurship. At the same time there has not been an increase in paid posts as full-time counsellors, but an increase in sessional work leaving many counsellors needing to do some additional private counselling to have an adequate income. Of course this increase in numbers of private practitioners brings with it increased competition for work, particularly in the large conurbations. In most of the large cities, for instance London, Manchester and Leeds, it is increasingly difficult to find sufficient clients to be able to work full time as a private practitioner. This is also true of some smaller cities such as York and Norwich. This leads to more counsellors becoming freelance and doing some private or independent work, some work for Employee Assistance Programmes (EAPs) and possibly some sessional work for a GP Practice. On the other hand there are places where the current BACP directory has very few counsellors listed: examples are Cumbria, Devon, Cornwall and North Yorkshire. This under-provision brings a different set of problems in its wake for counsellors. With a very small number of counsellors it is difficult to find supervisors and therapists without creating dual relationships. There also appears to be an under-provision in Scotland, Northern Ireland and Wales. However, this may be because counsellors choose not to put their name in a register that is perceived to be English.

In many respects working in private practice is the most difficult setting and this is reflected in the United Kingdom Register of Counsellors

(UKRC), where the Independent Counsellors have to be accredited counsellors, either with BACP or the Confederation of Scottish Counsellors Associations (COSCA) or with one or two other organisations whose standards have been recognised as of equivalence by the UKRC. It is for similar reasons that BACP insists that inexperienced trainee counsellors on BACP Accredited Training Courses should not be in private practice except in unusual circumstances (BAC, 1996). I would recommend that this should be the approach taken by all courses. The particular demands of private practice are that, apart from the counselling work, there is a business to be set up and run, which demands organisational and entrepreneurial skills (see Chapters 3 and 13). In addition there is the danger of isolation and loneliness (Syme, 1994), the need to contain clients without any institutional support and often without a secretary or a receptionist, possibly the necessity of earning sufficient money, which could lead to overworking, and if working from home there may also be the management of the practice so that it does not intrude into the private life of other people living in the house (see Chapters 8 and 13).

## Training

There has been a considerable increase in the number of training courses during the 1990s so that there are more counsellors being trained than there are salaried posts. With no regulation the standard varies enormously from course to course. This is a minefield for a student, who will often have no idea what would constitute a 'good' course. A further problem for potential students is that the standard cannot necessarily be deduced from the title of the course. There are certificate courses, diploma courses, undergraduate and Masters degrees in counselling and some may be of a similar standard, though some training organisations offer a graduated training starting with an introductory course followed by a certificate course and then a diploma or advanced diploma (for example, Westminster Pastoral Foundation). Some courses in counselling studies and others in research methods may not have any requirement for students to have undertaken client work in the past, to be a practising counsellor during the course, or to have to undertake supervised client work to complete the course. A further complication is that at one time no differentiation was made between counselling and counselling skills courses. This is not now true: a counselling skills training is recognised as being different from a counselling course.

In 1987 BAC endeavoured to clarify the confusion by introducing a recognition scheme, later renamed an accreditation scheme, for courses. This scheme outlines the basic requirements of a satisfactory training. It should have a minimum of 400 hours staff/student contact and is unlikely to last less than one year full time or 2–3 years part time. Nine basic elements are expected of any training course. These are outlined in considerable depth. Briefly they are as follows:

1   Admission procedures that are transparent and directed towards selecting students who will have sufficient maturity to become counsellors and not to use the course as a substitute for personal therapy.
2   A component of the course focused on self-development throughout the course.
3   A minimum of 100 hours of supervised work with 'real' clients.
4   Skills relevant to the theoretical model should be practised with regular opportunities for observation and feedback.
5   Regular supervision of at least one hour to every eight hours client work.
6   There should be a core theoretical model underpinning the course and this should be augmented by the introduction of material from the relevant social sciences to put the counselling into its social context. Other theories of counselling should be introduced for comparative purposes.
7   Professional development should include such components as developing an understanding of the work of other key mental health professionals, introducing codes of ethics and practice, and teaching research methods so papers can be read and understood.
8   The assessment should be congruent with the core theoretical model.
9   Course evaluation should take place regularly and should be ongoing throughout the course.

This accreditation system has been very demanding and somewhat daunting, though many trainers have been glad of the rigour once their course has been accredited! Perhaps as a result of this rigour relatively few courses have been accredited. In 1989 two courses were recognised, increasing to 24 in 1995, 49 in 1999 and 64 in 2000. This sharp increase may be the product of the competitive market.

In the BAC Training Directory (2000), 568 organisations offering courses were registered and this does not include all the courses in the UK. One way for students to assess whether a course is of a good enough standard is to apply to study on a BACP accredited course. Apart from being of a known and agreed standard, the hours of taught theory and skills training meet the requirements for accreditation as an individual counsellor set by BACP. Other requirements for accreditation are 450 hours of counselling practice with at least 1.5 hours supervision per month and 40 hours of personal counselling or an equivalent experience. Many students completing a BACP accredited course can fulfil these requirements within six months of completing their course.

BACP does not stipulate a curriculum for accredited courses to follow but relies on the staff to design a course that is congruent with their core model and containing the main elements necessary to train a counsellor. The assessors would be looking at both the course content and its congruence during the assessment for accreditation. Few courses, if any, have a unit on private practice. I believe this is correct because private practice should only be undertaken by experienced practitioners who have been accredited or are eligible for accreditation by a body such as BACP. In general this is likely to be someone who completed a diploma in counselling at least three years earlier. If a diploma course were to have a unit on private practice it would tacitly be encouraging its members to enter private practice straight away. Though it is not appropriate to have a unit on private practice in a diploma course, trainee counsellors should be made aware of the difficulties involved in running a private practice and the inadvisability of a newly trained counsellor working in this setting. I would suggest that counsellors should attend a short course on setting up in private practice as part of a Continuing Professional Development requirement (see Chapter 8). BACP has occasionally run day workshops on this topic, as have a few enterprising individuals. Some training courses also address the implications of working independently. There are three books available that are well-worth reading. These are written by Syme (1994), McMahon (1994) and Thistle (1998). While there is some overlap, these books are complementary because different topics are covered in depth.

## Costs of training

I mentioned earlier that I believe that before counsellors move into private practice they should be an experienced practitioner and be accredited by BACP or an organisation setting similar standards. Nowadays this means having undertaken and graduated from a substantial course, having worked with at least three clients a week and completed a minimum of 150 hours per year for three years with adequate supervision. In addition to being accredited one must have had a minimum of 40 hours of personal therapy or an equivalent experience. All of this costs money with no subsidy available unless a training therapist or supervisor is prepared to offer students lower fees. Many courses, although not all, include the cost of supervision while training, in the course fee. This rarely happens with personal therapy though many courses insist on their students receiving therapy, and thus it is an additional cost during training. After graduation the counsellor has to fund supervision and may wish to continue in therapy, which will have to be self-financed. It can be seen that the training will be expensive (at least £5000 in 2000). The actual costs of courses vary considerably. It is a very competitive field with colleges of further education and of higher education, universities and privately run organisations all competing for a finite number of people. This makes it imperative to read the small print and know what is required to become an accredited or registered counsellor.

Without this knowledge students may choose a cheaper course and then find there are many extra hidden costs involved in reaching the level of experience to equip them for private work.

This level of expenditure raises issues of equal opportunity of access to training. One of the recent developments is the development of a National Vocational Qualification (NVQ) at level 3 in counselling. The method of assessment is using a portfolio presentation to give evidence of having gained the necessary experience to practise as a counsellor. It is hoped that this will be a considerably cheaper way of training and BACP has developed a route of accreditation for people with an NVQ qualification. This will not remove the costs of personal therapy and supervision but there are counsellors who have a sliding scale of fees or concessionary fees for those on a low income.

## Availability of work

I indicated earlier in this chapter that in some areas of the UK there are more counsellors than work because of the increase in number of people who have been trained as counsellors without an increase in salaried posts. In addition, up to now the natural wastage of counsellors through retirement or death has been low for two reasons: first, because counselling is a relatively young profession and therefore the majority of counsellors trained in the last 25 years are still practising; second, this is exacerbated because there is no retirement age and many experienced counsellors continue to do a small amount of private work long after the statutory retirement age. Younger counsellors should take heart, as no one lives for ever! Over the next 20 years the older counsellors will cease to practise and therefore there will be more work to go round even if there is no increase in the number of people seeking counselling. There is likely to be an increase in people seeking counselling as it has and continues to become more acceptable to seek help. There has been a noticeable trend in the last 20 years of the British being less repressed and more able to express emotions publicly. A particularly powerful example was when Princess Diana was killed: this is not an isolated example, though by far the most public.

The result of the increase in people being trained as counsellors, without significant numbers leaving the profession, has been less private work and therefore greater difficulty in earning a living through this alone. This lack of private work has been partly compensated for as a result of increased use of sessional counsellors by GPs and by the formation of many more EAPs subcontracting work to accredited or registered counsellors. This encourages many more counsellors to become freelance in order to earn an adequate income for their needs. It is common for a counsellor to do some private counselling, and supervision if they are sufficiently experienced, along with sessional work for a GP and some contract work for an EAP. I think this trend will continue and it may be a good thing because it decreases the isolation of the private practitioner. However, there is a danger of increasing the overheads disproportionately so that the increased income does not balance out the costs of travelling and the loss of income-generating hours while travelling.

There was a clear growth in counselling in GPs' practices in the 1990s and it is probable that this will continue. In 1993 about a third of family practices in England and Wales were employing at least one counsellor (Sibbald *et al.*, 1993). This has now grown to over 70%. There is much circumstantial evidence that patients appreciate counselling because they like being listened to. Randomised controlled trials do not indicate that counselling is effective, though the methodology of much of this research is highly questionable (Rowland and Goss, 2000). However, there are an increasing number of naturalistic studies which reveal a satisfactory outcome with either reduced referrals to psychiatric services or a reduced drug bill for a practice. This evidence is becoming increasingly important from the point of view of generating more work for counsellors.

A recent publication by the Department of Health (1999) stated that 'at any one time around one in six people of working age have a mental health problem' and for 'every one hundred individuals consult[ing] their GP with a mental health problem, [only] nine will be referred to specialist services'. This means the remainder have to be seen by other mental health professionals, which includes counsellors (see Chapter 11 for working in the NHS).

In 1996 a social worker successfully argued that his employer was liable for his nervous breakdown and received compensation of £175,000. Subsequently there have been a number of other cases of workers successfully arguing that their employers' work practices caused their stress and receiving compensation. It has been estimated that in 2000 mental health and stress problems were costing employers in Britain about £5 billion. This has resulted in some companies setting up in-house occupational health departments but more commonly they subcontract this work to EAPs, who in turn subcontract the counselling work. It is likely that this will increase further unless the working practices of British employers change radically (see Chapter 13 for working with EAPs).

## The future of freelance counselling

There are many counsellors who are highly critical of freelance counsellors, believing that all counselling should be free at the point of need (Pilgrim, 2000). If they had their way private practice would cease. I think many counsellors would prefer to be able to offer counselling free at point of delivery and this would be possible if the way the health service was funded was altered (Syme, 1994). Meanwhile the UK is a mixed economy and there will always be people who prefer to pay for their care. While private work may not grow I think it likely that freelance work will continue to expand, with counsellors surviving financially with a 'pick-and-mix' type of practice. It is to be hoped that this is stimulating rather than stressful. This will only be so if counsellors are realistic about what can be achieved in a day when working in a variety of settings, and protect themselves from overwork.

## References

Bond, T. (2000) *Standards and Ethics for Counselling in Action*. London: Sage.

British Association for Counselling (BAC) (1996) *Code of Ethics and Practice for Trainers*. Rugby: British Association for Counselling.

British Association for Counselling (BAC) (2000) *The Training in Counselling and Psychotherapy Directory*. Rugby: British Association for Counselling.

Department of Health (1999) *National Service Framework for Mental Health: Modern Standards and Service Models*. London: Department of Health.

Freud, S. (1927) *Postscript to 'The Question of Lay Analysis'*. Penguin Freud Library, Vol. 15. Harmondsworth: Penguin.

Jones, E. (1953) *The Life and Work of Sigmund Freud*. Harmondsworth: Penguin.

McMahon, G. (1994) *Setting up your own Private Practice in Counselling and Psychotherapy*. Cambridge: NEC.

Pilgrim, D. (2000) Social class. In C. Feltham and I. Horton (eds), *Handbook of Counselling and Psychotherapy*. London: Sage.

Rowland, N. and Goss, S. (2000) *Evidence-Based Counselling and Psychological Therapies*. London: Routledge.

Sibbald, B., Addington-Hall, J., Brennerman, D. and Freeling, P. (1993) Counsellors in English and Welsh general practices: their nature and distribution. *British Medical Journal*, 306: 29–33.

Syme, G. (1994) *Counselling in Independent Practice*. Buckingham: Open University Press.

Thistle, R. (1998) *Counselling and Psychotherapy in Private Practice*. London: Sage.

Thorne, B. (1984) Person-centred therapy. In W. Dryden (ed.), *Individual Therapy in Britain*. London: Harper & Row.

Tyndall, N. (1993) *Counselling in the Voluntary Sector*. Buckingham: Open University Press.

# Chapter 2

# The internal dynamics of freelance

*Jean Clark*

The three words, collaboration, competition and collusion, floated into my mind in the early 1990s—and somehow would not go away. They were a shorthand for what appeared to be happening as training courses proliferated, and counselling was increasingly being spoken about in both positive and negative ways by the general public and by the media. How would I and my colleagues react in an increasingly competitive situation? Would we be willing to acknowledge and work realistically with what was happening?

By then I had been working freelance for five years, though my history as a counsellor and trainer went back to 1971, when I was appointed 'to undertake some student counselling' at Leicester Polytechnic. At that time there was no one to collaborate *with*. It was lone pioneering work, setting up the first student counselling service in an institution. I was aware of a few other student counsellors in different parts of the country, and I had no sense of competition. It was the tutors at the polytechnic who seemed to see me as a competitor!

I spent 10 years as a salaried student counsellor; then came a marital break-up, and in 1985, aged 59, I moved to another part of the country and began to work freelance as a way of earning my living. It was challenging, but there were not many trained counsellors at that time, I was not aware of competition. My internal dialogue at this time was about practical things. Can I cope with schedule D income tax? How do I find an accountant? How do I keep business accounts?

It was not until I was supervising students on a counselling training course in the late 1980s, most of whom lived locally and were coming to the end of their training, that I began to recognise there was a new dimension to my experience of freelance working. I had been using the metaphor 'aquaplaning—it is alright so long as you don't look down'. Now I might lose my balance if I looked round to see who was coming up behind me.

There was beginning to be competition for clients and increasingly I found myself hearing about my newly qualified supervisees' efforts to find paid work. I began to talk to them about the fact that we were now in competition with each other for clients, which initially seemed to be a shock to them. I found myself exploring with them the facts of life around working on a freelance basis. It felt then, and still does feel, a healthy thing to do, during what I see as the mentoring stage of supervising students who are coming towards the end of their counselling training.

I recall my own, well-concealed, feelings of anxiety at that time, as more courses equipped more counsellors to come into the field of competition for clients. I tried not to acknowledge that I might be an object of jealousy because I could be seen as successful. After all I had been a practitioner for a long time. I comforted myself with thinking 'Well, they probably see me as an elder', and then imagined them saying 'When is she going to stop working and make more room for *us*?' I was now becoming conscious of the un-spoken, unacknowledged, sometimes destructive dialogues which occasion-ally went on inside my head, and the unspoken conversations with peers.

One of my (now) very experienced colleagues recently wrote to me about her feelings during the first months after she ended her training:

> During the first years I lived on the edge of fear as far as earning a living was concerned. I did not know if it was possible and I certainly had no preconceptions about how it could happen. I lived for the moment and drove myself relentlessly, enjoying the challenge. The fear was my spur, as was a newly found competitive energy. These two powerful feelings were, I think, well hidden from most people; though I could acknowledge them to myself easily, I did not believe they fitted in with the expected image of a caring and competent therapist. What was not so comfortable to admit to myself, let alone anyone else, were the deep feelings of anxiety, anger and envy.
>
> I found that if I heard of a peer getting work that I could have done, I would be furious, because they didn't need the money to live, and I did; or I felt I could do the work much better than her/him. I was envious of peers who got 'proper' counselling jobs, even though that was not what I wanted. I was sometimes despairing that things would ever work out.
>
> (Gilchrist, A., personal communication, 1999)

Listening now to recently qualified trainees and supervisees, I hear very similar concerns:

- 'Now the course has ended my partner keeps saying "Well, when are you going to start earning some money?" I have done all I can. The counselling room is ready, I have put out publicity, but where are the clients? Will I ever get started?'
- 'Yes, it is a vocation, it *is* what I really want to do, but will I ever get through the hoops and be accredited? Will I be good enough? What are they looking for? It all takes so long and it costs!'

- 'I have spent so much money on my training but they don't really tell you how difficult it is to get started.'
- 'It seems like the only way I can reach this 450 hours supervised practice and apply for accreditation is to do a stint as a voluntary counsellor somewhere, yet I need to be earning—I have used up all my savings.'

Over the last few years, experienced colleagues were facing the implications of more competition for clients, and occasionally sharing their frustrations in supervision or therapy:

- 'I either have too much work or not enough. It really is hard to keep a balance and pay my way.'
- 'This week it seemed that all my clients sat down and said "I think I have got flu!" If I am ill, it means a week or two off work and no income.'
- 'I know I can be competitive and that's alright, but it means I can take on too much and work too hard, and things get out of balance.'

There can be periods of feeling insecure and afraid:

- 'There was this article in the newspaper about counselling . . . one unethical counsellor and we all get rubbished, and when I feel tired I can get quite paranoid about it all.'
- 'There is more and more in the journals about complaints and litigation. It could happen to me and that's scary!'
- 'It can feel like a knife edge; erratic earnings, occasional very disturbed clients, needing to get away from it all sometimes, yet it's what I want to do!'
- 'I am competing for clients with colleagues who may be my supervisor or my therapist. We meet in professional groups and workshops, and then we compete for the occasional salaried post! How do I hold all that together?'

For the recently qualified therapist, just setting out on their journey, such thoughts as these may feel like paranoia, and therefore not to be spoken about. Fear, a sense of isolation, feelings of rejection, jealousy, envy, anger, pain—are they a lapse into primitive sibling rivalry? Does the sometimes acute anxiety indicate an infantile longing for dependency? I would suggest that these painful emotions are often appropriate to the situation we find ourselves in. They are the shadow side of working as a freelance counsellor or psychotherapist, and I believe it can be healthy to bring them out into the light of day. Then they may be openly discussed with peers and with more experienced colleagues. We might then be able to ask some important questions. How may these conflicting emotions be held in a creative tension? What will happen if we openly acknowledge them, bring them out of the shadows and speak about them, even though they may not fit in with the expected image of a caring and competent therapist?

Participants at a conference, when invited to suggest metaphors for the experience of being a freelance practitioner, suggested the following:

- A ballerina in a circus, riding two horses, one bigger than the other.
- Journeying through a tangled forest.
- A sailing boat (and sometimes the wind fails).
- Serious hill walking (needing at least one companion, or even a group, with maps and resources).
- Gardening (things take time to grow, it is cyclical, we need help sometimes, there can be times of drought).

All of these metaphors convey a sense of freedom, of journey, of uncertainty and risk. Will I lose my balance, will factors outside my control create difficulty or even danger? Yet implicit in them all is the satisfaction which can come from hard work, struggle and the need for some pre-planning.

## Starting out on the journey of freelance

People are attracted to counselling courses for a variety of reasons. They may have had a good experience as a client, and so develop a fantasy of being a wise, serene, powerful person like their therapist. They may be seeking personal growth, or have a strong desire for a career change. They may be seeking a peer group with whom they may find trust, understanding and a shared philosophy of helping. Or they may see counselling as an extension of their work as a nurse, or a manager or a carer. Their training course may have prepared them well for the challenges ahead, or it may have focused upon the skills, values and psychological understandings of being a counsellor, and neglected the more practical matter of work possibilities, realistic potential earnings, and when it might be ethically responsible to consider setting up in private practice.

When the course is over, the qualification has been gained, and the support and challenge of the training group has dispersed, what follows can be a time, which is both lonely and stressful. And yet in a strange way perhaps it can be trusted. I have permission to quote from a letter written by a counsellor who qualified two years ago:

> I finished the diploma course, thought I had sorted myself out and now expected to find paid work as a counsellor. . . . I had given up a secure career. There was no going back to previous employment because the

excitement for me was in counselling. . . . As for that elusive employment, I am still searching. What does the future hold? I do not know and strangely it is no longer important. This year I have learnt to live with uncertainty and maybe this is my future path.

(Dansey, R., personal communication, 2000)

I am minded of the film *Field of Dreams*, where a farmer, walking in his field of corn, hears a voice saying 'Build it and he will come.' And as an act of faith he builds a baseball pitch, and the ghosts of Shoeless Joe and his team mates do come. To set out to work freelance can be just such an act of faith but of course there are no guarantees that the clients will come. Part of the experience of the newly qualified practitioner is that at the beginning of an adventure we do not know what we need to know.

The poet David Whyte takes poetry into his work with change in organisations. He writes words that might well have been written for those who are trying to build up a freelance practice:

In my experience, the more true we are to our own creative gifts the less there is any outer reassurance or help at the beginning. The more we are on the path, the deeper the silence in the first stage of the process. Following our path is in effect a kind of going off the path, through open country. There is a certain early stage when we are left to camp out in the wilderness, alone, with few supporting voices. Out there in the silence we must build a hearth, gather the twigs and strike the flint for the fire ourselves.

(Whyte, 1997: 73)

Being a counsellor, like being a poet or a creative person in industry, means being willing to tread a lonely road. I feel that it is important to know this from the very start for it requires of us a particular kind of stamina and certain survival skills. This is particularly true for those who do not have the security of earnings from other work, or do not have a partner who is in paid employment.

We may visualise the act of setting out to work on a freelance basis in terms of innovation: the creation of a new way of life that is as yet unclear. 'The act of innovation is both cognitive and emotional' (Goleman, 1998: 100). The cognitive phase involves preparation, gathering data and information, looking at possibilities. Then comes the incubation phase where we let the mind play with the material, allowing connections, possibilities, ideas to simmer . . . until hopefully the time comes when there is an intuitive sense of how to begin. The hard work comes with the following through.

We may find support from various sources. Sometimes when a training course has ended, a group of ex-trainees decide to meet on a regular basis, to share their efforts to find work and offer peer support, as well as exploring personal and professional development issues. Such a group might also be open enough to be able to face the experience of competition when one member manages to secure regular work! Some people seek out an experienced practitioner who may be willing to act formally or informally as a mentor for a period.

## Mentoring: a green 'L' plate'

The words 'mentor' and 'mentoring' have recently emerged in the counselling vocabulary. Here I am using the concept in relation to the immediate post-qualifying period, in the sense of an experienced driver accompanying a driver who has just passed their test, and wants for a little while to use a green 'L' plate. The role of mentor also now appears as a formal requirement in the BACP re-accreditation procedure (see Chapter 9).

Kim Pearl, who works both as a supervisor and a therapist with students during the final stages of their training, through qualifying and beyond, remembers her own post-qualification experience of disappointment and abandonment, and decided to undertake a small piece of research on this theme. She found that some of the responses seemed to mirror her experience:

> I wasn't prepared for the lost empty loneliness . . . that I experienced. I believed I would feel amazing about having accomplished so much, but that got lost somewhere.

> I felt a big loss and isolation following qualification—I would have welcomed a support network of other peers for learning and, maybe, further development of self.

> I still do not see myself as qualified. My training provided a grounding and a focus for me; the rest of the training is up to me. I was quite frightened when I first left the course; since then I have jointly set up a person-centred counsellors' support group with two other ex-course members.

> I felt incredibly alone at the end of the course and after numerous attempts to get the group together—felt as though I was out there totally alone thinking, I'm qualified, what the hell do I do?

She writes, 'Talking to recently qualified counsellors, many identified with the idea that it felt as if, having conquered this huge mountain of learning, they were suddenly dangling over the edge of a cliff and beneath them lurked dragons of fear and chasms of loneliness' (Pearl, K., unpublished paper, 2000).

It appears that for some counsellors there may be a need for some form of support during the post-qualifying period, which might be different from supervision or personal therapy and that this might be termed mentoring. A colleague, who was a teacher before her counselling training, clarified and named the role I have played in her journey. Our infrequent yet significant contact was happening during that crucial period following the end of her course, which has been described as moving from a position of *unconscious incompetence to unconscious competence*. She writes:

> When I decided you were going to be my mentor I don't know where this thought came from. Is it a term used in counselling? It *was* in education but usually you were allocated a mentor rather than choosing one. The Oxford Dictionary definition is 'an experienced and trusted advisor'. It has helped me to (be able to) write to you to clarify what is going on in my life. If you remember, you were the person I decided to contact when I was lost at the end of my initial training. Perhaps I am greedy needing a counsellor to explore my personal development and hold me in moments of crisis, a supervisor to clarify what is really going on in the counselling process and a mentor who gives me the opportunity of exploring future directions, to share apprehension and excitement.
>
> (Dansey, R., personal letter)

Clearly many people are relieved to reach the end of training, are clear about how they are going to move ahead and would not wish to have a mentor. Certainly I do not think it should be a formal requirement for the newly qualified. But for those who do feel lost and deskilled, it could be that to be able to talk with an experienced colleague of their choice from time to time would give support during a vulnerable period.

Johns (1996: 49) quotes Bridges (1933), who identified three phases of transition. There is an ending, followed by a period of confusion and distress, leading to a new beginning. Johns suggests that this process inevitably means 'a loss of something, letting go of an aspect of life or self that matters, in order to move on to something else . . . So often courses, even those where students have a great deal of control and self-direction, have the effect of deskilling people, especially where a degree of unlearning and of abandoning former perspectives on oneself are necessary' (p. 50). It seems paradoxical that students may attain qualified status just at the moment when they have most fully unlearned old ways, and are in that stage of confusion before reaching a new beginning.

Having decided to find a mentor, who would they be and what might they offer? They would be a senior, experienced, probably freelance colleague, who would be willing to share ideas from their experience on a range of practical and emotional issues. It might be a paid or unpaid arrangement. The mentor would be offering encouragement and colleague support through the initial post-qualification period; a companion during the transition from ex-trainee to new professional. How might this be negotiated? Does it just happen? It may take courage to ask a senior colleague to be available from time to time in this way. Are qualified and experienced practitioners willing to do this, paid or unpaid? They will be supporting their potential competitors. Are they prepared to share their hard-won experience and wisdom?

Another possible model might be for a group of ex-trainees to come together to form a mentoring group for an agreed period, say six months, with an experienced practitioner who would be able to facilitate their emotional and professional journey at this stage. Its purpose would be negotiated, and the work might include discussion of practical and professional issues as well as offering peer support.

There is a wider recognition of the place of mentoring in society at this time, in education, nursing and in schemes where young people are helped to get back into employment and need support from a person further along the road. Perhaps it is a helpful concept to bear in mind in the sphere of counselling and psychotherapy, but *not* as a requirement.

## Living with the dynamics of freelance

How we may meet the challenges of freelance working will depend upon a number of factors: our organisational ability, the emotional skills and stamina we bring to the task, the capacity to make connections, to network, to be patient—and perhaps an element of luck.

Among counsellors and psychotherapists there will be different personality traits. There are those who by nature appear to be organisers or managers or teachers. There are those who are introverts and perhaps loners, and extroverts who may thrive on competition. We may be the oldest or youngest members of our family of origin with all that may mean, or like myself, an only child who was not used to collaborating or competing with siblings. We will have developed our own unique coping strategies for dealing with anxieties, which are likely to have originated in childhood. All these factors may inhibit or enhance our capacity to innovate, to 'build a hearth' and to discover ways of inviting potential clients to come.

I have a feeling that those who live most satisfactorily in the world of freelance are those who have worked through early insecurities, jealousies and resentments possibly in their own therapy, and come to the work with awareness of the inevitable stresses, and therefore with positive energies, not with unconscious unmet emotional needs. It helps to be well rooted.

Brady *et al.* draw attention to the physical, social and emotional isolation, which may be one of the tensions most keenly felt by counsellors:

> Few anticipate the physical isolation that stems from conducting psy-
> chotherapy in the same small room, hour after hour . . . Whereas most
> other professions have a fair degree of social give and take in their work
> settings, psychotherapy affords limited interaction among peers. While
> there is much interpersonal contact with clients, it cannot be compared
> to the mutuality and sharing that can occur between colleagues.
>
> (Brady *et al.*, 1995: 10–11)

As well as an internal dialogue, there are complex dynamics which can exist
between ourselves and our colleagues as we compete for available work. We
may make comparisons and feel jealous or insecure or superior. 'Why did
they ask *her* to become a co-trainer?' 'My supervisee has just talked about
their new client, and it was someone who ended with me about two months
ago.' That can be hard to take! When we are envious of a colleague's
'success', we may get into a cycle of resentment and self-doubt, or we may
gossip about them as a way of boosting our own morale.

We may hold misconceptions and prejudices about counsellors and
psychotherapists who work from different orientations to our own or
whose training appears more or less adequate than our own. Dare we
discuss these issues or do we stay within our own theoretical enclave? How
do we deal with the fact that counselling can in some quarters be seen as
inferior to psychotherapy? This can be reflected in the level of fees which
clients may expect to pay, and yet experienced counsellors will be doing
very similar work. How the various professional bodies distinguish between
counselling and psychotherapy is a matter for ongoing debate, while it
remains to be seen whether this will be clarified or confused by the decision
to rename BAC as the British Association for Counselling and Psychotherapy (BACP) (Annual General Meeting, September 2000).

These are all areas where we may experience anxiety and discomfort, and
I believe that the issues can only be worked through if we begin to name
them. Then we are able to explore the necessary tension of freelance
working, between competition and collaboration. One definition of competition is 'a friendly contest in which people try to do better than their
rivals' and 'the action of endeavouring to gain what another endeavours to
gain at the same time'. To collaborate is 'to work in conjunction with
others, to cooperate' (*Oxford English Dictionary*). How do counsellors
working as freelance balance these two modes of being? It is seldom, if ever,
discussed in the counselling literature.

We collaborate, because when we work alone we need professional support, and often emotional support too. For BACP-registered or accredited
counsellors, supervision is a requirement, and so we are likely to be supervised
by a colleague, and in due course some counsellors go on to supervise other
colleagues. This is inevitable in those parts of the country where there are few
counsellors. Is there sometimes a kind of collusion in this situation, as we try

to pretend that we do not feel jealous about each other's work and income, while perhaps concealing our anxieties about our own practice?

I have found it strangely difficult to find anything in the counselling literature about the theme of competition and collaboration. It was in a collection of women's writing, *Competition—A Feminist Taboo?* (Miner and Longine (eds), 1987) that I eventually found some helpful and relevant material.

Writing about her experience as a freelance proof-reader in the Bay Area of California and comparing it with a previous salaried post, Debra Matsumoto writes, 'I have to hustle to obtain assignments and must prove myself anew with each one. The competition is continual, and the competitiveness within the competition can be destructive' (Matsumoto, 1987: 90). Plain speaking, and yet she has experienced solidarity and networking among her freelance colleagues. Despite acknowledging the existence of petty feelings towards competitors, she suggests that 'the nature of the business strongly requires *ethical networking and cooperative competition* in order for a freelancer to function and continue to work successfully' (my emphasis). There seem to be strong parallels here with the experience of working as a freelance counsellor in Britain. Matsumoto is not afraid to acknowledge aspects of her own competitiveness. She notes that she is discriminating in her networking, and that she is more guarded in passing on information about companies she particularly enjoys working with: 'I feel possessive of certain companies'; and her initial response to a freelancer who is not a friend and is seeking information about a particular company is 'to reveal as little as possible' (p. 90). All this feels familiar; dare we be as open about our own competitive behaviours?

I feel that the implications of her phrase 'ethical networking and cooperative competition' could provide the material for at least one valuable seminar on any counselling training course, if we are to be open to the shadow side of freelance counselling and psychotherapy.

I have used the word 'collusion' earlier. It is a more sinister word—the meaning implies conspiracy, intrigue, machination, and yet it feels appropriate to some of the issues around freelance working. I wonder if part of the illusion we engage in is that we are all nice people who support each other. Yet this is not the reality. There is a secrecy around fees and earnings and a general reluctance to admit to financial worries. We may complain about the apparently ever-growing number of training courses, and yet many of us collude in the system and are glad to be invited to teach on those same courses, and to be therapist or supervisor to trainees.

How do we react to the situations in which low-cost counselling can be offered to clients by agencies, who depend on trained counsellors who are willing to work as volunteers? For some recently qualified counsellors, it seems the only way they may gain the requisite number of hours of supervised practice to be able to apply for accreditation. For others, a period of voluntary work offers opportunities for working on a long-term basis with clients presenting a wide range of issues, thus widening the base of their professional experience. One may say that this benefits both counsellor and client, but it can also be seen as a political matter, for it offers a low-cost way of ensuring that at least some help is available for clients whose needs cannot be adequately met by the NHS. Trained counsellors working as volunteers in agencies may well be holding conflicting feelings; an altruistic desire to give to those who might not otherwise receive the help they need; gratitude for the opportunity to gain wide experience and to receive in return the support of a peer group and free group supervision; the opportunity to gain specialised experience in a specialist agency, e.g. for drug and alcohol misuse, rape crisis or bereavement—and yet anger at not receiving financial recompense for their counselling, when they have already spent so much money, time and effort preparing to do this work. For some there is the frustration of finding that they must still serve an 'apprenticeship' as volunteer counsellors, in order to gain the necessary hours of practice before they can become accredited and begin to establish themselves. However, it can be argued that this period of unpaid counselling should be seen as part of the initial training process, and in fact should be budgeted for from the beginning.

Working in an agency can be viewed as a transition between the training course and readiness to work independently. In fact work with Employee Assistance Programmes, with the NHS, and most salaried posts increasingly require accreditation and two years' work experience. For the counsellor trying to get started, this can seem like a 'catch 22' situation.

There can appear to be a collusive situation, between overstretched mental health staff and general practitioners, who refer patients to 'low-cost counselling centres' and the reality that those same counselling centres depend for their survival upon trained volunteers, and even then, find it increasingly difficult to obtain adequate funding from statutory or voluntary sources to enable them to remain solvent.

## Areas of insecurity

How do established counsellors and psychotherapists feel about the ever-increasing number of counsellors who are emerging from training courses and who threaten their livelihood? And how do newly qualified counsellors handle their jealousy of those who appear to have more than enough work? How far do trainers take notice of these dynamics? And above all, what do we do with frustrations about our often unrecognised role in sustaining the mental health of many people?

There are issues around power. As in every profession, there is a kind of hierarchy. Those who have worked in the field for a long time; those who devise and teach training courses (and sometimes change the goalposts!);

those who write books, who sit on committees, give public lectures; those who have higher qualifications than we do. We may ask ourselves 'Where am I in the pecking order when all I do is solid, responsible work with clients?' or perhaps 'Am I afraid to put myself forward?' I know from many counsellors who are just starting out what a huge step it can be even to have business cards printed with name, address and qualifications. Counselling is such a private activity, yet whether we like it or not we are increasingly in the public arena.

There are other disquieting areas. How honest am I willing to be about uncomfortable or embarrassing professional issues when I meet with colleagues in supervision and as co-learners in workshops and training groups? Where do I place my fears and angers about financial insecurities? Clearly these must not be shown to the client, and I may not wish to show them to colleagues either. Am I willing to acknowledge my areas of vulnerability and ask for help? And perhaps the most difficult area of all, what do I do when I hear about seemingly unethical practices by a colleague?

In their research paper, 'The supervisory relationship', Webb and Wheeler (1998) quote Salzberger et al. (1983), who suggested that 'sibling rivalry between peers in a learning situation may make it more difficult to admit to one's failings when approval is being competed for'. Qualified counsellors were more likely to discuss sensitive issues when their supervisor was not a senior work colleague, and trust was likely to be greatest when they were able to choose their own supervisor. It was also found that supervisees were less likely to disclose in a group than in individual supervision. For both trainees and experienced counsellors, supervision is seen as a crucial learning experience. When we add the dimension of competition for clients to the possible sibling rivalry in the supervisory relationship, we can see areas where collusion may exist (see Chapter 5).

David Whyte (1997: 25) suggests that 'the price of our vitality is the sum of all our fears' and that as our illusions of immunity and safety are shattered, we can discover that 'we do have a place in the world, but that it is constantly shape-shifting, like the weather and the seasons, into something at once new and beautiful, tantalising and terrible'. These words, for me, describe the risks inherent in our work as therapists. For as well as developing our professional competence, the journey is deeply personal, and the challenges offered by both our clients and society can indeed touch and shake our illusion of safety. Poets sometimes use powerful, accurate language which meets me as an expression of profound empathy and helps me to live with my vulnerability and insecurity as a counsellor with vitality and trust.

## Challenge and change

We, as well as our clients, mirror the insecurities of the times. Political and social structures shape-shift. Violence, wars and the threat of irreversible climate change touch us all. I believe that if I am to be of real help, I must acknowledge these global fears and uncertainties as well as my personal anxieties, and try to hold them in some frame of balance. Particularly for those of us who live and work alone, this can be difficult sometimes. Yet maybe I can use it all as a resource for the journey alongside those who have lost their own spark of hope. And perhaps I can decide to become part of a peer group, such as Psychotherapists and Counsellors for Social Responsibility, where we can agree to discuss the social and political implications of our work.

The challenges are many. How may we create ways in which, as individual freelance practitioners, we can be ethically accountable, give and receive personal and professional support, appreciate our ideological differences, be part of the 'political world' and have a voice in it? Can we develop a positive relationship with the statutory mental health services? How can we maintain a space of creativity in the sphere of the personal, the professional, the political? How can we care for ourselves?

In a world of constant, sometimes turbulent change, we and our clients are involved at many levels, as also are our professional bodies and training institutions. While I would expect that our personal philosophy as therapists would be one of growth, development and self-renewal, involving body, mind, emotions and spirit, it is equally important that institutions concerned with counselling and psychotherapy are willing to look at their processes of change in similar terms as they seek to ally themselves with other caring professions.

We live in a measurement-oriented world where outcomes and throughputs and cost-effectiveness are inevitably becoming part of our experience and our thinking. As organisations like BACP grow in complexity, inevitably they take procedures and concepts from business. But we must not neglect the shadow. David Whyte suggests that 'The corporation needs the poet's insight and powers of attention in order to weave the inner world of soul and creativity with the outer world of form and matter' (Whyte, 1997: 8).

Edwards and Sen (1999) explore the inseparable link between personal or inner change and social or outer change. They remind us that all social systems—and counselling is a social system—rest on three bases, rather like a three-legged stool, and each base needs to be understood and taken into account (and hopefully held in balance) when we are creating processes of change. The first base is the accepted set of principles which form a basis of ethics and values (our codes of practice and ethics); the second is the institutional base which undergirds the system, the professional bodies like AHPP, BACP, BPS, UKCP, who carry out various tasks and procedures for a growing membership; and the third base, the third leg of the stool, is about the individual, 'the subjective states which constitute our inner being—our personal feelings and intuitions in the deepest sense' (Edwards and Sen, 1999: 2).

The first two bases describe how we understand and rationalise the workings of the social order, while the third describes how we understand ourselves. The interaction of these three will determine the different ways in which power is exercised. In the social system, which is counselling, too great an emphasis on counsellors' personal freedoms may create unsafety for our clients; too great an emphasis on regulation and codes may threaten the creative environment in which counsellors and psychotherapists seek to work. Too much power in the hands of institutions, and they may lose touch with what the day-to-day life and work of freelance counsellors may bring, in terms both of stress and of learning. In times of social change we need to be aware of the relationship between our value systems, institutional processes and subjective states. To integrate these is an exercise in rebalancing, not the wholesale replacement of one set of procedures by another.

Edwards and Sen suggest that to create social change requires 'compassion, and tenderness of heart and toughness of mind, courage and flexibility'—all of which are qualities we may need in our work as therapists. And their paper ends with these words: 'the willingness to confront the shadow of the Self is the secret of all sustainable progress' (Edwards and Sen, 1999: 13).

For many counsellors and psychotherapists, 'The therapeutic relationship is the agony and the ecstasy of our work' and within it 'there are fleeting moments of realisation that we have genuinely assisted a fellow human being' (Brady et al., 1995: 15–16). These are the times when the insecurities of working freelance are set aside for a while, but they may still be lurking in the shadows.

Gilchrist writes:

> The fear is real, as although I did well last year and this year seems OK, how do I know next year will be the same? The truth is, I don't. None of us in private practice do, whether we are just beginning or have been working for ten years. At some level I enjoy the uncertainty and it stimulates me, suits me.
>
> (Gilchrist, A., personal communication, 1999)

I have suggested that if we can acknowledge and express the competition, collaboration and collusion, which we experience in working freelance, we may begin to face 'the shadow of the self' and release energies which are held there. What can help us to hold the paradox in a healthy and creative way? I have some suggestions:

- To develop and sustain a sound ethical base for our practice.
- To be aware of our own needs and ensure these are met, so that we do not fall into neediness and lose a sense of balance.

- To name the tensions held within collaboration and competition, and to speak about them with our peers, for to name the paradox is to bring energy out of the shadows.
- To be aware of the dynamics of social change and to be able to live in and with its processes.
- To find our 'political' voice so that the imbalances and dilemmas of freelance may be spoken about, heard and respected.
- To see with a poet's eye and find metaphors which express our unique personal experience of working freelance. For several years my metaphor was aquaplaning, keeping my balance as I moved, sometimes quite fast over deep water. Now I feel more like a sturdy wooden fishing boat, which has voyaged both in rough seas and calm waters and is good for a while yet!

Perhaps it is only in metaphor that some of us can find that place where we may 'weave the inner world of soul and creativity with the outer world of form and matter' as we face the challenges and freedoms of working as a freelance.

## References

Brady, J. L., Healy, F. C., Norcross, J. C. and Guy, J. D. (1995) Stress in counsellors: an integrative research review. In W. Dryden (ed.), *The Stresses of Counselling in Action*. London: Sage.

Edwards, M. and Sen, G. (1999) NGOs, social change and the transformation of human relationships: a 21st century civic agenda. Paper for the 3rd International NGO Conference on 'NGOs in a Global Future'. University of Birmingham, UK, 10–13 January 1999.

Goleman, D. (1998) *Working with Emotional Intelligence*. London: Bloomsbury.

Johns, H. (1996) *Personal Development in Counsellor Training*. London: Cassell.

Matsumoto, D. A. (1987) One young woman in publishing. In V. Miner and H. Longino (eds), *Competition—A Feminist Taboo?* New York: Feminist Press.

Miner, V. and Longine, H. (eds) (1987) *Competition—A Feminist Taboo?* New York: Feminist Press.

Webb, A. and Wheeler, S. (1998) The supervisory relationship. *British Journal of Guidance and Counselling*, 26(4): 516–517.

Whyte, D. (1997) *The Heart Aroused—Poetry and the Preservation of the Soul at Work*. London: The Industrial Society.

# Part II

# Setting up as freelance

This section explores the practicalities of beginning to work freelance in ways which are ethically sound. There are important choices to be made initially, about where to work, how to find clients, setting up a small business, supervision, accreditation and registration, matters concerning money. The chapters in this section explore these choices from a number of different perspectives: practical, emotional, ethical, professional.

Training courses vary widely in the ways they prepare students for what can be a period of confusion, anxiety and financial hardship once the course has ended and the reality of working independently has to be faced. Supervision provides a necessary ethical framework. Professional bodies including the British Association for Counselling and Psychotherapy, the Association of Humanistic Psychology Practitioners, the United Kingdom Council for Psychotherapy and the British Psychological Society have criteria for accreditation and registration and also offer support and information, and opportunities for further professional training among their members. The Independent Practitioners Network provides peer support and challenge.

Some of the issues discussed in this section may provide material for training and post-training seminars, particularly the chapter on financial dynamics in freelance therapy. The contract between counsellor and client inevitably involves the matter of fees, yet it can be an uncomfortable area for those setting up as freelance.

# Chapter 3

# Starting in private practice

*Colin Feltham*

In what follows, I attempt to raise issues for consideration when starting as a freelance, independent or private practitioner (I mainly use this latter term); these are based on my own and others' experiences and are intended to be of interest and possible usefulness but they do not in any sense constitute a comprehensive recipe for 'how to start in private practice'. Since I am not now primarily a counsellor who relies on private practice for a livelihood, my writing this chapter requires some explanation. Currently, I am a full-time university lecturer with a very small private practice in counselling and supervision, which keeps me in touch with the essence of counselling. But I have had an ongoing private practice of varying size for about 15 years, I am aware of many of the problems involved and have written a little about them (Feltham, 1993, 1995). I am also frequently confronted with the problems involved, by trainees seeking advice and clarity about private practice. Indeed, increasingly trainees and those newly qualified rightly complain that training courses typically do not include sufficient (if any) material on these bread-and-butter issues. Also, from time to time, I reconsider my position and wonder about the feasibility of undertaking a greater amount of private practice work. I will first say a little about my own experiences before going on to discuss some of the practical, financial and psychological issues facing all who contemplate private practice.

The factors that drove me into a private practice were as follows. I found it very hard to get employment as a counsellor, having gained my diploma in 1981. (The difficulty of finding employment is still just as much the case for newly qualified counsellors, as I write, in 2001.) I worked in a probation hostel for several years, doing some counselling alongside a variety of other tasks. I changed to a job in a mental health agency where I was promised a role in setting up a counselling service. Although that role eventually transpired, it was still only a minor part of my work. I was frustrated with organisations. At about this same time, we (my family) moved house and I had a room available for counselling. I also had two small children and we needed any extra income I could get. Within a couple of years I left my job and became entirely self-employed. In retrospect, this was a mistake. Although I started with a large contract for counselling-related work (gained via networking and chance), after a year this was gone, and money became an acute problem. Later, I picked up some more lucrative work and made a decent living, although never primarily from individual fee-paying clients. But I hated the insecurity of this way of life and, too, the loneliness, and jumped into academia (about which I had utterly incorrect fantasies; but that's another story for another book!). It should be noted that the insecurities of livelihood in this field can be traced back at least to Freud himself and his own economic agonising before starting to practise privately in 1886 (very soon after he was married) and later at Berggasse 19, Vienna, in 1891.

## Practical issues

Different views exist on the earliest suitable time to begin in private practice; these are evident elsewhere in this book (Chapter 1). For the most part, I advise trainees not to commence practising independently until well after the end of their training. This is simply because I believe that a grounding in counselling in an organisational context gives most practitioners the necessary background, integrity and confidence. However, I am personally persuaded that many mature trainees with backgrounds in other professions are probably well able to undertake private practice from the later stages of their training.

The most concrete aspect of private practice concerns premises. Do you have a suitable room in which to practise? I have twice used attic rooms in my house and I would not choose to repeat this, since it necessitates providing access through the rest of your house. Often this will involve stressful or tedious checks on general tidiness of thoroughfare areas, closing doors and trying to ensure that other inhabitants of the house are not wandering semi-clad (or not at all!) to the bathroom at just the crucial moment, that children or pets are not lining the route, that guests are not entering or leaving the house at just the wrong, coincidental moment that clients arrive and so on. There are many variables on what can go wrong domestically, and I do not wish to labour the point. No doubt some practitioners prefer a reasonably naturalistic approach to all this, while others will want to guard all boundaries and their possible breaches (see also Chapters 8 and 13).

The question of suitable premises is also tellingly about the house itself and its location. I remain convinced that most clients are more impressed, reassured or contained by smart, middle-class houses in quiet, middle-class neighbourhoods than by houses in neighbourhoods that are poor, dense and noisy. The ideal, arguably, is a detached or semi-detached house with a separate entrance. Think twice if you live on a noisy and/or densely populated and/or obviously working-class housing estate. I state this baldly both because I have had this scenario put to me by a client who was clearly repelled by it, and also in order to raise the issue of class and appearance. Counselling is now regarded as a professional activity in a way that clairvoyance, for example, is not. Very few people would expect to see a professional in a run-down area. (I am *not*, incidentally, saying that working-class neighbourhoods are necessarily run-down!)

But here is an actual personal example: as part of my divorce I was forced to move from a typical middle-class area where professionals live into a slightly 'less desirable', more terraced, less 'professional-class' area. Although I had access to separate basement accommodation for my counselling, I soon became aware of problems of unpredictable noise, neighbour curiosity and aesthetic disadvantages. Fee-paying middle-class clients are unlikely to feel comfortable or confident in such circumstances. Although I have no real evidence for it, I suspect that some of my recent trainees and supervisees benefit from the simple fact of living in smart, middle-class areas and being able to offer reassuringly comfortable counselling rooms whose furnishings reflect clients' own backgrounds. This example may also serve to remind readers that the life of the counsellor is not necessarily more stable than anyone else's and that living and working arrangements are sometimes susceptible to unexpected or uncontrollable changes. These may include change of address, alteration to telephone numbers and promotional material, and changed financial circumstances.

Consider too how house style, size and so on can affect counselling practice and clients' circumstances. It had not occurred to you before but suddenly in the middle of a session your neighbour starts mowing his lawn and the noise makes counselling almost impossible. Do you negotiate with your neighbour, or move your counselling to another room in the house, or move house? Another example: you have a modest house with no space for a waiting room, no porch, etc. Just as your client is leaving, she realises it is pouring with rain, and she asks if she can phone for a taxi. You could tell her that she can't or let her, but then she has to wait somewhere for the taxi: but where? These are, in a sense, trivial but real examples. But beneath the triviality are serious questions about the counsellor's philosophy and politics: is counselling/therapy primarily a 'boundaried' professional activity or a friendly, humanitarian undertaking? Can these be combined, or not?

An alternative to this home-based working scenario is, of course, to rent accommodation elsewhere, with or without other practitioners. It is often possible to rent a room by the hour or half-day, with or without services such as a receptionist. I know of a few successful such arrangements but I am also aware of these kinds of arrangements proving costly and often folding up. Making the transition into any kind of substantial practice based outside the home requires careful thought and financial planning. In some cases, counsellors have found it possible to buy into existing practices, although this of course entails a certain financial outlay, and therefore risk.

If you have a suitable room and an income independent of your proposed private practice (a job, a pension, a partner's generous income, etc.), and presumably if you have already trained, there is nothing to prevent you from simply putting word about that you are available for clients. A good deal of work comes from word-of-mouth contacts. So, a room, a mechanism for getting clients, a telephone (and preferably, if not essentially, an answerphone)—these are the most basic and among the cheapest elements of the enterprise.

## Storage of confidential papers and records

Working independently means that the practitioner is solely responsible for all matters concerning confidentiality, a prime case being the safe storage of records and notes. Readers should refer to appropriate texts for details of the law relating to records, data protection, etc. (Jenkins, 1997). Physical safe-keeping of all written records is, however, quite crucial in several ways. The practitioner should have a lockable cabinet to which access is available only to themselves, and possibly a named person able to take over in the event of the practitioner's death. No family or household members should be able to find keys; nor should they be able to find or stumble on computerised records. This applies to the possibilities of discovery of records accidentally or otherwise. Additionally, all records of clients should be stored in such a way that even in the unfortunate event that they might be discovered by third parties (for example, by a burglar or intruder), no identifying details would be available; this can be achieved by keeping separate coded notes and identifying details. Independent group practices obviously need to give careful thought to the complex variables of how these matters are handled, always bearing in mind the necessity to guarantee confidentiality. Further pointers may be found in the relevant sections of Feltham and Horton (2000).

## Financial and business issues

Alongside these arrangements, the next most significant considerations are financial, including possibly a business plan, registering yourself for tax and national insurance purposes, and remembering that you need to plan for sickness, holidays and pension arrangements. These are well covered in Syme (1994) and Thistle (1998) and I do not propose to go into them here, except to stress that working in private practice is a small business requiring related skills. Since it is known that many therapists dislike these business aspects (which include invoicing, bookkeeping, and possibly even debt recovery), sometimes intensely, it is important for practitioners to consider in advance whether they can handle such matters or at least engage book-keepers or accountants who can. Related business and professional issues may include expenditure on stationery, an additional telephone line, adver-tising, supervision, professional body membership fees, insurance, personal therapy, any continuing professional development (e.g. workshops, con-ferences, journals and books) and so on. Costs can be considerable. I was recently shocked to receive an invoice for annual membership fees of £113 and an invitation to advertise my services in a professional directory for £43—money that I simply had not been able to put aside; in themselves modest sums, perhaps, but add to them the annual costs of all the above professional needs, and see how these mount up.

What I am attempting to convey here is that the financial aspects of counselling or therapy in private practice are much like those relating to running a small hairdresser's salon or any other commercial concern. A 'business brain' is needed. Now, I believe that many of us are attracted to counselling because we value individual autonomy, spontaneity, creativity and so on (perhaps even simple *kindness*—that threatened and almost unfashionable quality) and we may have more than an iota of the anarchist in our make-up. Many practitioners certainly wish to offer a sliding scale or even a proportion of free counselling places or sessions as part of their political or moral aspiration towards subverting the power and position of money in our society. This raises the interesting question of whether clients benefit more from therapy that they pay for. Some counsellors and ther-apists believe that payment enhances clients' motivation; some appear to believe that charging very high fees (I have heard of high fees of £60 to over £100 an hour, mainly in London) may enhance clients' motivation, or at least boost the placebo effect. In any case, anyone embarking on private practice must consider their own views on the practicalities of finance, which are in turn inextricably related to politics. Most counsellors appear to be moderates and 'realists' here, realising that neither the anarchist nor the conscienceless entrepreneurial modes are to their taste.

In this domain lie also the matters of work and income balance. Since it is usually impossible to make a full-time living from seeing individual clients, most realistic practitioners build a portfolio business or career. This may include a few regular, weekly clients, perhaps a more sporadic pattern of seeing supervisees and short-term EAP clients, teaching or training commitments, running a 'quit smoking' group, and perhaps even something completely unrelated to counselling and therapy. The challenge here is to examine how these fit together. Sometimes money is lost in travelling from one commitment to another; sometimes a commitment to one or two long-term clients inhibits the opportunity of taking on a more lucrative contract that arises unexpectedly. A carefully planned week or even annual schedule is undoubtedly more sensible than living hopefully from week to week.

Not all counsellors and therapists will want to be tied into the kinds of tight schedules that may be the very pressures they were trying to leave behind them.

I end this section with a brief look at a topic that may in fact be the most commonly expressed by trainees: how can I possibly take money from people for counselling them? This usually isn't heard from anyone who has been self-employed before. It is often heard from those whose main or only experience has been counselling in the voluntary sector or counselling as part of paid employment. There are two basic ways of answering such a question. The first is to assert that counselling is a valuable service like any other, that the counsellor is a trained professional supplying a desired and needed service and that she or he needs to value herself or himself, understand that time is money, and so on (see Chapter 6).

The other answer, which is usually quickly dismissed, is that perhaps it *is* very odd and somehow unjustified or distasteful to accept payment for counselling; that such a transaction is like prostitution. The scarcity of objective, non-exploitative and skilful, healing listening and responding in our society means that people are often willing to pay for this, or have no alternative but to pay, but this in itself is not a robust defence of private practice. Of course, we can and do desensitise ourselves to these objections, otherwise we would earn little or no money. But the fundamental dilemma remains. It is, in fact, one faced by many feminist therapists who acknowledge societal causes of women's collective distress but feel that they cannot simply refuse to offer individual help to those who are suffering acutely now; and it takes time and resources to be able to provide therapeutic help: inevitably someone must pay. Some feminist therapists claim that all institutionalised therapies fail women and that radical feminist therapies must be offered outside of mainstream structures (McLellan, 1999). These are thorny questions and the answers may not be in the form of an 'either–or'. For many practitioners, the 'answer' is involvement in a range of activities: individual counselling, group work, training, voluntary activity, political activity, co-counselling, etc. But still it has to be experienced: in private practice you will sometimes take directly from the client, perhaps at the end of a harrowingly emotional session or of a rather uneventful, unsatisfactory, session, cash or a cheque. It can feel strange and indecent; perhaps it *is* strange, this 'purchase of friendship'.

## Psychological issues

By psychological issues I mean the following. First, it has to be said that counselling and psychotherapy are *not* well-established, flourishing professions (compared, say, with medicine, law or even clinical psychology) and do not offer guaranteed employment or self-employment opportunities. In this sense, all potential trainees should consider seriously the precarious occupational position of the field before training. The kind of person with a psychological need for high levels of certainty and security should not enter the field at all. Secondly, anyone coming towards the end of training should weigh up carefully the pros and cons of employment versus self-employment. Private practice does maximise autonomy, if that is your psychological–occupational priority, but it also entails economic anxiety, physical isolation and a great deal of intensive, emotionally charged one-to-one work. Private practice in particular is lonely, with usually no direct colleagues to consult or to socialise with. (Supervision and peer support can of course offset this to some extent.) To some, it may be clear that this is not how they wish to spend most of their working time. Others may not foresee the potential problems of isolation. Combined with worry about income, the isolation and all the attendant stresses of private practice can add up to serious challenges that should be anticipated (Feltham, 1995).

A third kind of (subtler) psychological issue concerns the practitioner who is strongly attracted to private practice, who likes working alone, likes relating intensively with one other individual at a time, and perhaps enjoys unrecognised and unhealthy power and status from being in this position. Since there is no one to assess the suitability of qualified counsellors or psychotherapists to become private practitioners (as opposed to agency-employed and overseen workers), the scope is large for unintended or intended abuse of such a position. Although some training institutes have a significant say in who graduates, maintains an association with and receives referrals from them, and supervision offers some degree of protection (see Chapter 5), there is no really effective mechanism for detailed monitoring of the practice of sole practitioners. You can usually choose your supervisor, and choose which cases you present in supervision. No one can have a close ongoing view of all the work you do (Feltham, 1999a). Since it pays in private practice to maintain long-term clients, there must be a huge tempta-tion to do just that; in other words, to take on clients who seek long-term, possibly quite dependent relationships. Just a few private clients who come reliably for many months or years, possibly for one, two, three or even more sessions each week, are better for income purposes than many clients who come on a short-term or sporadic basis. For the practitioner who particu-larly likes such intimate and lengthy therapeutic relationships, the attrac-tions of guaranteed income may fuse with the psychological intensity so that it becomes hard to know whether the best interests of the client are actually being served. (See Sands, 2000, for a client's eye view of this kind of dynamic, and Mann, 1999, for a consideration of pertinent erotic nuances and potential traps and dangers.) It behoves the therapist or counsellor to strive for great honesty and self-awareness in such a scenario. But ultimately, where personal satisfaction meshes with the prospect of high or secure incomes, and oversight and accountability are low, risks must run high for consumers.

A fourth related issue, already raised but requiring emphasis, is the need for a critical quantity of entrepreneurial components in one's psychological make-up. This means that practitioners who seriously intend to 'make it' as freelance therapists or counsellors must believe in themselves and sell themselves. I am quite sure from my position as tutor, trainer, supervisor and observer of the field that those who make it are *not* necessarily more effective practitioners than others. I have seen some very able, competent counsellors fail to build or expand practices because in spite of their (in some cases) excellence as practitioners, they do not have the necessary belief and self-promotional flare, chutzpah (cheek, temerity, brazenness, effrontery, brass neck—as the thesaurus helpfully explains) and/or the business connections they need. Conversely, I suspect that some of those who make it 'big time' or 'do very nicely' are not necessarily, by that token, the most effective or sensitive practitioners. (There are no studies of these phenomena, as far as I am aware, and little research attempts to identify individually better practitioners, anyway.)

Ideally, this is an area in which collaboration between the more entrepreneurially and the more clinically oriented will pay off, yet the ratio of clients seeking counsellors appears to have reversed since about 20 years ago, so that counsellors and trainee counsellors are now more often 'chasing' and competing for clients and placements than collaborating. The exception to this may be small, collaborative group practices that have existed for many years in a specific geographical area, are well known and have cultivated a reputation for reliability and excellence. Such practices often demand high levels of group cohesion, attained for example through regular business and clinical meetings. Collaborative networking may also pay off but probably has similarities to family dynamics: the benefits of kinship and mutual aid exist in tension with Oedipal conflicts and sibling rivalry.

A fifth kind of psychological issue, of particular relevance to those starting a home-based private practice for the first time, concerns feelings about strangers entering the home, and the home becoming merged with the workplace. Although it is possible to try to attract mainly 'known quantities' (i.e. referrals via friends and colleagues), anyone working privately also runs the risk of seeing as clients people who are quite unknown. If we accept that there is no such thing as watertight assessment, it seems probable that from time to time anyone will encounter and find themselves working with a client who is experienced as hard to like, or worrying, or difficult (Norton and McGauley, 1998). In principle it is possible and sometimes advisable to screen and if necessary exclude such clients, especially from a home-based private practice; especially perhaps one in which a woman lives as the only adult. (Many female counsellors are somewhat wary of counselling male clients in these circumstances, for example.) But in reality, occasionally you may have a difficult, perhaps even dangerous client. I have certainly known of a few cases of clients harassing their counsellor with late-night telephone calls, silent calls and other nuisance activities. To some extent these eventualities may be anticipated and forestalled, but 100% safety and comfort cannot be guaranteed and one must be psychologically robust enough to live with this uncertainty, and assertive and quick-thinking enough to deal with any emergencies.

Home-based practice also means that clients may have to use your bathroom, may incidentally meet your children, and so on (Chapters 8 and 13). It also means that the temptation to work all available hours can be hard to resist (for example, seeing early-morning, late-evening or weekend clients), often compounded by the facts of having to maximise income. The need for holidays, for example, can be too easily overlooked or denied (McMahon, 2000).

Finally, it is worth considering how fundamentally psychological disposition will affect all aspects of practice. Home-based sole practitioners have a huge amount of discretion in how they work, from furnishings to appointment variations, use of innovative techniques, session length and frequency, fee setting, choice of supervisor, even choice of professional or collegial body (e.g. BACP, Independent Practitioners' Network). Inevitably there will be a wide variation in details of practice, such as degrees of formality and informality, risk taking, liberal interpretation of ethical codes, etc. It is possible that more independently minded, creative counsellors and therapists will be drawn to freelance practice as part of their healthy exercise of the therapeutic use of self (Wosket, 1999). A possible shadow side of this autonomy is a rebellious, non-conformist, loner or guru mentality that shuns all or most collaboration. Although this point has been raised above, another twist to it is relevant here. This is that individual practices will reflect, perhaps quite critically, practitioners' personalities, for better and for worse, and in ways that can be only partly tempered by professional bodies' norms, such as those mediated by mandatory supervision. Some clients will experience very tight boundaries, for example, while others may experience very liberal boundaries (see Feltham, 1999b: 124–141). Consumers who are newcomers to counselling or psychotherapy cannot ultimately know quite what to expect and are exposed to a certain amount of pot luck.

## Conclusion

I think there are broadly two ways of conceiving private practice politically, economically and clinically: (1) as a liberating exercise for practitioners and clients alike, maximising autonomy and the freely chosen collaboration of individuals towards deep personal learning and transformation; and (2) as a conservative, adaptational and expedient exercise, making and defending one's living by participating in the climate, beliefs and myths of evidence-based practice (Clement, 1999). Broadly, those practitioners espousing cognitively oriented, symptom-removal models and practices are likely to be more attracted and attractive to NHS and EAP employment settings (see Chapters 11 and 12), while those favouring the radically humanistic, person and society-changing agendas will primarily practise privately as individuals and collectives. Anyone starting in private practice with the latter orientation is challenged to devise new forms of publicity, networking, rationale and practice. Many articles, books and workshops have been appearing on just these subjects in the USA for years, including those by clinical social workers seeking better pay and freedom from agencies (Linsley, 1996) and those commending the use of new techology as part of private practice (Binner, 1987). Indeed there is mounting evidence that Internet forms of therapy may be *the* big new market niche. Technologically mediated forms of therapy lend themselves naturally to home-based private practices and may fuel an increase in freelance work to compensate for the relative decline in long-term face-to-face therapy.

I suspect that there are clear (but very under-researched) links between the initial itch that starts anyone thinking about entering counselling or therapy and/or training, and eventual entry into private practice. Trainees are frequently attempting to escape from unsatisfactory, dehumanising jobs and/or to revitalise an overly domesticated (dull) life and/or to rediscover some richer meaning in everyday life and engagement with others. Private practice does essentially offer I–thou contact between free individuals beyond the constraints of the known and the oppressive (often ritualised family and occupational life). Whether those new to private practice can maintain their original motivation and integrity, or somehow create an authentic blend of profound interpersonal enquiry and commercial survival, remains an unanswered question. Some practitioners believe they have found an answer; for example, I know a few positive-thinking individuals who have knitted together a business bricolage of traditional therapy, neurolinguistic programming (NLP), solution-focused techniques, motivational workshop ideas and glossy promotional material into financially successful packages that they feel morally at peace with. They might see themselves as belonging in my category 1 above, as liberators. Readers must evaluate their own reactions to all such views and associated practices.

As an example of some of the dilemmas mentioned here, consider finally the case of Milton Erickson, the therapist who pioneered clinical hypnosis and helped spawn many strategic, systemic and brief approaches to therapy (Zeig and Munion, 1999). In 1949, at the age of 48, Erickson decided to move from his hospital-based position in Phoenix, Arizona, for occupational, health and financial reasons. For 21 years he then practised individual, couple and family therapy in an 'unprepossessing' room of 10 feet by 10 feet at the back of his family house. His family living room also served as a waiting room, in which clients would sit with his family and pets, and might sometimes be offered sandwiches. Since he suffered from polio, involving chronic pain, and was eventually confined to a wheelchair, much of this is understandable on health grounds. Yet Erickson was also very unorthodox in his methods, scheduling and fee arrangements, sometimes charging nothing or accepting bartered services instead of money. In spite of the brevity of most of his contacts with clients, he survived and prospered, in part by also teaching seminars from home. It seems that his success stemmed largely from his unique talent, dedication to clients and intrinsic interest in the work. He was, of course, exceptionally gifted and effective. He was certainly already very skilled and quite well known before entering private practice, and it may be that one cannot generalise from his example. But we can perhaps consider and compare our contemporary drift towards standardised, arguably low risk-taking and mediocre practice with his kind of inspired practice. I have seen the homes and practice settings of many practitioners, a few of them quite eccentric or domestically explicit, not at all the 'desirable', neutral, professional presentation that is often recommended. Who is to say who is delivering the most client-friendly, ethical and effective form of help to those who come to see them? Who is to say who will succeed, triumph over the undoubted obstacles, and who will fail in private practice? In this sense, starting in private practice must be regarded as something to be risked, tried out and tasted (without burning all bridges) in order to determine its congeniality and viability.

---

**Box 1: Questions facing those considering starting a private/independent practice**

1   Am I sufficiently well trained, and appropriately experienced, to commence private practice?
2   Do I have the necessary resources (premises, equipment, mechanisms, capital, etc.)?
3   Do I have the psychological temperament to be a lone practitioner?
4   Do I have the business mentality and skills to start and maintain a private practice?
5   Can I square my politics and/or moral temperament with the economics and implications of private practice?
6   What do I stand to lose or gain by commencing in private practice?
7   Am I going to do it, and if so when, how, etc.?
8   Exactly what are my (overt and covert) reasons for wanting to do it?
9   Who are my allies, my market and my competitors?

## References

Binner, P. R. (1987) Computers in clinical practice: the changing locus of the leading edge. *Psychotherapy in Private Practice*, 5(2): 115–122.

Clement, P. W. (1999) *How to Evaluate, Improve, and Market your Psychotherapy Practice by Measuring Outcomes*. New York: Guilford.

Feltham, C. (1993) Making a living as a counsellor. In W. Dryden (ed.), *Questions and Answers on Counselling in Action*. London: Sage.

Feltham, C. (1995) The stresses of counselling in private practice. In W. Dryden (ed.), *The Stresses of Counselling in Action*. London: Sage.

Feltham, C. (1999a) Counselling supervision: baselines, problems and possibilities. In B. Lawton and C. Feltham (eds), *Taking Supervision Forward: Enquiries and Trends in Counselling and Psychotherapy*. London: Sage.

Feltham, C. (ed.) (1999b) *Controversies in Psychotherapy and Counselling*. London: Sage.

Feltham, C. and Horton, I. (eds) (2000) *Handbook of Counselling and Psychotherapy*. London: Sage.

Jenkins, P. (1997) *Counselling, Psychotherapy and the Law*. London: Sage.

Linsley, J. (1996) The business of starting a private practice. *The New Social Worker*, 3(2). Accessed at http://www.socialworker.com/privprac.htm, June 2000.

Mann, D. (1999) *Erotic Transference and Countertransference*. London: Routledge.

McLellan, B. (1999) The prostitution of psychotherapy: a feminist critique. *British Journal of Guidance and Counselling*, 27(3): 325–337.

McMahon, G. (2000) Holiday cover. *Counselling*, 11(5): 298–299.

Norton, K. and McGauley, G. (1998) *Counselling Difficult Clients*. London: Sage.

Sands, A. (2000) *Falling for Therapy*. London: Macmillan.

Syme, G. (1994) *Counselling in Independent Practice*. Buckingham: Open University Press.

Thistle, R. (1998) *Counselling and Psychotherapy in Private Practice*. London: Sage.

Wosket, V. (1999) *The Therapeutic Use of Self: Counselling Practice, Research and Supervision*. London: Routledge.

Zeig, J. K. and Munion, W. M. (1999) *Milton H. Erickson*. London: Sage.

# Chapter 4

# Regulation, registration and accreditation: some issues

*Ian Horton*

## Introduction

Without some form of statutory regulation it will always be possible for anyone, with or for that matter without any form of training, to call themselves counsellors or psychotherapists and to offer counselling or psychotherapy to others and be paid for doing so. Whether you think this matters or not depends on your point of view. The chapter starts with an overview of some of the issues and then discusses the existing forms of registration and accreditation.

In the UK, support for some form of regulation is by no means unanimous. If you want to make a living as a counsellor or psychotherapist you may see the regulation of who can practise as the ultimate step to full professional recognition and status which will safeguard and enhance career opportunities. Understandably, many practitioners want at least to recoup the often enormous investment of time and money they have put into training and may resent what can seem like unfair competition from others with little or no training or those whose activities and behaviour bring counselling and psychotherapy into disrepute—yet seemingly without any lines of accountability. More altruistically, views about regulation are concerned with client or patient welfare and depend on whether counselling and psychotherapy are seen as having any potential to cause harm, or whether, if not always beneficial, then at least benign. Counselling and psychotherapy may be defined, for example, by the humanistic growth movement, as a form of personal growth and self-development, and the regulation of who can practise may be seen as unnecessary, if not actually detrimental. However, if counselling and psychotherapy are seen as forms of treatment for people who are not dealing effectively with life and who are vulnerable to financial, psychological and sexual exploitation, then regulation to protect clients seems more relevant, although it cannot provide any absolute guarantee of safe and effective practice.

Many counsellors and psychotherapists are ambivalent about the need for regulation, and a few are very strongly opposed to it (Mowbray, 1995;

House and Totton, 1997). Yet despite this, professional bodies, presumably reflecting the views of the majority of practitioners, either accept the inevitability of some form of regulation or welcome it as an important milestone in the evolution of the profession.

In general terms the regulation of who can work as a counsellor or psychotherapist would normally be achieved through the setting up of a register of practitioners who have completed an accredited training and a specified number of hours of supervised clinical practice and who adhere to a particular code of ethics and are subject to the complaints procedure of a professional body. Regulation rhetoric is usually expressed primarily in terms of consumer protection, with any advantages to the practitioner as secondary. Consumer protection is a concept of the 1990s. In an increasingly litigious society people are almost encouraged to complain about poor or inadequate products or services. Alongside this is the growing emphasis on quality assurance and the increasing demands from employers for accountability through annual audits and monitoring of performance standards. Counsellors and psychotherapists are not immune from this trend. The number of complaints against counsellors and psychotherapists has escalated dramatically over the past decade. Most practitioners are well aware of the pressure on them to develop evidence-based practice (Rowland and Goss, 2000) or now more accurately referred to as evidence-informed practice, to account for what they do and why they do it. Accreditation and registration are often seen as integral components of quality assurance and accountability. It could be argued that freelance practitioners may not be as vulnerable or need not be as concerned about these trends as those counsellors and psychotherapists who are directly accountable to their employers or agency managers, but aspiring freelance practitioners may find it almost impossible to get established if they do not have some form of accredited training, and are not demonstrably accountable to a professional body.

This chapter is about the regulation, accreditation and registration of counsellors and psychotherapists. It tries to side-step the ongoing debate about any possible differences between counselling and psychotherapy— and the related claims of superiority and status—by assuming that the activities are essentially the same. The very existence of separate professional bodies continues to feed this debate. Prior to 2000 it meant that clearly separate standards and procedures existed for the accreditation and registration of counsellors, counselling psychologists and psychotherapists. However, since the British Association for Counselling (BAC) incorporated the word 'psychotherapy' into its title in September 2000, the situation is less clear. It seems possible that at some point in the future they will seek also to accredit their psychotherapist members, who can, at least in theory, already apply for accreditation as counsellors and be included on the UK Register of Counsellors. Similarly, the UPA (Universities Psychotherapy Association), which registers its members through the UKCP (United

Kingdom Council for Psychotherapy), has now incorporated the word 'counsellors' into its title, to become the Universities Psychotherapy and Counselling Association (UPCA). UPCA intends to explore the possibility of establishing links with what is now BACP for the accreditation and registration of its counsellor members.

The next part of this chapter outlines the various types of regulation and the implications for practitioners. Many professional bodies, usually representing particular psychotherapy orientations, accredit their members but register them through UKCP, for example the British Association for Behavioural and Cognitive Psychotherapy. The current forms of registration and accreditation provided by three of the main professional bodies only—BACP (formerly BAC), BPS (British Psychological Society) and UKCP—are described here. The components of regulation are identified and a summary of the common arguments for and against regulation are then discussed. Finally, the chapter reflects briefly on the future of regulation for counsellors and psychotherapists. Contact details for BACP, BPS and UKCP are given at the end of the chapter.

## Types of regulation

At the present time there is no statutory regulation of counsellors and psychotherapists in the UK. Anyone can offer counselling or psychotherapy and call themselves counsellors or psychotherapists. However, UKCP (and BPS) are proactive in moving towards some form of statutory regulation. In late 1999, Lord Alderdice, a psychiatrist and psychotherapist, produced detailed proposals for a Private Member's Bill, modelled on that for the regulation of osteopaths, that would provide statutory regulation of psychotherapy. In his statement during the second reading of the Bill (19 January 2001) Lord Burlinson said 'I cannot accept that where counselling is offered by a trained practitioner to the high standards set by the leading professional bodies it is distinguishable from psychotherapy in anything but name'. While this Bill did not go any further, it may have been at least partially instrumental in getting statutory regulation onto the government's agenda.

Burley (2000: 322) provides a very useful explanation of the legislative context for statutory regulation. He states that any regulation of psychotherapy (or counselling) will take place within the framework of the 1999 Health Act, primarily intended to abolish GP fundholding but which includes 'a clause which gives the Secretary of State for Health Order-making powers to repeal, amend and introduce regulatory legislation in any health professional area'. This includes counselling and psychotherapy. At the time, and without any high-profile public scandal, which demonstrated clearly the potential for counselling or psychotherapy to cause harm to clients or patients, it seemed unlikely that the government would take any initiative to regulate the talking therapies. More invasive therapies, even aromatherapy or reflexology, were likely to be higher on the list of activities that might be considered for statutory regulation. However, driven by concern about public protection, the government made it clear that the psychological therapies—including counselling—should be regulated.

UKCP and BAC (now BACP) have already established voluntary registers which provide a type of self-regulation, but with very limited powers to protect clients or patients because the only legal force is through Trading Standards legislation. This is generally regarded as an inadequate form of consumer protection.

In addition to voluntary self-regulation, Burley (1999) identifies five other types of regulation:

- Functional closure by Act of Parliament. This makes it a criminal offence for anyone not registered to practise the activity, irrespective of how they describe themselves or what they do. In the UK this type of regulation is available only to midwives and Burley thinks that it is unlikely to be offered to counsellors or psychotherapists.
- Closure by common title by Act of Parliament. This makes it possible only for registered practitioners to use a common title, e.g. dentist. It is this form of regulation that seems to be favoured by the UKCP (and is implicit in Lord Alderdice's Psychotherapy Bill). It would mean that only registered psychotherapists could call themselves psychotherapists.
- Closure by 'indicative' title by Act of Parliament. This protects the use of an indicative title such as 'registered' or 'chartered' in association with an unprotected title. For example, State Registered Arts Therapists (combining art, music and dramatherapy) obtained state registration in 1997 through an extension to the Act of Professions Supplementary to Medicine (Waller, 1999). However, Burley suggests that this type of regulation may not provide strong enough protection and may be of limited value outside public sector employment in the health field. It would mean, for example, that non-registered counsellors could still call themselves counsellors, albeit not *registered* counsellors, and could still work as counsellors.

  Closure by indicative title is the most likely form of regulation for the psychological therapies and would involve the registration of individuals.
- Chartered status by Royal Charter would confer a protected title, usually 'Chartered' and bye-laws for self-regulation. This option is favoured by the BPS and would enable suitably qualified practitioners to register as Chartered Counselling Psychologists.
- Agreement between employers. Burley defines this as an agreement between employers in a particular occupational sector to abide by a common recruitment standard. He gives ambulance paramedics as an

example. Employers of counsellors and psychotherapists are a wide and very disparate group who in any case may also employ clinical psychologists, counselling psychologists, health psychologists, psychiatric nurses and others to provide some form of psychological or 'talking therapy' for clients or patients.

## Registration and accreditation

UKCP is the largest organisation concerned with the registration of psychotherapists. A 'National Register of Psychotherapists' is published annually, but seems to function largely as a trade directory. UKCP is not a professional association in itself, but more of a trade association or umbrella body that represents the interests of over 70 Member Organisations divided into eight largely autonomous Sections. It is the Sections that function as professional associations, representing the main traditions in the practice of psychotherapy. The registration of individual psychotherapists is possible only after the successful completion of a UKCP accredited training with a Member Organisation. While there are a small number of Member Organisations which may register individuals who have not trained with a Member Organisation of the Council, UKCP registration essentially excludes even those practitioners who may have completed an equivalent or more extensive training elsewhere.

BACP holds currently the legal and financial responsibility for the UKRC (UK Register of Counsellors), although it is proposed that the register will eventually become a subsidary company of BACP. The day-to-day operation of the register is carried out by UKRC staff located in the BACP offices in Rugby. Governance of the UKRC includes lay representatives. The UKRC is a multiple register which includes Registered Independent Counsellors (RICs,) but with separate sections for Registered Sponsoring Organisations (RSOs), which provide counselling services and which can sponsor their counsellors onto the register as Registered Sponsored Counsellors (RSCs)—but only for their work with the UKRC validated organisation—and a section for Registered Occupational Affinity Groups (ROAGs), which can register counsellors who work in a specific occupational field as Occupational Registered Counsellors (ORCs), for example primary health care. The Register of Independent Counsellors (RIC) is the most relevant section of the UKRC to freelance practitioners and entry is through BACP or COSCA (Confederation of Scottish Counsellors Associations) accreditation. However, alternative routes onto the register are open to practitioners with comparable counselling or *psychotherapy* training accredited by other professional bodies, for example UKCP, BPS or the Association of Humanistic Psychology Practitioners (AHPP), which are recognised by UKRC as having equally high standards of training and practice and whose practitioners adhere to the code of ethics of the particular professional body.

Both BACP and UKCP accredited training courses satisfy certain well-established standards and criteria. For example, training organisations are required to publish details of their selection criteria and selection procedures, their code of ethics and appeals and complaints procedures, an equal opportunities statement and full information about the course requirements, course curriculum and assessment scheme. Accredited courses tend to have very similar components. Typically, students or trainees are required to study in depth the theory and practice of a particular model or approach to counselling or psychotherapy and at least be aware of alternative ways of working. They also have to complete a specified number of client hours and related clinical supervision, undertake a minimum number of hours of self-development work including personal counselling or psychotherapy consistent with their core model of training and to complete satisfactorily the assignments that assess their understanding of relevant theory and their competence to practise. Assessed theory and practical course work is subject to external moderation. Psychology remains the core academic discipline for all counselling and psychotherapy training, although sociological perspectives on multicultural or social context issues are often included, especially in some counselling courses. Counsellor training also puts much greater and more explicit emphasis on the acquisition and development of skills and the application of theory to practise.

The length of an accredited training course may vary, but the minimum length of counselling and psychotherapy courses seems broadly comparable, although is described differently. BACP accredited counselling courses are required to provide not less than 450 staff–student contact hours, not including the time spent on such aspects as personal therapy, client hours, private study, assessed course work or tea breaks! The number of years of training is not specified. The length of UKCP accredited courses is defined as not less than three years' part time and the end of course qualification may not necessarily coincide with eligibility for UKCP registration. Similarly, completion of a BACP accredited course seldom coincides with eligibility to apply for individual counsellor accreditation. Practitioners have to complete not less than 450 hours of supervised client work in a period of not less than three years and satisfy other criteria before they can apply for BACP individual counsellor accreditation.

A booklet, *The Recognition of Counsellor Training Courses*, first published by BAC in 1988 and now in its third edition, describes the standards and criteria for all BAC accredited courses, irrespective of theoretical orientation. While UKCP publish some general guidelines for the accreditation of psychotherapy training, there seems to be an enormous variation between the requirements of each Section which produces its own training standards and criteria.

Bond (2000: 218) has produced a comparison of BAC (BACP), BPS and UKCP published professional guidance on a wide range of requirements of training and practice. While the general standards seem relatively comparable, only BAC (BACP) requires 'clarity about the terms of contracting' to be communicated to the client and emphasises the requirement for regular and ongoing clinical supervision, even after qualification and registration.

The latest buzz phrase to impact on the whole field of counselling and psychotherapy is *Continuing Professional Development* or CPD. Until 2000, a BAC accredited counsellor had to make a full reapplication for individual counsellor accreditation every five years, but this has now been replaced by an annual return demonstrating not less than 30 hours of CPD activities (see Chapter 9). Generally, once registered, UKCP psychotherapists seem to need only to pay the annual subscription to their Member Organisation in order to maintain their registered status. However, it seems likely that UKCP will introduce some form of CPD requirement in the future. CPD is already a part of ongoing registration for some UKCP member organisations, for example, BABCP (British Association of Behavioural and Cognitive Psychotherapy), which also requires ongoing supervision, and may include the presentation of audio-taped work and supervisor observation of practice. CPD may also become a requirement for maintaining registration as a Chartered Counselling Psychologist. What is clear is that all forms of registration will, if they do not do so already, require evidence of ongoing personal and professional development. The existing registers for counsellors and psychotherapists are the basis of the current systems of voluntary self-regulation.

## Features of self-regulation

Pyne (1994) argues that there are four major features of professional regulation. The first, and possibly obvious feature, is the existence of a register that can be readily accessed by employers, members of the public or anyone who needs to confirm that a practitioner who claims to be registered is in fact registered. A register provides the reference point for taking action against anyone who makes a false claim to registration. The second feature is about establishing standards of conduct and standards of practice and approving entry criteria and entry routes onto the register, including initial grandparenting which 'protects the position of bona fide but unqualified practitioners on a one-off basis at the opening of the register' (Burley, 2000: 324). If a register is capable of serving its purpose of protecting the public, then Pyne suggests that it must also have the authority and fair, efficient and widely known procedures for removing the names of practitioners who are found to be guilty of professional or ethical malpractice that may put the public at risk. The fourth feature Pyne identifies is the need to inform practitioners of what is expected of them. This is especially important if the regulatory body has, as he puts it, 'the awesome power to remove a person's name from the register and prevent them working at the same level within their chosen profession' (Pyne, 1994: 3). However, it is not only important to inform but also to educate practitioners, some of whom may, quite reasonably, have false expectations of the regulatory body and may not understand the philosophy and purpose of registration, seeing it as protecting and enhancing their own rather than public interests.

## Case for professional registration

The central premise of regulation is that it is the best way of anticipating and preventing major incidents of unethical and unprofessional conduct. The purpose can be summarised as follows:

- To offer protection to the general public and information on reputable practitioners.
- To give both employers and insurers information regarding professionally competent and ethically responsible practitioners.
- To provide a system of accountability and procedures for dealing with malpractice.
- To extend the professional status and recognition for practicioners.
- 'One of the hallmarks of an occupational group seeking to espouse the title "profession" is that it is willing and able to accept the responsibility of regulating itself, not in the profession's interests, but those of the public which the profession exists to serve' (Pyne, 1994: 1).

Pyne's passionate support of professional self-regulation is a view held strongly by very many counsellors and psychotherapists—albeit for a variety of reasons and not all to do with consumer protection. It can be argued that the image and reputation of a profession would be enhanced if it is able to demonstrate that practitioners face rigorous scrutiny before being admitted onto a professional register (Barlow, 1998). Any enhanced professional status is often perceived as increasing work opportunities for those practitioners who become registered.

It is hard to argue that the increasing number of training organisations that are applying for professional body accreditation for their courses are not motivated primarily by market forces and the need to attract trainees or students to maintain economic viability. Why do so many private sector counselling and psychotherapy courses seek university validation, often in addition to professional body accreditation? The answer, at least in part, may be connected with the prevalent climate in education, training and professional practice for better quality assurance and greater accountability at all levels. Registration is part of this too. It seems to be the thing that professions need to do! Burley (2000: 326) concludes that 'No profession in regulation at the moment in any sector is trying to become deregulated, and there has always been a queue of professions outside CPSM's (Council of

Professions Supplementary to Medicine) door wanting regulation . . .'. While seeking regulation because others are doing it is not a valid reason for doing so—and some counsellors and psychotherapists might argue it is a reason for not doing so—nevertheless, for many professions regulation seems to be regarded as imperative.

The case for regulation is strengthened by the fact that in some European countries psychotherapy is regarded as part of psychology and psychiatry. This powerful influence within the European Union, which could effectively sideline psychotherapy in the UK, could be resisted by statutory regulation and, ipso facto, the recognition of psychotherapy as an independent profession in the UK. In many European countries counselling is either not recognised as a form of psychological therapy or is seen as something more akin to guidance and advice giving, so the same argument could apply.

Few practitioners would argue, at least publicly, that they should not be accountable for what they do and why they do it and that they should not be subject to certain standards of conduct and practice; neither would they argue that emotionally vulnerable people should not be protected against abuse and exploitation. This is the *raison d'être* of professional regulation. However, the controversial issues are: what should be included in the code of ethics and can one code apply to all types of counselling and psychotherapy, and most importantly, who should be responsible for enforcing it (Tantum, 1999: 219)?

The implications for practitioners are described, according to Browne (2001), by Sally Aldridge, Head of Accreditation BACP, who said that 'when they bring registration in, it will be individuals who will be registered. It will be registration by title which means that only those who are registered will be able to call themselves counsellors and psychotherapists'.

## Some problems and issues

The principle of professional regulation may be regarded as eminently laudable, but it is not without its problems. Pyne (1994: 1) refers to an 'occupational group seeking to espouse the title of profession', but can counselling and psychotherapy ever be defined as an occupational group? There are many who hold strong, sometimes almost virulent views, but there is absolutely no consensus on the differences between counselling and psychotherapy (Syme, 2000; Thorne, 1999). Indeed, the differences between the various models or approaches to psychotherapy, as illustrated by the eight separate UKCP Sections, seem much greater than any substantive differences between counselling and psychotherapy (Iniss and Bell, 1996). Wheeler (1999) revisits the seemingly perpetual debate in a particularly refreshing and challenging way. She discusses the definition of a profession and points to the competition between professional groups for jurisdiction or legal, social, political and practical influence, over work with different client groups and questions whether counselling (*and psychotherapy*) can be a profession or just part of a disparate and fragmented occupational group. The credibility and acceptance of counselling and psychotherapy may be lost if there is not a unified and coherent understanding by the general public (Palmer Barnes, 1998: 7). All the talking therapies, that is, counselling, psychotherapy and counselling psychology, as one united profession would be in a much better position to apply for statutory regulation, but as Syme (2000) reports, sadly an attempt to set up joint negotiations between BAC, BPS and UKCP failed and remains, at best, a very remote possibility in the foreseeable future.

Setting up and operating a system of regulation costs money, but the only people who have a vested interest in self-regulation are the professional bodies themselves. This causes a problem. It can be argued that the regulatory and professional functions are incompatible. The former seeks to protect the public interest and is intended to safeguard vulnerable clients, while the latter serves the professional interests of the practitioner. Obviously there are degrees of overlap, but where the two functions are contained in one professional body there may be a perceived conflict of interest and the apparent lack of independence may prejudice the credibility and integrity of a professional register. The professional body would be open to accusations of protecting its own rather than the interests of the consumer. The medical profession resolved this issue by creating the BMC (British Medical Council) and the GMC (General Medical Council) to deal separately with the professional and regulatory functions. An alternative is for a professional body to hold the function of regulation, but with the authority of Parliament. This is how the Bar Council reconciles the two functions and is the model proposed for the BPS register. BAC is sensitive to this issue and has a strong lay representation on the UKRC Executive. Nevertheless, existing types of self-regulation for counsellors and psychotherapists are maintained and financed by two of the main professional bodies.

The financial cost to professional bodies of maintaining a register has further implications. It will have to be met from members' subscriptions, which, especially for freelance practitioners, will inevitably be passed on to their clients in the form of higher fees.

The registration of counsellors and psychotherapists, even through statutory regulation, will not provide a guarantee that no client will ever suffer from unethical or unprofessional conduct or practice, but there does not seem to be any other generally accepted or viable alternative—a view challenged by Mowbray (1999: 212).

Even after 150 years, the GMC does not seem to have got it right. 'Doctors stand accused of putting their interests ahead of their patients as divisions have emerged within the profession over how they should be regulated' (Laurence, 2000: 4). In 2000 a series of widely reported and successful prosecutions and further allegations of medical negligence and malpractice against doctors in the UK resulted in GMC proposals for doctors to provide continuous evidence of their competence to practise medicine, with detailed checks on their performance every five years. But this is not seen as an argument against regulation, but a call for tougher and more rigorous regulation. However, there are other, perhaps more valid arguments against the regulation of counselling and psychotherapy than the fact that registration in the medical profession does not necessarily guarantee that dangerous practice will not happen.

## Arguments against regulation

Postle (2000: 344) provides a compelling, albeit sometimes almost vitriolic case against regulation. He asserts that the proponents of psychotherapy professionalisation generally, and of regulation in particular, 'deny, avoid, side-step, absorb, ignore, but do not generally engage with the body of argument against their project'. Postle's polemic argument centres around what he sees as the abuse of power, dominancy, coercion and the use of sanctions to ensure compliance, exerted by the professional bodies over not only their registrants, but also over dissenting practitioners and ultimately over clients. 'Any fear in practitioners over the potential sanctions of regulation will', Postle (2000: 344) claims, 'inevitably contaminate their work with clients.' The 'body of argument' against regulation, to which Postle refers, is outlined by Mowbray (1999) in a clear, cogent and well-referenced account (which is elaborated further in Mowbray, 1995). He starts by listing the 'preconditions for licensing: valid criteria for the establishment of a statutory profession' and then discusses why these criteria cannot apply to the regulation of counselling and psychotherapy. He concludes that there is a complete lack of any sound research evidence to suggest that the risks to clients are actually any higher with unregulated compared with regulated practice. He argues further that not only is regulation ineffective in achieving its purported aim of consumer protection, but that it is likely to have a negative impact on both practitioners and their clients. Mowbray (1999: 208–209) summarises the albeit unintentional, but potentially detrimental side effects of statutory regulation, which are adapted here:

- Fees paid by clients will be inflated to cover the cost of regulation, thus restricting further access to counselling and psychotherapy for poor and less well off people.
- Similarly the costs of providing counselling and psychotherapy services will be increased.
- Higher than necessary academic standards and irrelevant entry criteria may restrict the supply of practitioners and exclude those without the required academic entry qualifications, but who possess the personal qualities that would otherwise make them excellent practitioners.

- Cost and length of training may discriminate against the poor and those who cannot afford the already escalating course fees.
- Paraprofessionals who have hitherto made a valuable, if not essential, contribution to the provision of counselling and psychotherapy services may find it more difficult to work effectively.
- Accreditation systems, disciplinary procedures and ethical standards derived from conventional wisdom rather than from empirical evidence of effectiveness may suppress innovation and flexibility in education and training and in the delivery of psychological therapy services.
- Clients may gain a false sense of security by assuming, wrongly, that they can depend upon regulation to ensure safe and effective practice and as a consequence become more vulnerable.

Mowbray (1999: 208) argues that professions generally tend to 'raise the barriers to entry under the banner of raising standards' but that the research literature on counselling and psychotherapy fails to indicate any correlation and only a very tenuous association between professional training and therapeutic effectiveness. Academic qualifications seem almost irrelevant. Mowbray points also to the consistent findings in outcome research, that it is client qualities and characteristics rather than practitioner knowledge and skills, acquired in training, that account for around 85% of the variation in therapeutic outcome. Yet, he suggests, regulation implies that the practitioner is the potent change agent and, ipso facto, the main source of harm to the client—an assumption he strongly refutes.

Anyone interested in the arguments against the professionalisation and regulation of the talking therapies may find much of interest in the IPN (Independent Practitioners Network) website (www.lpiper.demon.co.uk). IPN represents a seemingly growing minority of practitioners. It claims to provide a structure for self- and peer accreditation and continuous monitoring of members' work. IPN does not believe that any one organisation has the right or ability to decide who should practise the psychological therapies.

## Conclusion

What is the future of statutory regulation of counselling and psychotherapy? The drive towards statutory regulation shows no signs of abating. Despite the fact that it seems impossible to arrive at an operational definition that distinguishes adequately between the activities of counselling, psychotherapy and counselling psychology, UKCP and BPS seem determined to pursue their own sectarian interests.

It seems almost certain that the BPS will eventually achieve chartered status for its counselling psychologists. UKCP seem equally determined to establish statutory registration for psychotherapists, although its position as the body which represents psychotherapists might be open to challenge by other professional associations such as BACP and BCP (British Confederation of Psychotherapists), which broke away from UKCP soon after UKCP was established in 1993. The position of BACP seems less clear. BACP, who hold legal responsibility for UKRC, seem to favour continuing with voluntary self-regulation, accepting that at some stage in the future statutory regulation may be imposed on them by the government. BACP values the contribution of people who provide counselling and psychotherapeutic services at all levels and seem reluctant to disenfranchise any who do not have the qualifications and training that are required for registration, yet who provide often a very specialist and important service. However, BACP may not be able to resist the pressure from an increasing number of its members, especially freelance practitioners, who aspire to statutory registration and the perceived, if not actual, professional status it would give them. The future regulation of counsellors and psychotherapists may not, however, depend only on the activities of the professional bodies. A consultation paper produced in August 2000 outlines government proposals to replace the existing Council for Professions Supplementary to Medicine (CPSM) with a new Health Professions Council (HPC). It is intended that the HPC should provide a mechanism for regulating professions not currently regulated by the CPSM and establish the highest UK-wide standards of conduct, competence and public protection. The paper emphasises that 'recent events have dented public confidence in professional self-regulation and have led to an expectation that regulatory bodies should work in a more open, responsive and publicly accountable way' (NHS, 2000). BAC (CAP), BPS and UKCP have been consulted, but it remains unclear how the proposed HPC will affect the regulation of counselling and psychotherapy.

The regulation of professions, through the setting up of statutory registers of practitioners who are permitted to practise, seems to be the generally accepted way of demonstrating that public interests are paramount, even if motivated by professional self-interest. The main professional bodies have already invested enormous amounts of time and money in establishing voluntary self-regulation. The argument that at some stage statutory regulation is inevitable remains strong, however flawed, and despite the dissenting voices. Freelance practitioners may need to apply for voluntary registration if they are to survive in the increasingly competitive marketplace and, if or when statutory registration is introduced, will not be able to practise unless they are registered.

## References

Barlow, N. (1998) Scrutiny of applicants for registration as Chartered Psychologists? *Psychologist*, September: 443–445.

Bond, T. (2000) Professional issues: codes of ethics and practice. In C. Feltham and I. Horton (eds), *Handbook of Counselling and Psychotherapy*. London: Sage.

Browne, S. (2001) Regulation coming soon. *British Association for Counselling and Psychotherapy, Counselling and Psychotherapy Journal*, 12(2): 4–5.

Burley, P. (1999) *Types of Regulation*. Unpublished paper presented to the UK Register of Counselling Executive Committee (adapted from CPSM Guidance on regulation).

Burley, P. (2000) The statutory registration of psychotherapists. *British Journal of Psychotherapy*, 16(3): 321–326.

House, R. and Totton, N. (eds) (1997) *Implausible Professions: Arguments for Pluralism and Autonomy in Psychotherapy and Counselling*. Ross-on-Wye: PCCS Books.

Iniss, S. and Bell, D. (1996) *Final Project Report for Therapeutic Counselling, Couple Counselling and Psychotherapy Competencies* (Report 39, May). Welwyn: Advice, Guidance, Counselling and Psychotherapy Lead Body.

Laurence, J. (2000) BMA on the verge of gravest split in its history, say GPs. *Independent*, 24 June: 4.

Mowbray, R. (1995) *The Case Against Psychotherapy Registration: A Conservation Issue for the Human Potential Movement*. London: Trans Marginal Press.

Mowbray, R. (1999) Professionalisation of therapy by registration is ill-advised. In C. Feltham (ed.), *Controversies in Psychotherapy and Counselling*. London: Sage.

NHS (2000) *Modernising Regulation: The New Health Professions Council. A Consultation Document*. Leeds: NHS Executive.

Palmer Barnes, F. (1998) *Complaints and Grievances in Psychotherapy: A Handbook of Ethical Practice*. London: Routledge.

Postle, D. (2000) Statutory regulation: shrink-wrapping psychotherapy. *British Journal of Psychotherapy*, 16(3): 335–346.

Pyne, R. (1994) The case for professional registration: practical considerations. Unpublished paper presented at the Walker Martineau Seminar, City of London Chamber of Commerce, London, 17 January.

Rowland, N. and Goss, S. (eds) (2000) *Evidenced-Based Counselling and Psychological Therapies*. London: Routledge.

Syme, G. (2000) Psychotherapy and counselling: what's the difference? *Counselling, British Association for Counselling Journal*, 11(6): 332–333.

Tantum, D. (1999) Registration benefits and is necessary to the public and the profession. In C. Feltham (ed.), *Controversies in Psychotherapy and Counselling*. London: Sage.

Thorne, B. (1999) Psychotherapy and counselling are indistinguishable. In C. Feltham (ed.), *Controversies in Psychotherapy and Counselling*. London: Sage.

Waller, D. (1999) The arts therapists open their register. *British Journal of Therapy and Rehabilitation*, 6(3): 110–111.

Wheeler, S. (1999) Can counselling be a profession? A historical perspective for understanding counselling in the new millenium. *Counselling, British Association for Counselling Journal*, 10(5): 386–391.

## Further information

*British Association for Counselling and Psychotherapy (BACP)*
1 Regent Place, Rugby, Warwickshire CV21 2PJ
Tel: 01788 550899
Fax: 01788 562189
Email: bac@bac.co.uk
Website: http://www.counselling.co.uk

*British Psychological Society (BPS)*
St Andrews House, 48 Princess Road East, Leicester LE1 7DR
Tel: 0116 254 9568
Fax: 0116 247 0787
Email: enquiry@bps.org.uk
Website: http://www.bps.org.uk

*United Kingdom Council for Psychotherapy (UKCP)*
167–169 Great Portland Street, London W1N 5FB
Tel: 020 7436 3002
Fax: 020 7436 3013
Email: ukcp@psychotherapy.org.uk
Website: http://www. psychotherapy.org.uk

# Chapter 5

# Sorting out supervision

*Sue Wheeler*

## Introduction

The task that I have been allocated for this chapter is to consider aspects of supervision as they affect the freelance counsellor or psychotherapist. The subtitle of the book includes the words *collaboration* and *competition* and the Introduction names *collusion*, all of which have some relevance for the supervisory relationship. It is quite possible that therapist and supervisor might collaborate to work as a team in some settings. It is equally possible that supervisor and therapist might find themselves in competition with each other, either for clients if they practise in the same area or on an intellectual level as they work together to unravel the intricacies of the unconscious world of the client. Collusion is possible in any supervisory relationship and warrants close scrutiny. It is all too easy not to see or hear difficult or painful communication, not to challenge or confront when something seems to be amiss. Counselling, psychotherapy and the supervision of clinical practice are all complex tasks that need to be conducted by competent, emotionally secure, well-trained practitioners who adhere to relevant ethical codes. Difficulties must be recognised, acknowledged and worked through for the sake of all concerned and supervision has a crucial part to play in that process.

While recognising that some would argue that there are substantial differences between counselling and psychotherapy, this is not a debate for this chapter and the words counselling, therapy and psychotherapy will be used interchangeably throughout. There are some substantial differences in the codes of ethics that are adhered to by various professional groups, particularly as they relate to supervision. While the British Association for Counselling and Psychotherapy (BACP) includes a requirement for all members to have regular supervision for their clinical practice as a condition of membership (BAC, 1996a), the United Kingdom Council for Psychotherapy (UKCP) expects members to involve themselves in professional development activities and to seek consultative support when necessary. They stop short of making supervision a requirement.

This chapter focuses on a range of issues that freelance therapists might need to consider with respect to supervision. It seeks to identify needs, to consider ways of choosing a supervisor and to raise awareness of the problems inherent in dual or multiple supervisory relationships. The process of developing a good working alliance with a supervisor is given attention, together with thoughts about evaluating and reviewing supervision. Expectations of supervisory responsibility are scrutinised and the fraught topic of managing an ending is discussed. Freelance therapists may themselves consider becoming supervisors and the chapter is concluded with some suggestions about taking that next step on the career path.

## What it means to be a freelance counsellor/ psychotherapist

A freelance counsellor or therapist may find work in several diverse settings. Private practice may be one option, but referrals may come from a multitude of sources including employee assistance programmes, staff support services or particular organisations such as general practice surgeries or public services of companies with which the therapist has developed contacts. The freelance therapist might gain some part-time employment in a company, school, university, general practice or other organisation. They might see individuals, couples or groups, or might even work with organisations in a consultant capacity. There are lots of options that call for both generic and specific skills and experience.

For the newly qualified practitioner, gaining experience is essential. However, there is sometimes a catch-22 to be overcome. Organisations seek therapists with experience of a specific type of work, but the only way to gain the experience is to practise (see Chapters 2 and 10). This problem can sometimes be overcome by working as a volunteer for a while, or by opting for regular close supervision by someone with relevant expertise. To take on the roles and responsibilities of being a freelance counsellor or psychotherapist, there is no substitute for a sound, well-regarded training course, practice with real clients under regular supervision and substantial practice in an organisational setting, working closely with others who can offer guidance and support. Freelance work is not for the untrained novice. There are too many pitfalls with grave consequences for self and clients, for the lone practitioner who rushes unprepared into the realm of private practice. Counsellors and therapists who have gained a good reputation for themselves while training and on placements, who sustain good relationships with their tutors, colleagues and clients and who use networking opportunities will find work in many parts of the country. Private practice should not be the place to start, but a mode of working chosen by a mature practitioner when they are ready to take on its complex responsibilities (see Chapters 1 and 3).

Independent practice can be a lonely activity. It is sometimes possible to work closely with others to develop a freelance practice or consortium. This has many advantages. It might involve renting or buying premises for a group practice, joint publicity and marketing, pooling of contacts and extending networks, a built-in support system, opportunities to gain experience in new areas by working with others or using skills and expertise appropriately by teamwork, referring clients to the therapist with the relevant experience. Collaboration affords many opportunities if the anxieties about competition can be overcome.

## Supervision requirements

Supervision requirements will vary according to the professional allegiance of the counsellor or therapist. BACP accredited counsellors are expected to have a minimum of one and a half hours of personal supervision per month (BAC, 1997). This is seen as an absolute minimum that pertains to an experienced counsellor with a relatively light caseload of clients who are not very demanding, perhaps working part time. BAC (1998) advise that more supervision would be necessary if the counsellor has a high caseload, works with clients whose emotional needs are intense and complex, who takes on work with a new client group, who lacks experience or who encounters personal difficulties related to their personal or working life.

The UKCP does not make such explicit demands on its members but there is a culture of intense supervision in psychotherapy training programmes, where ratios of one supervision session per two or three client sessions is not unusual. After such intense supervision, the culture is embedded and supervision is likely to continue, if not under such intense arrangements.

The freelance therapist may find themselves working in several different settings, each with its own culture and demands.

### Example

Jane works for two days each week in the student counselling service, having been taken on there when she finished her training three years ago. She has a private practice in which she specialises in Employee Assistance Programme (EAP) work, taking referrals from several local companies, which takes up about seven hours each week. She has recently taken on a role in a local hostel for young people with learning difficulties, running a support group for staff, and continues with her voluntary Relate work that she started many years ago.

Jane has three supervisors: one paid for by the student counselling service to cover the work undertaken there, another with whom she has a private contract to cover her private practice and the support group work, and the supervisor provided by Relate for her voluntary work there—as well as the fortnightly supervision group she is required to attend. Her supervision sessions total four individual hours per month on average and three group hours, and all are necessary.

It might be possible that Jane could find one person to supervise her work, who had all the necessary skills for the diverse work settings, but that would not be acceptable to organisations she works with. The student counselling service want to ensure that the supervisor they employ looks at the work with their clients. Relate require their clients to be supervised by their in-house supervisors and the employee assistance programmes require counsellors to have supervision on the clients that they refer. Jane's needs for supervision with each client group are met, but there is no one who has an overview of her whole workload.

The *Code of Ethics and Practice for Supervisors of Counsellors* (BAC, 1996b) is liberally peppered with the word 'responsibility'. For example, supervisors are responsible for:

- A contract with their supervisee (B1.1).
- Ensuring that the best use is made of supervision time (B1.3).
- Maintaining boundaries between the supervisory and other relationship (B1.4).
- Enquiring about other relationships supervisees may have with their client (B1.8).
- Taking action if they are aware that the counsellor is not competent (B1.11).
- Ensuring that their emotional needs are not met by the supervisee (B1.16).
- Seeking ways to further their own professional development (B2.2).
- Making arrangements for their own supervision (B2.3).
- Working within the limits of their own competence (B2.4).
- Not working when they are unwell (B.2.5).
- Clarifying contractual obligations when working in the same agency as the counsellor (B3.1.1).

In addition, the word, 'must' appears in many of the paragraphs of the codes, such as:

- Must encourage the supervisee to belong to a professional organisation (B.3.3.1).
- Must ensure that supervisees engage in professional development (B3.3.4).
- Must not reveal confidential information about the supervisee or their client (B.3.2.4).
- Must discuss their policy regarding references for the supervisee (B.3.1.6).

With three or more supervisors, the professional role of the counsellor is well observed but there is the potential for assumptions to be made that an issue is being dealt with by one of the other supervisors and for problems to be ignored.

## Legal issues

Freelance therapists are vulnerable in many ways and need to be fully appraised of legal issues that affect their work. Therapists are required by the Consumer Protection Act 1987 to provide a fair and accurate description of the service they provide and will need to be competent in delivering that service. They must publicise their practice appropriately and provide correct information about themselves. They could be sued for negligence by clients who employ their service, if the service is not deemed to be adequate. Many therapists keep records of their sessions, which could be subject to the Data Protection Act 1998, even if the records are not computerised, should a client demand to see them. Therapists owe a duty of care to their clients and action can be taken against them if that duty is breached resulting in harm to the client. Such a breach might be bad advice, sexual abuse or failure to recognise physical illness. They must publicise their practice appropriately and provide correct information about themselves. Therapists should also be aware that the standard of care expected of them is the same whether they are an experienced practitioner or a trainee (Jenkins, 1997). Lack of experience does not hold up as an excuse for incompetence. It is important that counsellors work with a supervisor who is fully conversant with legal requirements, who can provide guidance on these issues.

Hence there are numerous implications for the supervisor in private practice, supervising a counsellor in private practice. There is no organisation for either party that can act as a buffer for complaints or legal difficulties encountered. Any litigation will affect the individual who is held responsible. Supervisors must ensure that their own practice sets an example for the counsellor, being competent to practise, with appropriate qualifications, training and experience for the role. Counselling is still an unregulated profession, without clear legal legislation that dictates who can and who cannot practise; nonetheless, there are laws that govern aspects of counselling practice, which can be invoked when relevant. Awareness of laws such as the Consumer Protection Act and common law related to negligence may, in itself, inhibit ill-trained and inexperienced counsellors from opening their doors to clients, or supervisors taking on such a role before they are ready to do so.

## Business issues

In private practice the counsellor is running a business, and incurs all the responsibilities and liabilities that such an undertaking requires. Typically, counsellors are not prepared for business management as a part of their training and may have much to learn. Supervisors can provide considerable help in this matter by providing a model of good practice for the counsellor. Issues related to the counsellor's business practice will be of interest and concern for the supervisor, who needs to ensure that their own practice is beyond reproach. This invites a discussion about a whole range of issues pertinent to a counselling business including contracts, fees, accounting, income tax, insurance, pension, marketing, publicity, personal presentation, premises, record keeping, recovering fees, time management, personal security, sickness and death strategy, monitoring and evaluation of the service, training and professional development that are beyond the scope of this chapter but are discussed elsewhere in this book (Chapters 3 and 13).

## Choosing a supervisor

Probably the most difficult and the most important task for the freelance therapist is to find a suitable supervisor who is willing to take them on. A good relationship will enhance good practice. A bad relationship will cause anxiety and stress. There are many factors to be considered, including therapeutic orientation, relevant experience, personal compatibility, distance, time and fees, to name but a few. It is tempting to choose someone you have already worked with, perhaps on a training course, but it can be beneficial to work with someone new, who can provide a new perspective on your work. Finding someone that you don't already know has its own difficulties by definition.

There are numerous practical ways to find a supervisor. There are directories such as the *UK Counselling and Psychotherapy Directory* (BAC, 2000) or the *Register of Psychotherapists* (UKCP, 2000). The training course you attended might be able to provide a list of suitable supervisors or you can ask around other colleagues or therapists for recommendations of people they know or have used.

Making a contract for supervision is a two-way process. You might find someone who you think would suit you, but it is up to them whether they want to take you on. Several studies that I have been involved with (King and Wheeler, 1999; Wheeler, 2001) have highlighted how cautious experienced supervisors tend to be about taking on inexperienced freelance practitioners, particularly those who work from home in private practice. In interviews with well-known supervisors who have published work on supervision, the general feeling was expressed that supervising counsellors in private practice is a big responsibility. They were concerned that such counsellors are easily swayed by inexperience or economic considerations to behave unethically, either by working when they are unwell physically or mentally, or by taking on inappropriate clients. They were also concerned about the lack of an organisational buffer between the therapist and the client. The supervisor needs to have an overview of the counsellor's caseload in order to provide adequate support. The inquiry into the Anthony Smith case (SDHA, 1996)[1] criticised the supervisor of the counsellor involved for not providing appropriate support and guidance for the counsellor in managing the case. This result of the case has added to the apprehension with which responsible supervisors approach working with recently qualified freelance counsellors.

In the second study mentioned (Wheeler, 2001) supervisors were asked the following question: 'When approached by a counsellor in private practice for supervision, what would be the most important issues to consider before agreeing to take them on?' Most respondents replied that they would need to consider their qualifications, training and experience, the premises in which the counsellor worked and the code of ethics to which they worked. They were also asked, 'How would your sense of responsibility for the work of a counsellor in private practice be different from how it would be if the counsellor were working in an agency?' In response to this many supervisors commented that providing they had good supervisees, the work was easier than working with counsellors in agencies, where organisational issues often added complications. However, they were keen to know the supervisee was accountable to a professional body and to ensure that the contract with the supervisee was carefully and thoroughly negotiated.

Hence the implication of this for the freelance counsellor is to ensure that they have thought through all aspects of working freelance, particularly in private practice, and to wait until they are suitably qualified and experienced to do so.

---

1  Anthony Smith was a client in a GP counselling service. He had a psychotic breakdown and murdered his mother and stepbrother. The court of inquiry criticised the supervisor of the counsellor involved for not helping the counsellor to manage this case appropriately.

*Example*

> Miranda made an appointment to see a potential supervisor. The
> supervisor asked her numerous questions about her training and
> experience and allegiance to a professional body. Miranda had com-
> pleted a counselling skills course and the first year of a diploma
> course, which she had decided to leave as she was not satisfied with
> the teaching. She had not undertaken a placement in a formal coun-
> selling agency, although she had been a voluntary Cruse counsellor for
> two years. She had set up in private practice and currently had three
> clients. The potential supervisor asked to hear something about the
> work she was doing with one of the clients. The supervisor quickly
> recognised that the client Melanie was talking about was quite
> disturbed and in her judgement was unsuitable for counselling with an
> inexperienced therapist in private practice. Melanie was not pleased
> to receive this feedback. The supervisor declined to take Melanie on
> for supervision and recommended that she seek further training.

As counselling is an unregulated profession, Melanie may have continued in
private practice and she may also have found a supervisor. Someone may
have decided to take her on because they were concerned about her practice
with clients and wanted to offer her support. In my view, taking Melanie on
would be a risk on the part of the supervisor, because her lack of training
and experience could lead to all sorts of difficulties and even complaints. In
any complaint the supervisor could be implicated—hence the need for
caution when agreeing to work with inexperienced practitioners.

When you have found a supervisor who agrees to take you on, you might
find that they want to monitor your work quite closely for their own peace
of mind as well as supporting you until they are confident of your competence. A good supervisor will insist on agreeing a contract for the work
with you, which will be wide ranging, including agreement about how you
present your work, expectations for the sessions, mutual feedback, time
limits, arrangements for confidentiality and agreements about how to
handle complaints. Fees, times, notice of termination and holidays as well
as aspects of the relationship that require mutual respect, such as theoretical orientation, would also be on the agenda for discussion. It is in the
supervisee's interest to contribute to the discussion that leads to a contract
and a working alliance between you. Thinking through for yourself what
your needs are in supervision and issues that are important to you will be
helpful, so that you can contribute actively to the negotiations with the

potential supervisor and the subsequent contract agreed. For example, a match of theoretical orientation, ethnicity, gender and sexual orientation could be important, as indeed is experience in working within contexts similar to yours and with similar clients. Inskipp (1999) and Inskipp and Proctor (1993) both offer helpful suggestions about ways in which supervisees should prepare to use supervision.

Burton *et al.* (1998) looked into relationships between supervisors and their supervisees in general practice. They found that supervisees were often dissatisfied with their supervisors because they did not understand the organisational context in which they were working and the restraints that ensued. Counsellors in general practice are often required to adopt a short-term counselling model. If the supervisor is unsympathetic with such a model and continually recommends that the client be referred for long-term work, the counsellor will not feel supported in their work. Similarly if the supervisor is too rigid in their adherence to confidentiality when supervising someone who is supposed to work with the general practice team (Kell, 1999), a dissonance between supervisor and supervisee occurs. Someone may have a brilliant reputation as a therapist but be a lousy supervisor.

It might also be important to look for a supervisor who has had some training in supervision. Supervision training has been available for about the last decade. Many older practitioners have never had any training and may not feel inclined to take it up, but there is no excuse for more recently qualified therapists not to have undertaken training. All the issues discussed in this chapter, such as supervisor responsibility, contracting and assessing supervisees for suitability, are all part of supervision training, together with various aspects of professional practice, ethics, awareness of equal opportunities, organisational awareness and other issues. The response to your question about whether the supervisor has had any training will also tell you a lot about the person and their attitude to professional development.

## Individual or group?

When choosing a supervisor it is probably easier to find someone with whom you can work one to one, than to find a relevant and appropriate supervision group. Supervision groups are most often found in counselling organisations that can prescribe and organise supervision for the counsellors involved. There can be enormous benefits for the freelance counsellor who does not work as part of a team to have group supervision under the right circumstances. The group immediately provides a reference group, within which counsellors can receive feedback from peers as well as the supervisor on their client work. A group is more than the sum of its parts and the support gained from a group environment can offset the isolation and insulation of working alone. The group will generate more ideas and perspectives than one supervisor as well as offering a range of life and work experiences that could prove to be a valuable resource.

But group supervision can sometimes be a negative or even harmful experience. Jones (2000) looked into destructive experiences that counsellors had had in group supervision and had little difficulty in finding subjects willing to tell their stories. Such stories included experiences of becoming the scapegoat in a group, of being put down and ridiculed for not sharing the same theoretical perspective as other members, of being assessed negatively in public by the group supervisor, and of being ostracised by other group members. Hence there are issues to be considered when joining a group, such as the mix or heterogeneity of therapeutic orientation of group members. It would not be wise to join a group if you were the only person practising in a particular way. A great deal can be gained from diversity, but that must be balanced with the need to identify with other group members.

There might be opportunities to set up a new supervision group or to join an established group. With a new group, it would be crucial to spend some time negotiating a working agreement with the group, to set some ground rules for the way the group behaves. When joining an established group, work must be done to facilitate integration, which might involve a renegotiation of group rules and discussion of expectations and procedures. Although much is known about group dynamics, the need for supervision and to 'get on with the business of presenting clients' sometimes obscures the need for time to be given to group processes such as the integration of a new member.

## Imposed supervision

All too often, supervisors are imposed by the organisation for which you work. The *Code of Ethics and Practice for Counsellors* (BAC, 1996a) clearly indicates that if supervisors are also line managers then counsellors must have access to independent supervision. For some, supervision from a line manager is acceptable and works well. Webb (2000) investigated what counsellors were prepared to disclose in supervision and she found that counsellors were less likely to disclose sensitive issues to supervisors who have been imposed. She also found that counsellors were inhibited about disclosing their sexual feelings about clients in supervision and about discussing their feelings about the supervisor. Supervision can be threatening whatever the setting or the circumstances. Revealing anxieties, uncertainties, negative feelings towards the client, lack of knowledge or mistakes will inevitably make you feel vulnerable, but yet are essential features of the supervision process. Establishing a relationship of trust with any supervisor but particularly with one who is imposed is essential. If this does not happen, then the supervisory relationship is not viable and the counsellor is faced with making the decision about continuing to work with that organisation if an alternative supervisor cannot be provided. The issue to be considered here is personal integrity, illustrated in the following.

## Example

Steve was a freelance counsellor who gained some part-time work with a staff support agency in a social services department. All the counsellors in the department were required to have supervision with a local psychiatrist employed by the department. At first, Steve seemed to strike up quite a good relationship with this supervisor, but over the next few months he realised that there were big differences in the way that he and the supervisor viewed the world and particularly the mental health of clients. On one occasion Steve discussed one of his clients, who was having suicidal thoughts. The supervisor was insistent that the client be referred to a psychiatrist for an assessment, even though Steve felt that he could hold the client and work with her distress. Some months later Steve had a similar client, who was also talking openly of suicide. At this point Steve found himself choosing not to discuss this client in supervision, because the referral had not helped the previous client. He recognised that he was putting himself and his client at risk by not taking the work to supervision and felt considerable discomfort. Steve decided to discuss his anxieties about supervision with the counselling team leader, who was sympathetic but unwilling to make other supervisory arrangements. Steve decided to leave the agency.

This example raises another important issue that might need to be considered when choosing a supervisor: their attitude towards assessment and risk assessment. Therapists and supervisors are influenced not only by their training, theoretical orientation and experience, but also by their employment background and history. The settings in which they have been employed will have had considerable influence. For example, therapists who have been social workers are likely to be influenced by the rigid procedures that have been instigated in statutory agencies to protect children and the agency. Risk assessment would have had a high profile in that setting and may continue to influence their practice as supervisors. Counsellors and therapists have considerable autonomy to decide how to manage disclosures of abuse, suicidal ideation and threats to others. They are not required by law or even codes of ethics to disclose or break confidentiality in such cases. I am not saying here that risk assessment and very careful consideration are not necessary when clients present with something that puts themselves or others at risk. On the contrary, I see it as crucial. However, it is important for the therapist to ascertain from potential supervisors their value system and practice on these issues, to ensure that belief systems are compatible. It will be in dealing with critical issues in supervision that the relationship will be tested and it is also at those very same times that the supervisory relationship is most needed. It is better to explore the most difficult areas when contracting for supervision than to wait until challenging situations arise that threaten the relationship.

## The invisible supervisor

There may be some legitimate circumstances under which you might choose to have a supervisor with whom you cannot meet. For example, people who live and work in remote areas, or who are part of small counselling communities, may choose a supervisor with whom they communicate via telephone, electronic mail or video conferencing. Telephone counselling and supervision are already well established, to the extent that telephone counselling sessions can be included in the portfolio for BACP accreditation (BAC, 1997). Internet counselling has also found a place in modern society and supervision via the Internet is a distinct possibility. Given Webb's (2000) finding that face-to-face disclosure of some issues in supervision is problematic, the absence of visual contact might provide a more conducive environment for more intimate feelings to be revealed. As Goss (2000) says, 'A certain amount of credence can be given to the suggestion (that more is disclosed when relative anonymity is maintained) that we might begin to generalise to the supervision arena and explore whether counsellors actually gain support for more areas of their work when detailed discussion can remain anonymous in this way' (p. 180).

## Developing a relationship with a supervisor

Relationships are often made on the basis of mutual attraction, rather than on an understanding and agreement about shared values and beliefs and negotiations about expectations. Successful relationships are the result of ongoing negotiation, sharing of expectations and compromise. There is nothing magical about supervisory relationships. Such relationships also need to be negotiated and developed based on a shared understanding and expectations. There are power issues to be managed in supervision. Both the activity and the language *Super-Vision* imply that one person looks over the other. Power relationships can produce dependence and passivity, which is not helpful to the counsellor. Supervisees can be empowered in the supervisory relationship if they prepare themselves to share expectations and negotiate a working agreement/alliance or contract that enables them to fully participate in setting up the parameters of the relationship. The contract can also make provision for ongoing mutual review, so that a reminder is built into the agreement that renews and reminds both parties of the mutuality of the relationship.

There are some helpful texts that discuss in detail the elements of a supervision contract and the negotiation process. Inskipp and Proctor (1993) write about the working alliance in supervision, Sills (1997) provides insight into contracts for counselling and Hewson (1999) provides a template of contracts in supervision. Some of the issues that should form part of the negotiations for a supervision contract are listed below:

- Practicalities: frequency of meetings, time, place, payment, holidays, missed sessions.
- Range of presentation: organisational issues, client material.
- Mode of presentation: free association to client material, case notes.
- Assessment: feedback to organisations, feedback to therapist, complaints.
- Confidentiality: disclosure of abuse, complaints, known clients.
- Responsibility.
- Risk assessment: values, beliefs and practice.
- Issues of difference: race, gender, sexual orientation.
- Therapeutic orientation: congruence, working without congruence.
- Respect for difference in the supervisory relationship.
- Developing skills.
- Monitoring and evaluation of the relationship and the work.
- Managing the ending.

## Expectations of responsibility

There have been times in my counselling experience when I have felt great relief that a supervision session is imminent. After a difficult session with a client I have sometimes reassured myself with the knowledge that my supervisor will help me understand it. Sometimes that has relieved me of the weight of responsibility for a while and I have not mobilised my internal supervisor to work through the problems for myself. In short, sometimes I have become dependent and have expected my supervisor to take some responsibility for helping me to understand my client. I see that as the potentially negative aspect of supervision, that allows me to let myself off the hook of fully owning the responsibility that I have taken on in seeing clients. I use this personal example to raise the issue of who has responsibility for clients and to put the responsibility of supervisors into perspective.

There is no doubt that the freelance therapist working in private practice is fully responsible for their work with clients. Supervisors help and support, guide and challenge, but cannot take responsibility for clients that they never meet. Supervisors have a responsibility to the counselling/ therapy profession to ensure that the therapists they work with behave in a competent and professional manner and for their own practice as therapists and supervisors. The message is a harsh one. If you cannot fully bear the weight of responsibility that therapy and counselling entail, you should not be working in private practice. In an organisation some responsibility is assumed by the organisation, which provides a safer and more protected working environment. In private practice there is no buffer between the therapist and the client. Complaints and mistakes stick firmly with the therapist. Supervisors can and do provide support when the worst happens and may receive indirect criticism, but they are not responsible.

## Ending supervision

Having found a good supervisor with whom there is a good rapport, who meets the needs of the supervisee and who understands the work in hand, it is tempting to stay with that person for ever. Circumstances often change which might force an ending, but if that does not happen it is prudent to change supervisor every 3–5 years. Supervision can become too comfortable and the risk of collusion becomes greater with time. In a good working relationship an end date can be set some months hence, a new supervisor can be sought and an ending process can be negotiated. It is not so easy when the supervision is not going well, the relationship is poor and an end is sought by either party.

All supervision arrangements should be subject to regular review, which might be set in place during the original contracting phase. Typically a review of the work and the relationship might occur every six months or when requested by either party. When such an agreement has been made, at least there is a framework in which any difficulties encountered can be discussed, even if such discussions are stressful. Webb (2000) found that addressing issues in the relationship with the supervisor was uncomfortable and likely to be avoided. The power and authority of the supervisor are experienced as intimidating, which may in itself contribute to communication problems. However, if the relationship is not one in which there is sufficient safety to present all aspects of the work with clients, including personal thoughts, feelings and fantasies, as well as mistakes, it cannot fulfil the purpose for which it is provided. If the difficulties cannot be resolved in a review session in subsequent weeks, then there is little point in continuing with that supervisor. In organisations where the supervisor is imposed, this may have serious consequences but this is also a problem with which the organisation must engage.

## Supervision and self-esteem

Both Jones (2000) and Kaberry (2000) have written about aspects of abuse in supervision that were revealed through their research. The type of abuse reported includes violation of personal boundaries, harassment and lack of respect in a variety of forms. The result of an abusive relationship is lack of self-esteem and self-confidence for the supervisee. If you are consistently told that you are wrong, it is hard to hold on to a positive image of yourself and your work. If your theoretical model is trivialised or rubbished by the supervisor, it will undermine your confidence in using it. In effect, you can be persecuted for being different, for having a philosophy or frame of reference that does not match that of the supervisor. A little anxiety in supervision sessions is not a bad thing, but overwhelming anxiety that interferes with a capacity to think has serious consequences. A good test of whether supervision is working well is in monitoring the level of support and challenge experienced and the growth or demise of self-confidence. Swift action is needed when the balance tips in a negative direction.

## Becoming a supervisor yourself

A freelance counsellor or therapist may decide at some point to become a freelance supervisor, for which re-reading this chapter may provide some preparation. The supervisor may not be directly responsible for client work, but there are certainly times when they feel responsible. Supervision is not to be undertaken without adequate preparation. It often happens that someone comes on placement in an agency and you are asked to supervise them. If you are ready for this challenge, it can be an important growth point that triggers your continuing professional development, and an opportune moment to seek supervision training from a reputable organisation. Through the training, strengths and weaknesses in undertaking a supervisory function can be identified and addressed. Without such exposure to experiences that promote reflective practice, there is the risk of perpetuating styles of supervision that have been handed down from previous supervisors, which may not always be helpful.

## Conclusion

Supervision is an important function in the profession of counselling and psychotherapy. For the freelance therapist it provides a vital mechanism of quality control for the protection of the client and the reputation of the profession, as well as support and containment in what could be a fragmented and isolated working life. The choice of supervisor and attention to contracting and creating a working alliance with that supervisor are vital to establishing a professional arrangement that is satisfying and rewarding.

There are many pitfalls and no short cuts, but careful attention to the process of supervision can contribute to the development of a reputable practice founded on sound ethical principles, which offers a competent service to the public.

## References

BAC (1996a) *Code of Ethics and Practice for Counsellors*. Rugby: British Association for Counselling and Psychotherapy.

BAC (1996b) *Code of Ethics and Practice for Supervisors of Counsellors*. Rugby: BACP.

BAC (1997) *Scheme for the Accreditation of Counsellors*. Rugby: BACP.

BAC (1998) *How Much Supervision do you Need?* Information document. Rugby: BACP.

BAC (2000) *UK Counselling and Psychotherapy Directory*. Rugby: BACP.

Burton, M., Henderson, P. and Curtins Jenkins, G. (1998) Primary care counsellors, experiences of supervision. *Counselling, British Association for Counselling Journal*, 9(2): 122–133.

Goss, S. (2000) The impact of new technology. In B. Lawton and C. Feltham (eds), *Taking Supervision Forward*. London: Sage.

Hewson, J. (1999) Training supervisors to contract in supervision. In E. Holloway and M. Carroll (eds), *Training Counselling Supervisors*. London: Sage.

Inskipp, F. (1999) Training supervisees to use supervision. In E. Holloway and M. Carroll (eds), *Training Counselling Supervisors*. London: Sage.

Inskipp, F. and Proctor, B. (1993) *Making the Most of Supervision*. Twickenham: Cascade.

Jenkins, P. (1997) *Counselling, Psychotherapy and the Law*. London: Sage.

Jones, G. (2000) Destructive experiences in group supervision. *Counselling, BAC Journal*, 11(10): 648–649.

Kaberry, S. (2000) Abuse in supervision. In B. Lawton and C. Feltham (eds), *Taking Supervision Forward*. London: Sage.

Kell, C. (1999) Confidentiality and the counsellor in general practice. *British Journal of Guidance and Counselling*, 27(3): 431–440.

King, D. and Wheeler, S. (1999) The responsibility of counsellor supervisors: a qualitative study. *British Journal of Guidance and Counselling*, 27(2): 215–230.

SDHA (1996) *Report in the Case of Anthony Smith*. Derby: South Derbyshire Health Authority.

Sills, C. (1997) *Contracts in Counselling*. London: Sage.

UKCP (2000) *Register of Psychotherapists*. London: UKCP.

Webb, A. (2000) The difficulty of speaking. In B. Lawton and C. Feltham (eds), *Taking Supervision Forward*. London: Sage.

Wheeler, S. (2001) Supervision of counsellors working independently in private practice. What responsibility does the supervisor have for the counsellor and their work? In S. Wheeler and D. King (eds), *Supervising Counsellors: Issues of Responsibility*. London: Sage.

# Chapter 6

# The unspoken relationship: financial dynamics in freelance therapy

*Keith Tudor and Mike Worrall*

All therapeutic practice is underpinned by philosophy: 'one cannot engage in psychotherapy without giving operational evidence of an underlying value orientation and view of human nature' (Rogers, 1990: 402). Such philosophy is both personal and informed by the practitioner's chosen theoretical orientation. In addition, and as regards money, social philosophy informs and gives rise to different economic systems in which we live and work. Furthermore, therapists (a term which we use generically to encompass counsellors, psychotherapists and counselling psychologists) for whom congruence is a value and core condition of the therapeutic relationship are sensitive to the relationship between the personal and the contextual or environmental:

> there is, of course, a certain interplay between these two areas or elements in terms of how the environment we create or choose to work in fits with the self we bring to that environment: in other words, how congruent is our therapeutic environment with who we are? The environment or context we create is the precondition for our contact for our clients and reflects our congruence.
>
> (Tudor and Worrall, 1994: 202)

In freelance therapy, money is often a precondition for contact and ongoing work with clients and thus, as therapists living and working in a society in which services are predominantly exchanged for money, it is an important aspect of the therapeutic context. It can also be an area of difficulty, even embarrassment, especially, although not exclusively, for the newly qualified practitioner.

In this chapter we refer to the financial relationship as the 'unspoken relationship' between therapist and client since neither the psychology nor politics of money, let alone economics, are much if at all discussed in the context of clinical practice—or of training as a therapist. Mearns (1994) refers to the unspoken relationship as those aspects of the psychotherapeutic relationship which are not referred to directly by either therapist or client. He notes the paradox that, while client-centred therapy and, more broadly, the person-centred approach, emphasises open relationships, many thoughts and feelings—and particularly those of clients about their relationship with their therapists—remain 'unspoken'. Mearns also believes that it is those parts of the relationship which are the most difficult to access that may be the most therapeutically productive.

This unspoken or hidden psychology of economics is counterpointed by the hidden economics of the psyche—or, as Samuels (2001) puts it: 'the economic psyche'. In discussing a 'psychologically inflected approach' (p. 135) to politics and economics, Samuels advances three reasons for therapists to focus on economics: an *ethical* one, because anyone with a conscience has to evaluate the economic sphere, both the one within which they work and the wider one within which they live; an *influential* one, in that economics exerts a powerful influence on all of us; and, thirdly, one to do with *credibility*, as 'a psychotherapist who spends a good deal of time and earns most of his money doing clinical work is trying to say something about the wider world of politics' (p. 136).

In this chapter we discuss the dynamics which the exchange of money for services between client and therapist brings to bear on the relationship in freelance therapy; the action of such exchange often speaks louder than words. We consider the meaning of money and address practice issues with reference to the framework of competition and collaboration, understanding these both as internal dynamics *and* external dynamics in the context of a post-industrial, capitalist economy. Collaboration and competition are topical dynamics in the public sphere as represented by the 'docusoap' *Big Brother* and the TV gameshow *The Weakest Link*. Both shows require contestants *both* to collaborate (in certain tasks and in banking prize money, respectively) and *at the same time* to compete with each other (by nominating for exclusion). In the case of *The Weakest Link* the compere/interrogator even invites tactical voting which blends collaboration (of sorts) with competition. Playing games, however, is not confined to the world of gameshows. We may be clearly and explicitly competing and/or collaborating with colleagues; more problematic is the implicit process of collusion (*col ludere* = to play together) by which we make ulterior and deceitful contracts with each other. We view collusive relationships as an unspoken subset of competitive relationships.

## Money matters

'I don't believe money is no object. Money is the object' (James Gulliver). Money itself is inert, yet it is a powerful symbol. It has many uses and carries multiple meanings, many of which are most observable in the way in which we use it and exchange it. In their comprehensive work on *The

*Psychology of Money*, Furnham and Argyle (1998) identify and explore a number of issues, including:

- The development of understanding of social and economic world.
- Habits around money (spending, saving, gambling, giving it away, etc.).
- Attitudes to money, its psychological significance and symbolism (including personal and professional identity and self-esteem).

All of these, of course, are relevant to our current enquiry—as regards both clients and therapists.

Among its other processes and outcomes, therapy facilitates an understanding of the social and economic world and addresses some of the *mis*-understandings (misconceptions, misconstructions, distortions, defences) of that world—understandings and misunderstandings we develop in childhood and may maintain throughout life. Most of us internalise messages about money (see, for example, Matthews, 1991) from 'pocket money', saving and/or spending, to banking, possession and ownership, through to poverty, comfort and wealth. These messages then inform our attitudes to money and our habitual ways of using it. In practice, we often see these issues the other way around: someone presents a habit, e.g. giving a therapist a cheque in a sealed envelope, which may represent an attitude such as 'Money is dirty', 'It's impolite to give money (especially cash) openly for professional services'—attitudes which, in turn, suggest specific understandings about money, exchange, service, professionalism and class. One of us worked briefly with a client whose attitudes to sex and sexuality were confused following his teenage experiences of paying for sex. Every time he came to pay for a session he felt again and acutely the very ambivalences, uncertainties and shame which he had come into therapy to explore.

A lot of research has been conducted into attitudes towards money. Furnham (1984), for instance, developed a number of attitude statements regarding money which, through study, were categorised statistically into six clear, attitudinal factors:

- Obsession—'I feel that money is the only thing I can really count on.'
- Power/spending—'I sometimes buy friendship by being generous.'
- Retention—'I often have difficulty in making decisions about spending money.'
- Security/conservation—'I believe I think about money much more than other people I know.'
- Inadequate—'The amount of money I have saved is never quite enough.'
- Effort/ability—'I earn what I deserve.'

Such attitudes may be broadly summarised as representing plenty, poverty or sufficiency: some people, including therapists (although not many), make a lot of money; others live in debt (often exacerbated by easy access to credit facilities); and still others spend what they have and go without what they cannot afford—and people are either dissatisfied or make their peace with (integrate) these attitudes to money and what it brings. Obviously, our personal histories, including intergenerational family histories, influence our present attitudes to money.

Different approaches or 'schools' of psychology and therapy have their own theories about health and pathology (as regards the development of values, beliefs, attitudes, habits, etc.) which may be applied—and, indeed, should be examined in relation—to money and money matters (see Borneman, 1976, and Krueger, 1986, for discussions of money from psychoanalytic perspectives). For instance, from a person-centred perspective, the therapist's *unconditional* positive regard and acceptance is a central and necessary condition of therapeutic growth. As payment is a *precondition* for most freelance therapy, this constitutes an apparent contradiction which needs addressing—both in theory and practice. This is made more poignant by the fact that conditionality is viewed as the bedrock of a person-centred approach to psychopathology (see Bozarth, 1998).

## Case study (MW): The cost of conditional acceptance

I work in private practice, and I don't have any other source of income. I have rent to pay and food to buy and I charge people to see me. Even if I offer reduced rates and am as generous and accommodating as I can afford to be, it is still a condition of us working together that people pay me. This presents me with a dilemma. I aspire to accept my clients without any conditions. I believe that this is therapeutically crucial. I'm convinced by my own experience, and by Bozarth's argument, that it is a client's experience of unconditional acceptance that is the agent of therapeutic change. So, I want to accept my clients without conditions, and I want to eat. I therefore make it a condition of somebody seeing me, and continuing to see me, that they pay me. To the extent that an individual client experiences this as conditional acceptance, to that extent I believe I compromise my capacity to be therapeutically helpful (see Foundation for Inner Peace, 1996). Mostly (I imagine) my dilemma is a relatively abstract one, although the reasons for it being so interest me. I suspect that people are so used to paying for anything and everything that they expect it, and don't experience paying me as anything unusual. In so far as I go along unquestioningly with this social assumption, I'm colluding in it. Even though my fee, strictly defined, is a condition which somebody has to meet in order to get to work with me, I think many people don't experience it as such. It isn't even so much a condition of my acceptance of someone as a condition of the possibility of that person experiencing my acceptance: if someone can't or won't pay, I may not stop accepting them but I probably will stop seeing them.

I worked once for two and a half years with a client who didn't ever pay me a penny. When he first approached me he had money to pay his rent and buy his food and nothing else. He thought about approaching his parents for the money to pay me, and decided not to because he knew that he would be spending most of his time with me talking about the ways in which he felt they had betrayed him and let him down. He might have felt a certain ironic satisfaction if the people who had, in his eyes, damaged him most acutely had also paid for his therapy. There would also have been potential complications if he had accorded them or they had claimed for themselves any rights to influence the course, frequency, duration or content of his work with me. On balance, he didn't want to approach them for reasons which I understood and endorsed.

Even at this point, where I understood and agreed with his thinking and its consequences, I had to think for myself, and ask several questions. Was I both genuinely willing and financially able to work with him for nothing? If I wasn't, could I refer him elsewhere? If I was, could I work with him regularly and indefinitely? Could I foresee a point where the fact that I wasn't charging a fee would compromise our therapeutic endeavour? If either of us had found our circumstances changed, could we review our agreement? I agreed to work without charging a fee only after I'd asked myself these questions and come to satisfactory answers. Clearly, if he had come to me, a stranger, and asked me to lend him, or give him, a substantial amount of money, I'd have refused. Over time, however, and as our relationship progressed and deepened, the issue of money faded into the background of my thoughts.

Gradually, my client generated some income for himself and could have afforded to pay me something. As we worked together, however, and as he became financially self-sufficient, we recognised the therapeutic significance of the fact that he didn't pay me. He had expected unconditional love from his parents, and hadn't experienced it. He didn't trust anybody to accept him without conditions. We began to work at depth only as he came to know that I was working with him because I wanted to rather than because he was paying. For this man the fact that he could see me at no cost was therapeutically as well as financially significant.[1]

We now turn to consider financial dynamics in freelance therapy through the themes of competition and collaboration.

## Competition

> You can't have money like that and not swell out.
>
> (H. G. Wells)

> Her voice is full of money.
>
> (F. Scott Fitzgerald)

'In capitalist society, the leading ideological edge of Internalized Oppression is *individualism*—the set of beliefs which places the individual above the collective. Behavior inspired by individualism takes a certain form as well, and that form is *competition*' (Costello *et al.*, 1988: 55). Competition creates individuals and individualism is inextricably linked with competitiveness as we think (or are encouraged to think) about everyone else as competitors. As an internal process competitiveness is one of comparing oneself *against* (rather than alongside) others and then judging negatively ('I'm OK, You're not OK' or 'You're OK, I'm not OK'); competitiveness then (as distinct from positive competition for survival and 'intense joyfulness') is a form of internalised oppression—which may, in part, explain the embracing of inequality. In the external world, competition creates scarcity and hunger (literally) through 'winning' rather than 'running alongside'.

1  There is, of course, no such thing as a free session. There was a cost here, which I bore. I calculate that if I had been charging this client my normal rate, or seeing paying clients instead of him, I would have earned somewhere between five and six thousand pounds. Although I'm committed to the principle of available therapy, I can't afford to do that kind of work very often.

In a private sector economy freelance therapists, in competition with each other, are in collusion with such societal and economic norms which endorse competition as a legitimate, if not *the* legitimate, *modus vivendi* and *modus operandi*. There is a finite number of clients and any client who comes to one individual therapist and pays them is not going to someone else and paying them. We know many therapists, particularly (although not exclusively) less experienced ones, who are struggling to find enough work and are afraid for their livelihood. We know therapists who have felt obliged to take other work to subsidise their income, and some of these therapists have faced clinical repercussions. One therapist, for instance, worked behind the bar of a local pub and found it impossible to maintain a helpful therapeutic relationship with her one client who drank there. Another therapist found work that demanded such irregular hours that he could not offer any of his clients a dependably regular session from week to week.

Therapists in training experience a similar pressure. Most training courses require students to see clients as part of their training. Some courses insist that students do this through a placement in an agency rather than in private practice—and, indeed, the BACP discourages trainees from seeing clients in private practice (BAC, 1996) (although it advances no substantiated argument in support of this recommendation). Given the number of therapists there are in many parts of the country, it is a 'buyers' market' and agencies can pick and choose who they take. Given the financial pressure most agencies are under, it is understandable that many, if not most, of them take not the most qualified or experienced therapist (who would cost more) but beginning therapists who need the hours and will work for little or nothing. This has clear repercussions for other therapists. Those who volunteer their services in this way are competing directly with experienced and/or qualified colleagues—and colluding with commonly held views that therapy is an indulgence or luxury and generally should not be paid for from the public purse.

As training fees and professional expenses increase, the only people who can afford to become therapists are those who have money already. Therapists therefore run the risk of creating an informal, self-perpetuating, unspoken and protectionist closed shop, open only to those who can afford its fees and closed to those who cannot. (Many professions, of course, are explicitly closed shops; we might even say that this is one of the ways in which a profession defines and delineates itself.) Some therapists and politicians are currently arguing that what we *do* (an activity) should be (more) professionalised through, for example, recognised training and statutory registration. We are sceptical of these trends and the arguments put forward in their support (for a critique of which see Mowbray, 1995; House and Totton, 1997). This process is paralleled at the practice level, such that therapists are most readily available to those who can afford them and less freely available to those who cannot. The implications of these states of affairs are ironic: we select out of our 'profession' by exclusion whole groups of people who could bring fresh and vitally challenging experiences, and whose presence would render us more fully representative of the society we serve; and, once trained, many therapists reach only a particular more or less monied minority of potential clients who might want and benefit from their skills.

The logic of competition is that we maintain inequality. Recognising this, Samuels (2001) challenges us to reflect at depth and to ask ourselves why we stay competitive and, therefore, why we continue to embrace inequality. As trainers on counselling training courses, we have noticed:

1  That students are both peers and also often competing for placements and for work.
2  That this situation also pertains to the trainers—both in relation to their own peers and, at times, to their students.
3  That, of course, training courses themselves are in competition with each other.
4  That these realities are rarely discussed.

## Collaboration

Money should circulate like rainwater.

(Thorton Wilder)

If collusion is a deceitful playing with each other, collaboration (*col labore* = to work together) is an active and purposeful cooperation. For Steiner and Roy (1988: 29), cooperation is 'a mechanism for facilitating alliance and intimacy' and, as a concept, is both visionary and practical. It is also central to the theory and practice of radical psychiatry. It involves a commitment to equality, which demands (in the language of radical psychiatry) 'no power plays', 'no lies' and 'no rescues'. It is clear from the above that collaboration about money matters, specifically in freelance therapy, runs counter to the prevailing (capitalist) culture, ideology, economics and organisation of society and to the increasingly protectionist culture, ideology, economics and organisation of therapy. It is significant that the literature deals less with the psychology or politics of collaboration or cooperation than with competition. It is equally significant that while Britain has a Competition Commission (to regulate monopolies), it has no national 'Cooperation Commission'.

For inspiration we have to look to earlier eras. Under Scots law, for instance, until the early nineteenth century tradesmen could petition for increased wages to their craft incorporations, to the town magistrates, to Justices of the Peace and, ultimately, to the Court of Session. In England, radical, often socialist, traditions have led to the establishment of the Co-operative Society and alternative practices such as bartering, Local

Economic Trading Systems and tithing. (For a discussion of these issues and systems as they relate to counselling see Tudor, 1998). In many ways such forms of individual or collective action are attempts to 'prefigure' a different (i.e. cooperative) politics, economics and psychology under a present economic system which is, at best, indifferent and, at worst, positively antagonistic to such alternative ideology and initiatives.

There are a number of restraining forces which act or militate against collaboration and cooperation: capital(ism), competition and collusion, as well as how we internalise our own experiences of money matters. Steiner (1971), for instance, develops the concept of the 'stroke economy'. (In transactional analysis a 'stroke' is defined as a unit of social recognition.) He argues that our emotional lives, analogous to our financial lives, are strongly influenced by the supply and demand of recognition. Discussing the importance of collaborative power in relationships, Natiello (1990) describes six qualities which enable or facilitate equality and mutuality in therapeutic relationships:

1 Openness (all information is fully shared)—'This is what I charge.'
2 Responsiveness (all needs and ideas are carefully heard)—'I hear what you say about what you can afford.'
3 Dignity (everyone is respected and considered)—'How can we agree?'
4 Personal empowerment (each person has both freedom and responsibility to participate fully)—'This is what I'm willing to work for. How about you?'
5 Alternating influence (the impact on process is shared)—'It matters to me that we both feel OK about what we've agreed.'
6 Cooperation rather than competition—'How can we make this work for both of us?'

We take these as guiding attitudes to dealing with and negotiating money matters in relationships between therapists and clients (and supervisors and supervisees, trainers and trainees). In relation to money matters in therapy, we take this to mean that we have a responsibility to establish clear financial agreements *before* we make a therapeutic contract and 'before the client incurs any commitment or liability of any kind' (British Association for Counselling, 1997, Section B.4.3.1). (For further discussion of the setting, changing and payment of fees, as well as rules and contracts about them, see Worrall, 1997; Tudor, 1998.)

## Conclusion

Nothing knits man to man like the frequent passage from hand to hand of cash.

(Walter Sickert)

A freelance therapist is a person who sells their services to various employers and is not employed by only one employer. (Interestingly and perhaps significantly, in the *Shorter Oxford English Dictionary*, a 'freelance' has a more pejorative and, historically, a more mercenary connotation—which may serve as a caution.) It is worth reminding ourselves of this contractual and economic relationship as, in clarifying that our clients are also our employers, we emphasise the mutuality of the therapeutic relationship as well as its broader economic context. This reminder may also help with our humility in relation to how we regard clients. The mutuality we advocate is best facilitated by dialogue (as distinct from monologue) about issues such as money, and by the collaborative approach to power in therapeutic relationships as described by Natiello (1990). This constitutes a move away from the unspoken relationship about money which, in turn, demands of us as therapists that we be aware of our own histories, attitudes and issues about money; that we make a commitment to continued personal reflection and development about these matters; and that, in our practice, we eschew relationships characterised by competition (and collusion) in favour of active, conscious and collaborative relationships with clients and colleagues.

## References

Borneman, E. (1976) *The Psychoanalysis of Money*. New York: Urizen Books.

Bozarth, J. (1998) *Person-Centred Therapy: A Revolutionary Paradigm*. Llangarron: PCCS Books.

British Association for Counselling (1996) *Courses Recognition Handbook*. Rugby: BAC.

British Association for Counselling (1997) *Code of Ethics and Practice for Counsellors*. Rugby: BAC.

Costello, J., Roy, B. and Steiner, C. (1988) Competition. In B. Roy and C. Steiner (eds), *Radical Psychiatry: The Second Decade* (pp. 55–67). Unpublished manuscript.

Foundation for Inner Peace (1996) *Supplements to a Course in Miracles. Psychotherapy: Purpose, Process and Practice*. London: Viking Penguin.

Furnham, A. (1984) Many sides of the coin: the psychology of money usage. *Personality and Individual Differences*, 5: 95–103.

Furnham, A. and Argyle, M. (1998) *The Psychology of Money*. London: Routledge.

House, R. and Totton, N. (1997) *Implausible Professions: Arguments for Pluralism and Autonomy in Psychotherapy and Counselling*. Llangarron: PCCS Books.

Krueger, K. (1986) *The Last Taboo: Money as Symbol and Reality in Psychotherapy and Psychoanalysis*. New York: Bruner/Mazel.

Matthews, A. (1991) *If I Think about Money so much, why Can't I Figure it Out?* New York: Summit Books.

Mearns, D. (1994) *Developing Person-Centred Counselling*. London: Sage.

Mowbray, R. (1995) *The Case against Psychotherapy Registration: A Conservation Issue for the Human Potential Movement*. London: Trans Marginal Press.

Natiello, P. (1990) The person-centered approach, collaborative power, and cultural transformation. *Person-Centered Review*, 5(3): 268–286.

Rogers, C. R. (1990) A note on the nature of man. In H. Kirschenbaum and V. L. Henderson (eds), *The Carl Rogers Reader*. London: Constable (original work published 1957).

Samuels, A. (2001) *Politics on the Couch: Citizenship and the Internal Life*. London: Profile Books.

Steiner, C. (1971) The stroke economy. *Transactional Analysis Journal*, 1(3): 9–15.

Steiner, C. and Roy, B. (1988) Cooperation. In B. Roy and C. Steiner (eds), *Radical Psychiatry: The Second Decade* (pp. 29–35). Unpublished manuscript.

Tudor, K. (1998) Value for money. *British Journal of Guidance and Counselling*, 26(4): 477–493.

Tudor, K. and Worrall, M. (1994) Congruence reconsidered. *British Journal of Guidance and Counselling*, 22(4): 197–206.

Worrall, M. (1997) Contracting within the person-centred approch. In C. Sills (ed.), *Contracts in Counselling*. London: Sage.

# Part III

# The dynamics of survival

The word 'survival' seems appropriate to freelance existence. There are no guarantees of security, of pension rights, or that short-term contracts will be renewed. Clients come and go, periods of sickness and holiday breaks are also times of no income. Yet for many people it is a way of life that offers independence, freedom, flexibility and a deep satisfaction. A definition of survival is 'continue to live' (*Oxford English Dictionary*). In the context of being a freelance therapist then, the matter of 'continuing' is both a very practical matter and a psychological state, which may involve endurance, persistence, satisfaction. And 'to live', for the person who has chosen to work as a freelance therapist, can be a statement of intent to live life as fully and creatively as possible.

This section explores the inner, psychological world of transitions, which is a matter of concern to the trainee, as well as the counsellor whose work inevitably involves some aspect of change for the client. The changing dynamics within family relationships, which inevitably occur when a family member becomes or works as a therapist, may or may not be explored during training; certainly it appears that the break-up of relationships can be an 'occupational hazard'. Continuing Professional Development underlies the ongoing work of the therapist; it can support the 'survival' of the practitioner by ensuring both that professional skills are kept up to date and that personal nurture is seen as an equal priority.

Part III

The dynamics of survival

# Chapter 7

# The loneliness and freedoms of change

*Jean Clark*

Some of the material in this chapter is taken from a paper which I presented to a small audience in 1988, and then in response to a number of requests for copies, eventually self-published under the title 'Change is boundaries dissolved' (Clark, 1988). It has had quite a history, with over 1400 copies printed to date, and each year this small booklet finds its way into people's 'travel kit' for that journey which is invited by a major life transition. A colleague in Rochester, New York State, regularly gives it to clients, and when I visited him in 1996 I was asked to meet with two women for whom it had clarified aspects of their life experience. Another copy had found its way from a client in Norwich, to her friend on Vancouver Island, who passed it on to a therapist in Alberta! When we met in Calgary, she produced her tattered photocopy of 'Change is boundaries dissolved'!

I have decided to include an edited version in this book, because it explores and names themes which are pertinent to the experiences of being a therapist who is working freelance, and of clients who are moving through transitions and trying to make some sense of their confusions.

The journey through a training in counselling or psychotherapy, which may last for several years, is for most people an experience of profound internal change. It is usually followed by a transition out into 'the market-place', which may be an unsettling and confusing time. I think it is fair to say that at the beginning we could not imagine or foresee the effects upon ourselves, both in our outer and our inner life, and the impact upon families and even some friendships. Contributors to this book are drawing attention to different facets of the journey and what may be required of us both personally and professionally.

In this chapter I want to offer some maps of the journey through change. To be a counsellor inevitably brings us face to face with change in its many aspects, as we work with clients on the impact of loss and transition in their lives, as clients come and spend time in the transitional space which we offer and then move on, as our workload and financial circumstances fluctuate, as losses and changes happen in our own lives and the lives of our family, and as we move through our own personal and professional development processes.

To work freelance is a way of being which places us on the edge of uncertainty. Counselling is about change and for the counsellor as well as the client this may be experienced as challenging, as confusing, even threatening, as well as bringing new perceptions, new insights. It can be lonely and yet a creative space of new freedoms.

We speak about *managing* change, but I believe that external change can only be satisfactorily lived through when we acknowledge the internal process. For me this means finding maps—not to tell me which road to take, but to show me the terrain as others have experienced it, and perhaps to be aware of those areas marked 'here be dragons'.

My conscious exploration, of what I came to call *the place between in the process of change*, began a number of years ago, when a client said 'I wish there was a better word for it.' Her marriage had just ended and people were using words like 'mourning' and 'bereavement' and for her these words were not appropriate, in fact they were positively unhelpful. She needed a special word for her time of transition and there did not seem to be one.

I began to reflect. I recalled a poem which had 'written itself' during a conference, 10 years before, a time when I was struggling with the risks of making major changes in my life. A time, I now recognise, when I was very afraid of moving into that transitional space. The poem is a series of images of that place between.

> Change is boundaries dissolved
>   space unlimited reaching stars
> Change is being lost in strange
>   unreadiness to end or to begin
> Change is fear of things unknown
>   approaching
> Change is water flowing under bridges
>   a leaf carried by the flood
>   to fortune or to oblivion
> Change is mourning for things ended
>   regret for things undone
>   now never to be known
> Change is challenge
>   to begin anew
>   a letting go, renouncing, moving on
>   to find an unpredicted life
>   now shaped

I did eventually trust myself to the 'water flowing under bridges' and crossed over into my personal unknown territory, as a woman alone who would now be working as a freelance counsellor. I wanted to reflect on the clues, the elusive images that seem to have given me some sense of that terrain. I realised too that I was often with clients when they were lost and incoherent, in a process of change and transition, and I wanted to see how I could be with them more fruitfully.

Journeys have always fascinated me, unexpected journeys and journeys made to new places and as I looked back over my life I began to see some of the clues to the mystery of 'the place between'. There was a Saturday at the beginning of September 1939, when my parents and I were on holiday, and war was imminent, and because we lived in London and there might be bombing, my parents decided to leave me with a family we had just met at the boarding house. I still remember how it felt, standing at Cromer station waving goodbye to my parents; being in a space between the known and the unknown. Later that day I journeyed with these strangers to Cambridge, a place where nothing was familiar. It was while I was living with this family that I discovered and devoured books of Antarctic exploration, of Scott and Amundsen's journeys to the South Pole; those archetypal journeys into the dangerous unknown.

Then six months later, another major, life-changing journey. I was now back in London with my parents, because there had been no bombing, and one Friday night my father came home from work and said to my mother, 'We are going to have to shut up the house and move to North Wales next Wednesday, for the duration of the war.' I do not recall the process of packing, but I do remember the journey, the long nine-hour train ride to an unknown country, where I was to discover that people spoke a different language! And I remember the brief space of time when my mother and I sat on our suitcases on Colwyn Bay station platform looking at the sea, while my father went to find where we could stay that night. That moment of being utterly between experiences has always remained vivid in my mind.

And I remember sitting beside my father in a large saloon car on the way to my wedding.

And I remember the two or three hours before my first child was born, when I was a wife and not yet a mother.

I can see and feel how it was on those particular journeys, but there have been other times of transition which were less clear, when I was aware of lostness and chaos, depression, fear and excitement, and a deep sense that somewhere in it all there was something of great value to be discovered. Gradually the search became more conscious; there was a journey to be made from the known to the unknown by way of a time and space that seemed to have no words. And I was aware sometimes of clues.

In 1971, when I became a student counsellor, it was a fairly uncharted profession. Looking back I recognise that very soon I fell into a crisis of

identity as I moved from the roles of wife and mother, working inter-
mittently and part-time, to full-time creator of a counselling service in a
large polytechnic. For a while I was very lost indeed. I was in a kind of
limbo. As a student from Yorkshire said one day of his own journey, 'It's
like crossing the moors by an unmarked path when the mist is down.'
Clearly for me it was about a process of inner change as I made this
transition; certainly it was a journey, but I too was in a mist and could not
find a map that made sense to me.

Then one day I picked up a novel by Morris West, called *Summer of the
Red Wolf*. One of the characters spoke some words that leaped out of the
page and have accompanied me ever since. The hero is walking on the
Appian Way, outside Rome, and somehow everything is stale and unprofit-
able, when he meets a chance acquaintance, a doctor, who says to him that
sometimes a man sees everything so clearly that he becomes blind and sees
nothing at all. 'It's time to go then', McKenzie says, 'time to stick a shell in
his hat, pick up the pilgrim staff and take the road . . . To the place of
unknowing . . . A place where you are strange and a stranger and lonely,
and because of that, perhaps afraid' (West, 1971: 8).

'The place of unknowing', the phrase was numinous, it was one of the
milestones on the map of my unknown country. It told me what I already
sensed, that there would be transitions in my life, when I would be lonely
and afraid. But clearly others had been there, and that was some comfort.

It is a journey which I see trainees on counselling and psychotherapy
courses making. There are those who give up the certainties of salaried jobs,
others who leave the securities of marriage, or priesthood, and they come to
recognise that there are no certainties ahead. They too are journeying to a
place of unknowing, and if they find themselves attempting to set up in
independent practice, there will be times when they experience loneliness
and fear.

Other clues emerged for me. Because in the 1970s I worked as a student
counsellor in a multiracial city, where some of my black and Asian student
clients were victims of prejudice, I became very involved in questions about
cross-cultural counselling, and about the culture shock endured by
immigrants to my city and the racism they suffered. I began to work in
this arena, and faced a quite shattering sense of culture shock myself, as I
moved from my safe, white, middle-class working environment at the
polytechnic out into the challenge and confrontation and conflict of working alongside black people, some of whom became colleagues as we
developed training strategies to combat racism in institutions. I was afraid,
yet excited, lost and insecure. I was in a strange country between two
worlds, where I now did not know the rules, and I was slowly learning what
it would truly mean to live in a multicultural society. I recognised too that
when I step outside of the established order, when I begin to challenge how
things are, then I may be rejected.

I found that these experiences and my work with clients from a variety of cultures challenged 'the traditional notion of therapeutic changes that take place in clients as a result of counselling. Transcultural counselling gives both parties a unique chance to achieve personal growth' (d'Ardenne and Mahtani, 1989: 100).

Now that I have worked freelance for a number of years, I have come to value the creative space which is available when one is not working within an institution, even though it can be a lonely place. Perhaps I was preparing for this phase of my life when in 1984 another piece of the map emerged, A booklet came through the post, from the Guild of Pastoral Psychology, the transcript of a talk by Bani Shorter. She was suggesting that a life change, a transition, is like a border crossing between two countries, one familiar and the other not yet reached. Part of being human is that although we may not want walls, yet we create them, or they are built for us. We tend to respect them and may live most of our lives within them, in our own familiar territory, rather than taking the risk of experiencing a world outside. From the beginning of our lives we are defined by others and by society, and perhaps we are not anyone or anywhere until we can acknowledge and claim our identity for ourselves. Is this 'the journey to the place of unknowing', the quest for our unique identity?

Sometimes we feel compelled to go beyond our walls, our borders, our limits. We abandon our secure job, or some traumatic loss occurs. We are cast out into limbo, and must dwell there for a while, until we again move to a place where we create new boundaries of who we are and where we might be, but with wider perspectives about what is possible. There, we build walls round our newly discovered identity (though hopefully with doors and wide windows).

So a life transition is like a journey from one country to another, from one kind of identity to another. From a country that is familiar, where we know our roles and status, we must cross over into no-man's land, where our passport is outdated and we have currency that now seems of little value. For a time we are in limbo, a place of unknowing, a border territory between the known and the not yet known. At frontiers we may feel powerless as our passport of identity is scrutinised, our luggage opened and searched and some things may be confiscated. We are no longer in control. Our laws and language may be of little use. Fear flickers. I could be lost in this place. I may never recover my identity. 'At the border we are exposed to two conflicting pulls; we want to stay behind but we are also prompted to leave and to arrive' (Shorter, 7).

Jung wrote of the border country, that the person 'is in process of becoming another but suffers imbalance because there is no longer purpose and significance in the former state. He has been uprooted from meaning, the logic of his soul, and consequently his life is in chaos without the ordering principle' (Shorter, 10).

I wrote my own description of the territory:

Limbo is the place where
there is no certainty of outcome
no point of reference
no expectation
that there are signposts
even a road . . .
chaos or chasm?

Limbo is no place, no person
upon the frontier between two worlds
one known and lost
the other yet to be . . . still inchoate.

Limbo is where nothing can be predicted
the hand that may or may not reach out
the word that may or may not be spoken
the life that may or may not be lived.

I was writing then about the border country of an ended marriage, but the words well describe those feelings of deep uncertainty which can occur for those stepping out into the world of freelance, where there is 'no certainty of outcome', where one is still upon 'the frontier between two worlds'. In transition we step across a threshold, a *limen*, and once we have taken this step we are in a state of limbo, of *liminality*.

It was Jung's insight that the crossing of the border was to do with initiation, and here I come to another set of images and to the word for which I had unconsciously been searching.

It appears to have been Van Gennep and Victor Turner, both anthropologists, who expanded the meaning and function of the word liminal and created the word *liminality*. The *Random House Dictionary* (1986) gave a very significant definition and examples of *limen* as: (Latin) 'threshold' and 'to make urgent the appetites and needs which are smouldering below the limen of awareness and are barely perceptible'; and *liminal*: 'of or pertaining to the threshold or initial stage of a process'. Victor Turner, in his book *Dramas, Fields and Metaphors* uses and gives a rich meaning to the word *liminality*, which further clarified my search.

Liminality is the second and central stage in a process of initiation, in the sequence: separation, liminality and reintegration. We have few clearly defined rites of passage in our society, apart from baptism, weddings and funerals. In the stages of our growing (up), at puberty, or midlife, or dying, or in the changes of status which occur in widowhood, divorce, redundancy or retirement, there is no recognition by ritual that marks out the stages and process of the transitions. They are assumed to be rational, private processes.

But if we look at rites of passage in traditional societies, we find there are three stages in the rituals, which are lived out by initiands.

1   *Separation* from the familiar. A group of young men or young women are literally led out of the village, away from the tribe, having said their farewells. It is clear that today a phase of life has ended.
2   Living for a period of time on the margin, beyond the boundaries of the village, a period of *liminality* prior to some ceremony of initiation into a new status.
3   *Reintegration*. Returning to the tribe changed, their new status acknowledged, accepted, valued.

'Separation comprises symbolic behaviour signifying the detachment of the individual or the group from either a fixed earlier point in the social structure or from an established set of cultural conditions' (Turner, 1974: 232). Crossing the threshold into a state of liminality can be experienced as being in a tunnel where things are dark and hidden. I am reminded of the Greek mystery religions and the descent into the dark cave, and the dark night of the soul, and my clients who talk of being in a black hole. 'The state of the liminar becomes ambiguous, neither here nor there, betwixt and between all fixed points of classification; he passes through a symbolic domain that has few or none of the attributes of his past or the coming state' (p. 232).

Looking back at experiences of liminality, I recall fear and excitement, desolate loss and potential gain, inertia and exhaustion; yet freedom, a sense that it was never like this before and it never will be again, the 'space unlimited reaching stars' of my poem. I sense that many recently qualified counsellors will recognise these feelings. A training course tends to change one's life in profound ways—there is no going back—and the way ahead is unclear, ambiguous, fraught with possibilities.

In the liminal state of a rite of passage, the symbols indicate that the initiate is virtually invisible in terms of their culture's classifications. They are stateless and set aside from the main arenas of social life. It is so in our culture. A client having a breakdown said he felt he was invisible to his employers; a woman newly separated from her husband finds she is *persona non grata* in some social settings—she is unlikely to be invited to dinner parties with couples for some time. Initiates have been reduced in status to equality with fellow initiands, regardless of their pre-ritual status, and it is in this space of liminality that a spontaneous expression of comradeship and equality can develop. On a training course, a doctor, a housewife and mother, a lawyer, someone made redundant and still unemployed, a psychology graduate, can come together unencumbered by status.

Victor Turner offers two views of society: as social structure, where the units are status and role; and as *communitas*, a kind of utopian place of free and equal comrades, which he describes as a modality of social inter-relatedness. 'Liminal states are often stressful and disorienting. The familiar is dissolving and a new place to stand has yet to be found' (Combs, 1995: 242). Yet it can be a space of time where we can be more open, where we can relate to each other in our brokenness, in *communitas*, where status is irrelevant, and through this experience we can grow. 'It is the flexibility inherent in liminal states that makes them rich ground for psychological and spiritual growth. It is their disorder, however, that may cause psychological disorientation, identity crises, and emotional upheavals' (p. 242).

Perhaps this is one of the profound learnings from our often painful and fearful times of transition, if we choose to be aware. Liminality is a space where we can gain some view of who and where we are in the cosmos, to reflect where we have come from and what we might be in the pattern of social relations, and who we are person-to-person in *communitas*.

Dare those of us who work alone, offering therapy to clients in *their* transitional space, sometimes put aside our roles as more or less successful competitors and more or less effective entrepreneurs and meet in *communitas*. There we can let go of status in the community of counsellors and psychotherapists, and acknowledge our vulnerability and our wisdom in the work we have chosen to do. *Communitas* has an existential quality; it involves the whole person in relation to other whole persons. It is a space where we may collaborate in profoundly creative ways, and may even talk openly about uncomfortable themes such as collusion.

There are risks and challenges. 'Liminal states hold great possibilities and also real dangers, because in them we are bound by neither the past nor the future, and our fate is open ended' (Combs, 1995: 242). There are no structures, emotions can well up from primitive depths. One moment I am standing on a mountain top, the next I have tumbled into the mire; mists come down and I cannot see where I have come from, let alone where I am going; paths peter out, there may be wild animals lurking. And we may meet unexpected significant people; or through images or dreams, something which has been confused becomes clearer.

We can distinguish different kinds of transitional state, all of which we may ourselves experience at some time in our lives, and the experience of which brings many clients into counselling:

- *A sudden loss* of a person, or a role or status (through death, illness, redundancy, a broken relationship).
- *A change of a role or status* which may be seen as positive, like getting married or starting a new responsible job, an adolescent or an adult becoming a student, parenthood, becoming a counsellor; or experienced as negative, through becoming unemployed, a widow, a retired person,

- *Life transitions*: child into adult, the midlife watershed, menopause, mature adult into old age.

A transition may be marked in some way by an event, or it may be a long deep process not consciously recognised. But I would suggest that the emotional and psychic processes involved are likely to be similar, and involve a letting go, an experience of liminality and reintegration into a period of more certainty and stability.

Perhaps one of the most confusing of transitions is the watershed of midlife, and interestingly enough this is a time when many people choose to undergo training as a therapist. Murray Stein's book *In Midlife* illumined more of the pieces of my map. He describes the psychological liminality of midlife as 'the condition in which the ego becomes unmoored from its former fixities of identification and identity and "floats"' (Stein, 1983: 41).

Midlife is a time when we are challenged to let go of our earlier perspective of life as an experience of continuous growth and expansion, and reach an acknowledgement that the second half of life leads ultimately to our dying. We may try to deny the reality of our ageing, but only when we can accept what has been and will never be again can we recognise the absurdity of our pretence that life is controllable and manageable.

Stein describes the territory in midlife transition as he sees it; 'recall that a person's sense of direction forward is beclouded and obscured during liminality; life's pathways to the future appear to be unmarked and even uncharted and the future itself seems unimaginable in every single direction . . . The person seems to stand perpetually at some inner crossroads, confused and torn' (pp. 85–86). There is a circling around which feels aimless, paths promise to lead somewhere, then come back to where we started. Yet the circling can become a spiralling down, until we become aware of our inner resources, and we are strengthened enough to be able to acknowledge that death is life's fated conclusion.

Liminality is a place of death and rebirth, and in many of the old rites of passage this is acknowledged and acted out. When our sense of identity is changing, there has to be a kind of death, so that the new self can be born. And it is a place of ambiguity, because, when I do move on to the next crossing of the border to the new country of reintegration, I may find that I have gained in status or that I have lost. I may find myself dispossessed of material things. It can go either way.

Think of a queen at her coronation, in a plain white garment, in her place of liminality, before she is invested with the robes and symbols of high status.

Think of the woman or man who is given a 'golden handshake' and walks out of the office, redundant and unemployed.

Think of the business woman who gives up a secure salary and pension rights, and trains as a psychotherapist.

Think of the client with a very stressful job, who enters therapy 'because I have a lot of tension headaches' who leaves work, buys an air ticket and goes travelling.

Liminality can be a time of creativity. People write poetry, paint symbolic pictures, create new concepts. For a little while we may be willing to experience 'space unlimited reaching stars' as we hold the awareness that we are poised between our birth and our death.

Those who deliberately move into innovative, prophetic and creative roles, which challenge the established and accepted norms of society, may always live near the border, and move often into that place where 'the appetites and needs [which] are smouldering below the limen of awareness' may be allowed to emerge and be given voice. Because we are less centred in ego consciousness, perhaps we are more open to the deep needs of the self, that archetype of the wholeness of our individual life which seeks fulfilment. When we live within the safe walls of our business and the demands of our roles, the self is often denied. Sometimes it seems that through dreams, or when we encounter the unexpected, or our logical plans are over and over defeated, or we have a series of accidents, or become suddenly ill, the self calls us to take up our pilgrim staff and travel to the place of unknowing, to cross over into liminality, where we may experience initiation into who we may become.

There is one last image which I found very moving and now recognise as part of my map. At a conference, a colleague used the phrase 'the sacred space where growth can happen'. He spoke of an American Indian tribe who, when the seeds of corn were sprouting in the earth, would sit silently around this sacred space and listen to the corn growing. He was suggesting that a small group can be such a space, and it now occurs to me that the border country of transition is also a sacred space where growth can happen. As a counsellor, I am sometimes privileged to sit with a client in such a place.

I realise that the pictures that make my map may not be yours. And anyway a map is simply marks on a piece of paper, which gives no real sense of the terrain. Nevertheless, for me, the mapping of my border country and my discovery of the word *liminality* and all that it conveys have enabled me to be more fully with myself and with my clients in their confusions and discoveries in their times of transition. It has also helped me during the years of working freelance, to understand and work within the tensions of uncertain workloads, erratic income, times of ill health and, above all, the loneliness which can sometimes afflict and daunt me.

It has also led me to reflect upon the ways in which I seek to be with clients, and supervisees, in their life transitions, personal and professional. How can I be most facilitative? To leave the familiar, whether planned for or unexpected, is to face loss and some feelings of shock, numbness, denial, pain, anger, and a 'strange unreadiness to end or to begin'. Moving into the unknown, the phase of liminality, their feelings are likely to be a mixture of confusion, floating, excitement, fear, even panic, lostness, chaos, boundaries dissolving. I want to be with them, and not be afraid, which is why it has always been important for me to continue to explore this territory for myself, and to have some sense of a map, even though vast stretches are still marked 'unclimbed peak' and 'here be dragons'. I want to be ready to hear and see with them the symbolic images, the synchronistic events which are clues to their map, and to be able to say sometimes 'Yes, that is how it is'; for such experiences can make us wonder if we are going crazy!

I have the deep belief that liminality is a time of discovery of who a person is, when familiar roles, status, power or good health are shed or stripped away. I want to be a companion on this process of discovery, and to offer a model of what it is to be part of the *communitas* of free and equal comrades seeking to become more whole; and to perceive with them new significance of events in their lives—both past and present. And I need to be aware, as a counsellor, that borders are also dangerous places and to be able to recognise where border is becoming borderline psychotic—those rare occasions where the sense of reality is quite lost for a while.

The concept of initiation into a new phase of life tells me something about timing. Maybe we and our clients need to stay in our place of unknowing long enough to learn what we need to discover, to take stock and decide what can be left behind and what will be of use in the journey to our new country; and to gain the strength and energy to move on when the right time comes. There can be a pull to stay in the liminal state, to become more and more aware, and yet have a reluctance to commit to who we are becoming. To be initiated is to take our place, in ways that can use the strengths and qualities we have discovered in the *communitas* of liminality. I want to give myself and my client permission to take all the time it takes to pass through the border country. Transitional processes, like initiations, have a natural rhythm. How can I become so much in tune with my client's timing that I do not get impatient, yet do not collude with inertia?

I hope I may enable them to find some meanings, some new strengths and insights, to be ready to reintegrate into their life as it is now. Then they will be able to take up new roles and different status, to extend and expand these to their full potential. Some may hang a rucksack on a nail by the door, with their passport in its pocket, ready again one day to take their pilgrim staff and travel to a place of unknowing.

I hope they will be more able to define who they are as *persons*, regardless of ascribed status, whether it be retired, divorced, successful professional, counsellor or psychotherapist setting out on a new vocation, unemployed, widowed . . . I hope they and we will have found some sense of *communitas* of free and equal comradeship. Hopefully too, they can carry some of the qualities of liminality into the new country. For to be able to step out of security and safety of role and prescribed thinking in acceptable moulds is to be able to be creative, and prophetic, speaking the truth as we see it. We need such people in society today. And we need as therapists to risk our truth.

## References

Clark, J. (1988) Change is boundaries dissolved. Lecture at Norwich Centre for Personal and Professional Development (privately published).

Combs, A. (1995) *The Radiance of Being: Complexity, Chaos and the Evolution of Consciousness.* Edinburgh: Florris Books.

d'Ardenne, P. and Mahtani, A. (1989) *Transcultural Counselling in Action.* London: Sage.

Shorter, B. Border people. *Lecture 211.* London: Guild of Pastoral Psychology.

Stein, M. (1983) *In Midlife.* Dallas, TX: Spring Publications.

Turner, V. (1974) *Dramas, Fields and Metaphors.* Ithaca, NY: Cornell University Press.

West, M. (1971) *Summer of the Red Wolf.* London: Heinemann.

# Chapter 8

# A therapist in the family

*Tania Barnett*

In this chapter, my aim is to integrate the personal with the general within the context of having a therapist in the family. The range of issues addressed here are those which have made a significant impression in my own life and some identified as pertinent by my colleagues and their families. These will be interspersed with ideas from the literature in psychiatry, psychology and psychoanalysis, as well as from counselling and psychotherapy. The reason for this is that issues raised by related professions such as those which will be illustrated here have been highly relevant to different kinds of practitioners and their family dynamics. The term therapist will therefore apply to this wider group of practitioners of therapy rather than counsellors alone.

There are a number of issues that confront a therapist setting up in freelance work which impact directly on the family, particularly when the therapist works from home. My own experience has been of growing up in a family where my parents were both psychotherapists, and of part-time counselling and counselling-related work in the context of my own family of two pre-school children and my husband. Since training I have fortunately spent some years in the same home. The fact that my husband has a secure public sector post has enabled me to work flexibly, for intermittent periods seeing one or two clients a week at home, together with contract work in the urban and suburban community in which I live. So I write about these issues from several different viewpoints.

I will explore these issues in relation to the tensions, challenges and dilemmas that have arisen for therapist practitioners. Some of these impinge on other close relationships beyond the family and are thus relevant to home-based therapists who do not have family living with them. I have found only a limited exploration of these issues in the literature, and so the main emphasis of the chapter has evolved into a consideration of my own experience and that of others around me, and a less detailed account of other writing on the topic of 'family dynamics' in relation to our work.

## Setting up a private space for the counselling relationship within the family home

I have been fortunate in having the use of a spare/guest room upstairs for my work. This room gives easy access to an upstairs lavatory and is two doors from the landing hallway. This structural feature has helped reduce noise substantially. The fact that I can use this spare room for counselling and consultations has reduced both the intrusion into family life of the sessions, and the family's intrusion into the counselling/work space. This situation helps to maintain a level of privacy for all.

However, there is still a need to expect the unexpected. On one occasion for instance, mid-session, my client and I suddenly heard from afar my two-year-old boy's shrill shriek, while his father carried him down the stairs. Another time my client and I were plunged into complete darkness for a minute or so. I found out later that my husband had been tinkering with the mains electricity during a DIY project. Despite these less than ideal interruptions, which are a part of normal family life, on the whole it has worked well to see clients in the upstairs extension room.

## Deciding on priorities and boundaries for family and for clients

I would suggest that as well as the location of the room, organisation and negotiation with the rest of the family and setting clear boundaries with each client can help a lot. Deciding on your priorities could include a number of diverse issues, at various levels, such as handling children's or other family members' illness, holidays and other unplanned or planned changes to the routine arrangements.

A problem that I came up against at the time I decided to work from my own family home was, to my surprise, solved in a straightforward way. My downstairs hallway is small and, like many others, leads directly into the kitchen, with no door between the two. My counselling room is upstairs, as described earlier. The boundary that I set for clients, which at first in the back of my mind I thought harsh, has actually worked out well. It is particularly helpful because it means that, apart from not answering the door around the time I am counselling, the rest of the family can use the downstairs freely, and the upstairs, quietly.

I explain to clients that since I work at home, there is no waiting area inside the house for them to use if they arrive early. So I ask that they wait in their cars if they come early. Indeed, many other decisions, which are not ideal for the clients, tend to be accepted by them if they have a rationale for my decision and know what to expect.

A common issue for daytime therapists is decisions over which partner will cancel work in order to be at home with a sick child or when there are school holidays or school 'teacher days'. These can usually be decided beforehand, but my partner and I have found flexibility as well as spontaneous renegotiation may be necessary at times too. I would stress that there is a need to have clearly thought out one's fundamental priorities around family versus work and personal versus professional needs. Also these need rethinking every so often, so that when conflicts occur, as they inevitably will, there is a framework for making decisions.

## Combining family and work roles at home

In addition to one-to-one and small group counselling, I have had planning sessions and other meetings with colleagues in my home. This has worked best when the children are at school, in childcare or, next best, asleep. I do not recommend trying to perform the roles of professional and parent simultaneously. Alternatives to meeting at my home have been useful, such as in a colleague's house, bar or café, bearing in mind issues of confidentiality and anonymity in public places.

Although my colleagues have always been friendly and flexible during times when our consultation was disrupted for brief periods, if for instance my son needed me to do something for him, inside I always felt to some degree torn between my two roles. At times I felt mildly guilty and emotionally stretched too far with switching between the two, in order to keep things running smoothly. Inevitably, at these times I have not done my best work in either role, as professional or as mother. These effects were not fully apparent to me at the time, perhaps because I did fulfil both my professional role and parenting role adequately.

There is a freedom in being a freelance worker, which I personally have been empowered by, in that I am my own boss who can organise work life around home life in the way that suits my family, my clients and myself. Flexibility is a benefit of short-term contract freelance work as is control over the number of clients and hours of counselling work taken on. Unfortunately there can be financial constraints that limit the flexibility of being able to take up and cut down on work hours and this can be stressful. These issues have a very different impact on some people, for example, a therapist who is the main breadwinner of the family, and another therapist who in fact does not need to earn a salary at all. Some colleagues could be placed in between the two ends of the financial continuum, including those for whom freelance counselling work is additional to another career.

## Having a parent who is also a therapist: the children's perspective

The challenges of being a child of a therapist change over time according to the age and level of maturity of the child. This needs to be borne in mind when considering the potential impact of the following issues.

I have significant memories of the time when both my parents were working at home as therapists, and I was required to be silent downstairs in the hallway outside the therapy rooms 'when the curtains were closed'. This acted as a signal, indicating that one of them was in session. The main feelings I remember were resentment and jealousy. As a peer-centred and oversensitive teenager, occasionally I felt embarrassed, particularly when I had friends round. Also, throughout childhood I felt a growing sense of curiosity to know what went on 'behind the curtain', the other side of my parents' lives. I was curious about who got so much of their attention, and in what ways did they help these people? Looking back, it now seems inevitable that I would follow a certain path and later seek to study psychology, and then enter the field of therapy. Both of my brothers also studied psychology at university, although neither of them have pursued careers in the field; even I have not put all my eggs in the one basket of a career in therapy.

My children are still young and thus far have expressed few feelings about my type of work or the fact that I sometimes work at home. One is pre-school and the other goes to primary school. They are both usually asleep during my client contact hours. They have both got used to their mother 'working' in and out of the house in a variety of freelance counselling and other work. So far my children have been more interested in my husband's work and my roles as teacher and lecturer than as a counsellor.

## The therapist's effect on their children

Difficult therapy sessions may leave the counsellor unable or unwilling to attend to the needs of their children. If this happens consistently, it can have a detrimental effect on the emotional well-being of the whole family: children may begin to feel unwanted or unloved. They may misunderstand the actual reasons for their therapist parent's inability to listen to them and to meet their needs. As with children who blame themselves for the break-up of their parent's marriage, so too neglected children may attribute their parents' lack of attention to them to their own misbehaviour or lack of self-worth. Guy (1987: 124) suggests that children may sense [I would add 'or interpret'] that the therapist parent is more invested in the lives of clients than in their children. This then leaves them resentful, jealous, hurt and angry.

Few children have the capacity at any age to understand and accept emotional depletion of their parents. Furthermore, they may be unable or unwilling to verbalise their needs. A particular difficulty is when the parent-therapist counsels other children, which can involve play and use of stimulating media. This problem was expressed poignantly by one child, who when asked what he wanted to do when he grew up, replied 'I want to be a patient' (Cray and Cray, 1977: 338).

## Emotional withdrawal, preoccupation and exhaustion

Researchers have identified a specific, occasional problem with emotional withdrawal, preoccupation and exhaustion among therapists (Cray and Cray, 1977). Therapist parents are at those times less emotionally available to their family. Their children sometimes will need more patience, nurture and guidance than the burnt-out therapist can provide. Unfortunately parental burn-out occurs in a number of families due to work-related stress in other careers too (Powell, 1999). So it is difficult to disentangle the particular effects of therapy work from other careers.

Time allocated to discuss problems with a partner or friend who will be able to challenge our behaviour may be a useful way to stay aware of how our behaviour is experienced by others; Guy (1987) suggests finding 'an intimate soul mate' who will confront the therapist's tendencies towards isolation and withdrawal, among other issues. I suggest this could be either partner or friend. Some issues might best be taken outside the home. Do we also need to bear in mind how partners cope with the deep relationships we may develop with colleagues/soul friends?

## From being the daughter of two therapists to becoming a therapist myself

From an early age I took on the values of both of my parents, which included aspects of their work. I think it was this set of values, together with feelings of exclusion from this secret world of my parents' work and a strong curiosity over what therapy was about, which led me to study psychology at university and later to pursue a counselling training. As a teenager and as an adult I have benefited from being in counselling myself. I may have been less open to this type of help had my parents not been in the field. However, in several counselling relationships during my late teens and early twenties I did not disclose the fact for a long time that my parents were therapists. Perhaps it was difficult for me because I was striving to separate from them to find my own identity, even in a counselling situation!

Gradually, indeed I have done just that—developed my own identity as an adult, to the extent that I feel comfortable as the daughter of therapists and a part-time therapist myself. The experience of collaborating with my mother, in a mother–daughter team for workshops, has been enjoyable and important for me: It reflects our closeness and friendship, with little rivalry occurring, to my surprise. In looking back over the years I find that it has become easier for me to accept my parents for who they are, as therapists and in other ways. I do think having my own family has helped me understand better some of the pressures, dilemmas and challenges they faced. My attitude towards counselling and psychotherapy has always been and continues to be ambivalent: I think there are many reasons for this, which I continue to discover and make meaning from, some of which are conveyed here in this chapter.

There may well be a large number of therapists' children who will need, as adults, formally to explore and discover the secrets of psychotherapy; the research does indicate this. As was the case in my family, it is not unusual for at least one child of a therapist to eventually pursue a career related to counselling/psychotherapy. For example, one study found that 6% of those therapists surveyed had a child who was also a practising therapist (Guy *et al.*, 1987). I would think there are many more who, like my brothers, explored the field of therapy, if temporarily.

I anticipate an increase in emotional impact of my counselling work on my own children as they get older. As they begin to understand the nature of counselling work and why people sometimes come to see me at home, I anticipate that they will gain more insight into the impact of the work on our family and vice versa. I also hope and trust that my attempts to love them unconditionally, shown through my behaviour towards them, as well as my lifestyle as a whole, will significantly impact on the quality of the relationships I have with my daughter and son. This will be fundamental and instrumental in overcoming emotional difficulties that arise throughout their childhood. My parenting role is a high priority, which demands compromises and sacrifices in relation to my other commitments, including professional therapy work. Indeed, from an adult perspective, I have come to a point where I can appreciate how my own parents succeeded in providing me with substantial love and security, which helped our family to overcome the emotional challenges of two therapists in the family as I was growing up. This has led to a situation where I have been able to collaborate in work ventures with my mother.

## A therapist in the family: the partner's perspective

There are some challenging issues to be confronted in relation to the impact on the therapist's partner. There are positive aspects too, particularly around the flexibility of working times available to the freelance therapist, which benefits the rest of the family. I will focus on four problematical areas described by partners of colleagues: home as a refuge from work, home as a family space, financial issues and work as a refuge from home.

Firstly, for some partners, home provides a refuge from their day-to-day work. This is particularly important when the partner has a conventional job outside the home. They may then struggle with the idea of home also being a place of work. Returning home after a stressful day at work to a hushed work-like atmosphere in the home may feel like an unwelcome extension to the working day.

A partner may find the idea of periods in which the children must be quiet or cannot play in the garden difficult, particularly if those times are part of the small period in which he or she gets to see their children. Unfortunately it is usually the same hours each week that are available for working clients to see their therapist and for working partners to see their family.

Financial issues are a vast area, with wide ramifications. Depending on the partner's occupation, they may feel that the efforts made by everyone in the family to support or enable the therapist's freelance work are not commensurate with the income generated. One partner of a therapist doing freelance work said 'It felt like my partner was working part time as far as running the house went, but earning almost nothing.' Both early on and further down the journey of a career in counselling, partners may find it very hard when so much money is spent on training, therapy, supervision, conferences, accreditation . . . and then after qualifying, their partner does not earn any significant amounts for months, even years, or consistently, if at all. As professions go, freelance counselling work is as insecure financially as many other small businesses. This is a huge challenge to a therapist, their partner and indirectly their children.

Work as a refuge from home is a complex issue. If the partner is used to viewing work as an external activity, whose processes are about something outside themselves, they may find some of the practices of therapy unsettling and difficult. Sometimes the idea of bringing the physical space used for the freelance work into the home may seem an unwelcome metaphor for the intrusion into the home of the emotional space within which the therapeutic interaction occurs. This can go too far into the emotional world of the therapist and their family. Some of the consequences have already been explored, including the rippling effects on the children, but the partner too can find themselves bearing the strain. Some individuals and some marriages can break under the strain.

## When your partner is a therapist too

The challenges may be very different when both partners work in the world of therapy, according to several colleagues. For both partners to be full-time freelance therapists has only been possible for one couple after their children had left home. This seems to be less of a problem when one or both do part-time counselling work. A tremendous advantage of having a partner who is a therapist too came across to me when a colleague spoke of her husband thus: 'He understands what is involved in my work in a way that I think no one working in a different field possibly could. There are many unspoken understandings.' There are also shared interests and values. There is a special companionship in this context, which also is the case when the therapist has a close friend who is in the field too.

However, from my perspective as a child, this situation meant a double shroud of mystery surrounding my parents' occupation. Storr described some of the difficulties from the therapist's point of view:

If the most important thing which has happened to one during the day is that a particular patient has shown a sudden improvement, or that another has broken off treatment, being unable to talk about this in front of the children may increase a parent's remoteness and make the children feel excluded.

(Storr, 1979: 183)

## Family relationships and emotional stress

The emotional stress of therapy work can be long-lasting and extreme at times. This can drain the energies available for family life. I would agree with others that the therapist's own private life relationships need to be a top priority, above the counselling relationships (Freudenberger and Robbins, 1979). Chessick (1978) suggests therapists' mature, loving personal relationships are the key to replenishing their own 'anguished souls' and to empowering them, as therapists, to be able to 'function effectively in the world of loneliness, isolation and distress' of their clients in the therapeutic encounter. Sensitivity towards the emotional impact on partners and friends who provide emotional support is needed. Unless counsellors live a full, satisfying life of their own, they will have little of substance to offer their clients (Freudenberger and Robbins, 1979).

## A lack of emphasis on family dynamics

A search of the literature highlighted for me a visible lack of value given to the connection between 'family dynamics' and being a freelance therapist, since I found so little mention of any of the issues. The texts tend to centre on the practical issues of setting up a small business, ethical considerations and other pertinent and useful topics (for example Syme, 1994). Guy's and Thistle's books are notable exceptions to this, in that they encourage a thorough consideration of the practitioner's emotional needs (Guy, 1987; Thistle, 1998).

This reminds me of when I did my one-year postgraduate training in teaching. It was full of all sorts of useful tutoring on, for example, curriculum content and organisation. However, when I began the real thing with my own class, I realised how little guidance or discussion there had been to help me with how to approach discipline and tackle behaviour problems; how to develop an approach to the relationship aspects of teaching that fitted with my value system. In becoming a professional counsellor, I have had to renegotiate and develop two sets of relationships—professional and family/personal—and deal with the inevitable conflicts that have at times arisen.

I take the position that the extent to which 'being a therapist' can enhance or impede a counsellor's other relationships is one detail of the larger picture of the quality of those relationships, including within the family. A counsellor's particular skills and values may well enhance, for example, their listening and responding skills with others. However, a person's work, family and other personal relationships are defined by many complex, interconnecting factors. The fact that I am a therapist does not necessarily stand out from the many other roles in my life. In this context, self-awareness, love and commitment, together with an openness and willingness to confront difficult issues, arising out of the therapy work background, can help to negotiate successfully with the rest of the family.

## Conclusions

A number of variables combine to determine the kind and extent of impact of having a therapist in the family. The topics explored here have been both practical and psychological/emotionally based. They have involved issues of space, privacy and boundary setting, combining family and work roles, the children's perspective both in childhood and as an adult, as well as the therapist's and partner's views. A therapist's emotional preoccupation, exhaustion and stress have been highlighted as key challenges.

There has been a lack of emphasis on 'family dynamics' in the literature. Moreover the range of issues need to be debated more thoroughly. It is important for a therapist to be alert to the challenges of family relationships in connection with their work. I suggest that many of the tensions can be successfully tackled if the family relationships are able to be kept emotionally secure and loving. A therapist parent, like so many others, is a juggler of roles to maintain a balance of work and family life, which will need to be adjusted, evaluated and creatively adapted over time, to keep in tune with family members' needs and interrelationships.

## Some recommendations

- Sufficient quantity and quality time to be spent together with each child, so that a close relationship is developed and maintained. Children can then be enabled to weather the storms of periods of problematic family dynamics such as our emotional withdrawal from time to time.
- General self-awareness and awareness of each child's and your partner's perspective, and any changes occurring over time.
- A need to be alert to the children's feelings and interpretations of the work, so that parents may sense difficulties as they arise and respond to them quickly and appropriately.
- Time allocated to nurture the relationship with the partner and to discuss problems with a partner or friend, who will challenge our behaviour.

- A need for further research, exploration and debate of the tensions, dilemmas and challenges to the 'family dynamics' of a freelance therapist.

## References

Chessick, R. D. (1978) The sad soul of the psychiatrist. *Bulletin of the Menninger Clinic*, 42: 1–9.

Cray, C. and Cray, M. (1977) Stresses and rewards within the psychiatrist's family. *American Journal of Psychoanalysis*, 37: 337–341.

Freudenberger, H. J. and Robbins, A. (1979) The hazards of being a psychoanalyst. *Psychoanalytic Review*, 66: 275–295.

Guy, J. D. (1987) *The Personal Life of the Psychotherapist*. New York: Wiley.

Guy, J. D., Stark, M. and Poelstra, P. (1987) National survey of psychotherapists' attitudes and beliefs. Unpublished manuscript.

Powell, G. N. (ed.) (1999) *Handbook of Gender and Work*. Thousand Oaks, CA: Sage.

Storr, A. (1979) *The Art of Psychotherapy*. New York: Methuen.

Syme, G. (1994) *Counselling in Independent Practice*. Buckingham: Open University Press.

Thistle, R. (1998) *Counselling and Psychotherapy in Private Practice*. London: Sage.

# Chapter 9

# Personal and professional development

*Jean Clark*

This chapter explores perceptions of professional development in the context of counselling and psychotherapy. It looks at a wide range of experiences, which can help to ensure that skills, awareness of self and others and ethical working practices create safety for our clients, as well as the importance of giving attention to our own personal well-being.

The British Association for Counselling and Psychotherapy (BACP) sets out very specific criteria for Continuing Professional Development (CPD) as part of the accreditation and re-accreditation process (Appendix). The UK Council for Psychotherapy (UKCP) requires that each of its member organisations 'will develop a CPD policy that is appropriate for its registrants and in a form that is consistent with the practice and ethical codes of the organisation' (UKCP, 1999). The Association for Humanistic Psychology Practitioners (AHPP) has developed its own requirements for CPD. In the Independent Practitioners Network (IPN) each group has its own position on personal development. (Totton, personal communication, 2001). Although there are differences in the way each organisation defines CPD, there is likely to be a requirement for a portfolio to be maintained, which will include a log of CPD activities, together with certificates of attainment or attendance for courses undertaken. These will be available for scrutiny from time to time to support continued accreditation and registration. For some organisations supervision and personal therapy are seen as part of CPD, while for BACP proof of regular supervision is a separate requirement. The goal of these procedures is that each counsellor and psychotherapist should continue to ask themselves 'Am I a safe, mature, accountable practitioner?'

The majority of those entering training in counselling and psychotherapy are mature students, who have made the choice to move into this profession as a *development* from their previous work experience, be it in business, nursing, teaching, social work, or in the home caring for children, or as a complete career *change*. They will already have a basis of life experience which has led them to want to become therapists. Whether consciously or unconsciously they will already be on their path of personal development.

Training courses, whether they last one full-time year or up to four years part time, will be focused on the trainees' professional development, and also (in contrast to many other professions) upon their personal development. The personal development element of qualifying courses may include the requirement for a number of hours of personal therapy, and/or membership of a personal development group or experiential group, which are part of the course programme.

The categories for BACP re-accreditation specifically include Personal development (Appendix, category 6). It has long been recognised that just as the work with a client will hopefully lead to change and development, and that this will continue after counselling ends, so for the counsellor or psychotherapist a training course is regarded as the beginning, the springboard to their professional development. When the course finishes, there is yet much to learn and discover.

One dictionary definition of development is 'grow to a mature state'. This speaks of a process within which I seek to bring my learning, my experience, my concerns and my skills to maturity, yet recognise that this is a journey which does not end. I believe that just as counselling at its best is the releasing in the other of a life process, which involves trust, hope, curiosity, risk and the ability to make choices, so too must the counsellor be challenged to undertake activities and seek times of reflection which will release qualities of respect, concern, integrity, creativity and discovery in themselves.

## Choices at the early stage of working freelance

For the recently qualified and for those who may be struggling to work freelance and develop a portfolio of work, which may include counselling in various contexts, the requirement for evidence of CPD can be regarded as a series of hurdles to leap across, and the expenditure of further money at a time when income may be erratic or almost non-existent. A conversation with a recently qualified colleague made me aware of this. 'How many courses shall I attend, which I can then put on my CV? How can I afford the fees for additional training, for I now realise that my counselling diploma (which once I saw as a passport to working as a counsellor) is really a basic qualification? How will I be able to pay for more training courses when I have spent so much already on my course, and am earning so little?' All these were very live issues for him, and raise many of the dilemmas faced by those competing for work 'in the market-place'.

Since there are not many secure full-time or nearly full-time salaried posts in the field of counselling, the matter of professional development through undertaking further training courses is likely to be linked with realistic goals. To work freelance is coming to mean developing a portfolio of work, which may include some hours working in a GP practice, for an Employee Assistance Programme (EAP) and in a specialist agency, perhaps working with young people, drug and alcohol abuse, or with mental health patients, and perhaps some work not related to counselling; and also having clients who want or need to work on a regular long-term basis and are willing to pay for this. Some training courses prepare students for longer-term work, but do not sufficiently explore the stresses and challenges of short-term or contract work.

At a workshop on the theme of Personal and Professional Development, and in dialogue with a number of recently qualified counsellors, in response to the question 'How do you currently make choices which will further your professional development?' I received a range of answers:

- 'My choices are "client led". I find that my basic training was not adequate to work with clients who may have been traumatised, or who have an eating disorder, and so I will seek further appropriate training.'
- 'I look in the journals and think "That course looks interesting", and follow my intuition.'
- 'My choices are money led. I want to widen my skills base to include, for example, an approach to brief therapy, since this is likely to be appropriate if I seek work with an EAP or in a GP practice.'
- 'Having only just qualified, perhaps the more courses and conferences I attend, the better my CV will look.'
- 'I want to deepen my study of a particular topic, by reading and perhaps writing, as well as attending relevant conferences.'
- 'I may want to follow an academic route, bearing in mind the increasing demands for research and evidence-based practice. Once I have achieved accreditation and registration, I may move on to a postgraduate qualification, an MA or PhD, with the possible goal of becoming a trainer at some time in the future. This will make use of my previous years of experience as a teacher.'
- 'I have to consider what I can afford. The diploma course took all my savings, and I am earning very little at the moment.'
- 'I need to further develop my awareness of the ethical implications of my working practices, the various codes of practice, which professional body I shall join. It is a litigious society out there and I must guard my back.'

Clearly some of these responses indicate levels of anxiety about the future, as well as the present, together with concerns about the financial cost which will be involved in the requirements for CPD. For a therapist whose partner is earning, and who is able to work part time, the choices may be wider than for the therapist who is dependent totally upon their own earnings. Yet the former may have a deep desire to remain financially independent.

## Personal and professional development: some perspectives

So what is involved in professional and personal development? It has been very simply defined in terms of:

- *'Inputs'*: courses attended (non-core training), seminars, workshops, lectures, conferences attended, books read.
- *'Outputs'*: lectures, training delivered, involvement and/or responsibilities in organisations, agencies, etc., papers written.

The newly qualified practitioner is likely to discover that their training course did not sufficiently prepare them for some of the issues, which clients may bring. They may want to undertake short courses on specific issues. They will need to keep up to date with current themes, by reading and attending conferences or training days. These are likely, in the early stages, to be experiences of *input*. At a later stage, having digested and reflected upon these inputs and upon what they are learning in their client work, the practitioner may be ready to share their experience with others—to design and lead workshops, to write articles, to do research, to become a supervisor—the *outputs* stage.

## A reactive and proactive model of self-development

Johns (1997) describes two modes of professional development, which she describes as *reactive* and *proactive*. At the beginning of the twenty-first century, we live in a society where there seems to be increasing stress, conflict and violence. Changing expectations and attitudes towards work, gender roles, age-related issues, and tensions in family life, all contribute to the uncertainties of life. Counsellors and psychotherapists are inevitably affected personally, as they as well as their clients seek to find meaning and significance in their lives and in society. It seems that as society becomes more consumer-oriented, more fragmented, more contractual, we are more prone to seek scapegoats to blame when something goes wrong. Counselling and therapy are increasingly being held to account in terms of their effectiveness (or not) and their ethical practice. Our response to all this may be one of defensiveness.

It can be argued that the main reasons for professional development are to do with the *protection* of both the client and the counsellor. The work of developing appropriate and adequate codes of ethics and practice, which provide broad guidelines and strengthen the frameworks within which counselling and therapy take place, have created demands upon the practitioner.

Writing about self-development, Johns (1997: 57) takes as her starting point the reminder that counsellors and psychotherapists 'are people who have particular needs to be self-aware and well grounded, yet open and sensitive to others'. Approved counselling training courses have personal development as a core element. When training ends there will be a need, and increasingly a requirement, for ongoing personal and professional development. Johns suggests two kinds of argument to support this. The first involves what she calls 'reactive responses to the range of critical attacks which bombard counselling and therapy, particularly in terms of accountability' (p. 57).

Reactive responses are those developmental activities which are in the interests of both client and counsellor, protecting the rights of both by supporting and strengthening the ethical frameworks within which counselling and psychotherapy operate. They are defensive of the client and also of the therapist, either of whom may need protection when there is abusive, inappropriate or manipulative behaviour within the therapeutic relationship.

Clearly regular ongoing supervision by an experienced colleague is an important aspect of professional development. John also includes in this category of reactive development the need for the practitioner to consistently widen their base of counselling knowledge and skills and to develop new approaches and techniques which will enable them to meet the needs of a wide range of clients. They will seek constantly to develop and deepen their awareness of their clients and the different contexts within which they live and work, including cultural and gender factors, and to be willing to look at themselves—their responses, motivations, blocks and prejudices—all those factors which may stand in the way of a client's development.

'Clients are likely to be most vulnerable to unaware practitioners who use inappropriately power, seduction, influence, pressure or emotion' (John, 1997: 57). Both individual and/or group supervision and the willingness to undertake training courses with an experiential component will offer opportunities to identify 'blind spots': those areas of incompetence or unacknowledged needs which may be inappropriately brought into the counselling relationship.

It has to be acknowledged that alongside a wider recognition and understanding of the value of counselling in some sectors of society comes more challenge, even attack, from other sources. Complaints to professional bodies are increasing. All these factors will support John's perspective that much self-development is likely to be at some level defensive and reactive. However, she does acknowledge that such a perspective can feel threatening and suggests that instead of feeling caught up in a 'drama triangle' of *persecutor, rescuer and victim*, therapists may instead reflect on their role in terms of another more positive triangle of *pressures* experienced, *resources* available to them and *vision* which is able to take a broader view of the situation.

Johns' second category of developmental activities are those she calls 'proactive and creative'. These involve those activities which nurture, sustain and renew us through our personal and professional life. At the early stages of building up a freelance practice, particularly when there are anxieties about financial survival, there is always the temptation to work too hard, never to say 'no' and so become drained and exhausted. In some areas of the country counsellors are isolated from professional colleagues who would offer support. The wise counsellor will build into their diary, and planning for the year, space for holiday breaks, for creative activities and for time with friends who are not therapists.

Creative self-development is likely to be more concerned with our needs for emotional and social learning. We may forget in our focus on professional development that we need time and space to flourish as human beings, to relate to friends and family, to find time to be alone, to discover and express our creativity. What Goleman (1996) calls 'our emotional intelligence' is likely to be enhanced by time spent with the arts, literature, film, theatre, music and dance.

A creative part of my own development has been through travel, where I may meet and talk with people from other countries, become aware of my own cultural assumptions, meet challenges and widen my vision. It may be a holiday journey, or an international conference where I meet colleagues and hear about different ways of working, different professional structures, and I may find myself healthily disconcerted from time to time. Or I may be with myself walking on the beach, or in the country, and creative ideas seem to emerge—all these different places and spaces where there can be an integration of mind, body and spirit, as we encounter 'the challenge of harnessing our emotions in order to optimise our thinking, acting, choosing, changing, leaving, loving and surviving—or flourishing' (Johns, 1997: 61).

I am conscious that my own experience of self-development, in the early 1970s when training was far less formalised, was a question of what was available. New and creative approaches to personal growth and group work, many of which were relevant to counselling, were emerging from across the Atlantic. Though I did not name it as such, my professional development was a matter of available choices and personal curiosity. Some of my most formative experiences at this time were participation in groups from different orientations. These included:

- Large group dynamics sessions, with Tavistock-trained staff in Nottingham and Leicester.
- A 12-day person-centred cross-cultural workshop in Madrid, involving 180 participants from 26 countries, with Carl Rogers and an international staff of facilitators.
- The annual conference of the Group Relations Training Association, where management trainers, educators and counsellors shared new and creative approaches to training group work in a variety of settings and were able to receive feedback from peers.

In each of these areas of experience I was later fortunate enough to be invited to become a facilitator in subsequent large group experiences. I also tasted a variety of approaches to therapy, from gestalt to transactional analysis, from psychodrama to art therapy. Looking back I recognise what a rich period of both personal and professional development this was, though I might not have named it as CPD. I found my curiosity, creativity and space to explore, in the phrase of the time, my 'human potential'. And here I want to acknowledge the contribution of my Jungian psychotherapist who enabled and encouraged me to explore and reflect upon these experiences, as well as the process issues in my life, and to bring what I learned into my work with clients.

## Continuing professional development (CPD)

The various accrediting bodies require members to undertake and to log CPD activities and to make their records available for scrutiny when requested. BACP requires that during each year accredited counsellors will undertake at least 30 hours of activities which will have contributed to their professional development. These hours must be spread over three or more categories (Appendix), and at least one activity must be from *input* categories which include short courses, further study, seminars and conferences. They are also required to look ahead and make an annual development plan, in collaboration with a colleague or mentor, which may help to ensure a balance in the range of activities undertaken.

It may be helpful to think of CPD in terms of a *process* of learning, stretching, discovering, reflecting and sharing with colleagues in a variety of ways and at different levels, over time. There are a wide range of possibilities.

### Short courses on professional issues

It is likely that, initially, in the first two or three years, most of the activities chosen will be short courses and training conferences undertaken in areas of special interest or concern, as experience is built up to meet the needs of the work situation. Both locally and nationally, there are a range of post-qualifying courses available which enable the freelance practitioner to widen their knowledge and skills base. We can place these in various categories.

### Courses on specific issues

Bereavement, eating disorders, addiction (alcohol, drugs, sex, gambling, shopping), sexual abuse, trauma (including working with post-traumatic stress, critical incident debriefing), stress management, are all issues which may be brought to us by clients in the context of a general counselling service, private practice or an NHS Primary Care counselling service. A short course on assessment will help the counsellor to decide whether short- or long-term therapy is most appropriate, to determine levels of disturbance, and indeed to identify those clients for whom counselling is contraindicated.

### Mental health issues

As counsellors, we will find ourselves working with clients who are depressed or anxious, but not severely so. However, from time to time we may see a client with a psychiatric diagnosis, and this is more likely when working in a medical setting. It may have been part of an initial training course to learn about mental health issues. However, as the work develops, we may want and need to deepen our understanding and attend a seminar or short course where we will be able to ask questions about diagnosis and medication, and engage in case discussion with colleagues.

### Methods of working

Whereas the majority of training courses will be based on long-term working with clients, many counsellors find that their client work is gained through EAPs or in GP practices and health centres, where the client is able to receive a fixed number of sessions of free counselling, maybe six, four or even two. If we are to work effectively in this context, we may need to undertake some training in brief therapy, so that the client will gain maximum benefit from the time available.

### Awareness of difference

Unless we have been fortunate enough to live or work in a diverse multi-class, multi-ethnic community, it is likely that only as our range of client work develops will we become aware of the rich diversity of difference there is in society. We may find ourselves being challenged profoundly, and it can take courage to undertake training courses which will confront us with our own prejudices—be they about different racial groups, different classes in society, attitudes towards the young, older people, those with disabilities, the handicapped, those of a different sexual orientation, a different gender.

One of the criteria for initial accreditation by BACP requires that the applicant 'can show evidence of serious commitment to working with issues of difference and equality in counselling practice' (BACP, 2000). This may have been explored in initial counsellor training, but it may further be addressed by undertaking a subsequent training, seminar or workshop as part of CPD. The *Multi-Cultural Journal*, produced by the Race and

Cultural Education in Counselling Division of BACP (RACE), is a valuable resource for articles, and forthcoming training days and seminars.

Such a commitment to difference and equality is wide ranging. It can be painful to recognise, then to work with, our prejudices about those who are different in some way from ourselves. It is challenging to be aware of those issues of power which can stand in the way of equality of respect and treatment. It needs to be an ongoing process in our counselling practice.

### Spiritual dimensions of counselling

In discussion with trainees nearing the end of a course, I have found that a number are drawn to further training in approaches using Transpersonal or Psychosynthesis theory, where they will be able openly to acknowledge their own and their client's spiritual journey, and to work with visualisation, drawing, dreams, in a theoretical context, which matches their own self-development. There seems to be an increasing interest in the spiritual dimension of counselling and some therapists will encourage clients to write poetry or keep a journal or paint the symbols which emerge.

There are a variety of short courses and workshops which may nurture our creativity and our spiritual journey. My own exploration has involved courses and retreats using art, drama, singing, meditation, writing and dance.

### Information technology

Counsellors and psychotherapists are likely to see information technology (IT) skills as part of their professional development. It is becoming more and more relevant, whether it be for business accounts, publicity, correspondence, writing articles or a book, or to have access to the Internet, to develop websites, or undertake email counselling with a client. Email has immense potential in reaching some client groups such as young males, who would not otherwise approach a counsellor.

### Independent practice

In Chapter 1 Gabrielle Syme suggests that for those who are ready to consider setting up in independent practice it is worth seeking out a short course on the issues involved. These are likely to include readiness to take private clients, the business aspects and considerations about premises, publicity and support.

### Group work

I have already described the wide range of my own learning during the 1970s through membership of groups, large and small, based in different theoretical orientations. I know that I continue to be aware of the different levels of experiencing when I join any new group, my internal dialogue (intra-psychic), the processes of communication between different group members (inter-psychic) and the process of a group as an entity. I find myself sometimes shocked when counsellors undertake to work with a group and yet have not had the focused experience of group membership with time for reflection on process, or the opportunity to be an apprentice group facilitator.

### Attendance at conferences and seminars

A further BACP criterion for CPD is attendance at conferences and seminars on topics relevant to professional practice. These may be organised locally, nationally or internationally, by individuals or by organisations, and can offer opportunities to meet with peers at different levels of experience and from different theoretical orientations. Listening to speakers who have had wide experience can put us in touch with current trends. Meeting in discussion groups can take us out of the narrowness of our individual counselling room, and open new perspectives. Meeting informally at break times can enable networking, a vital element of support for the freelance practitioner.

### To undertake further award-bearing training in a relevant professional field

It is likely, for some therapists, that they will reach a stage in their professional development when they may want to undertake a further award-bearing training. This may be a certificate or diploma in supervision, or brief therapy or trauma work, which will enhance and extend their practice. Some will choose to undertake research for an MA or PhD. At this time when there is an increasing demand for evidence that therapy 'works', research topics may be in the field of evidence-based practice.

### Encouraging the development of others

With experience comes the capacity to use what we have learned for the benefit of others. For some this may involve writing articles or books on themes relevant to counselling and psychotherapy. For others it may be giving lectures, or offering workshops at a conference. Or we may take an initiative, alone or with colleagues, to develop new ideas and themes relevant to counselling, and make these available to others in a workshop or seminar. Becoming a trainee trainer, a workshop facilitator, a mentor, a consultant to a staff team, a contributor to conferences, offering workshops or as a speaker, or writing letters to journals—all these are ways in which we may encourage others to develop their thinking and widen their experience in the field of therapy.

### Committee work/meetings

This aspect of our contribution to the development of our profession may occur at national and/or local level. It could mean involvement with some national committee work for a professional body, or an advisory role for a local counselling centre, becoming a committee member for a local BACP group, membership of an Independent Practitioners Network group, a Psychotherapists and Counsellors for Social Responsibility group or a local forum of counsellors and psychotherapists.

This work, in addition to enabling organisations to exist and function, offers opportunities to share what we have learned, to contribute to the development of our profession and what it stands for, and at a local level the encouragement of those who are just beginning their journey. Meetings with colleagues can identify areas of concern and opportunities for collaboration, leading to local initiatives. Attending meetings set up by other organisations may mean that we can fruitfully represent counselling to others.

### Personal development

It is accepted that the quality of the relationship between therapist and client is crucial for the process of healing. What is it that contributes to this quality? Psychodynamic theory would stress the capacity to offer insight, understand the influence of the past on the present and awareness of transference and countertransference; consequently training courses require a long period of ongoing personal therapy. Person-centred theory would stress the capacity to offer the core conditions of genuineness, acceptance and empathic understanding. Both will require an awareness of self in the relationship.

Training in counselling and psychotherapy will normally require either a period of personal therapy, which will vary from 40 hours to the whole duration of the course or, in a person-centred training, participation in a regular personal development group. When applying for BACP accreditation, one of the requirements is to 'show evidence of having completed a minimum of 40 hours of personal counselling or has engaged in an equivalent activity consistent with the applicant's core model' (BACP, 2000).

Some therapists will choose to continue with their own therapy beyond the period of their training, and many will feel that if they are to understand the complexities of transference and countertransference in their work and in their lives this is a long-term commitment. Then there will be times when our personal life involves stress. Bereavement, loss, separation, anxiety about what is happening for a member of the family, can touch any of us. Some counsellors will use therapy for themselves at such times of crisis. Others will continue in long-term therapy for personal growth and development and see it as an essential part of their ongoing professional development.

However, personal development needs to be seen in wider terms. Because the work of offering therapy can be draining, even debilitating, we need to create balance and find nurture in other aspects of our lives. This may require planning. There was a time when I had a piece of card beside my telephone which reminded me to say 'Give me time to think about it.' It was a very simple act of time management as I learned to rearrange my workload in a way which gave me some clear spaces in the week when I could meet friends, go to the coast or simply sit and read a book.

We may need time for our own creativity. 'Human existence is half light and half dark, and our creative possibilities seem strangely linked to that part of ourselves we keep in the dark' (Whyte, 1997: 29). New ideas, concepts, connections may only come when we allow ourselves quiet time and space. It may be a walk in the country, or time to write in a journal, or reflection on work with a client. It may be time and space to brainstorm and design a new training workshop with a colleague. We may join a dance group, an art group, a drama group. We may even take a break from counselling for a period.

We need to find a balance in our lives, time for family, time for friends, time for nurturing activities—exercise, massage, concerts, theatre, films, holiday breaks, a peer support group. To allow ourselves what we need, to avoid burn-out, to widen our relationship with the wider world, all this is part of our development as persons who are professionals.

## Charting progress

Wilkins suggests that 'to demonstrate personal and professional development it is necessary to have identified professional and personal needs, to have decided how they might be met and to be able to show what progress has been made' (Wilkins, 1997: 24). To maintain BACP re-accreditation, there is now the requirement to maintain an annual CPD log on a formal basis (Appendix).

Here are some extracts from the log which I kept during 2000:

| Date | Activity | Hours | BACP criteria |
|------|----------|-------|---------------|
| 18 April | Participated in workshop on Critical Incident Debriefing and Diagnosis. | 5 | (1) |
| 29 April | Designed and facilitated workshop on Supporting the Professionals (planning time and workshop) and | 3 | (1) |
| | attended conference on The Impact of Suicide, UEA. | 3 | (2) |
| 2 May | Reading *After Silence: Rape and My Journey Back* by Nancy Venable Raine. | 7 | (6) |

However, if I find that written reflection helps me to internalise my learning, I may choose to take my log a stage further, and explore what I discovered from these experiences—about the subject and about myself in the experience?

### Reflective practice

Schon (1983) describes two perspectives on professionalism. Traditionally the basis of a profession is a body of knowledge which is handed down to the aspiring practitioner. But over time the qualified practitioner will be building up a repertoire of examples, outcomes and understandings as they learn by doing. Intelligent action describes the area of professional working which arises out of reflection upon this accumulation of knowledge. We know more than we are able to say and this knowing arises from the whole of our experience, so far as it is accessible to us for understanding and action.

For the practising counsellor we may say that professional development is about taking time and space both to learn about new areas of knowledge and to develop the capacity for reflection in action. This will also be happening in supervision as we reflect upon our relationship and inter-action with clients and with our own understandings.

Such a habit of reflection upon practice is an important part of con-tinuing professional development. The CPD log will be a record of various activities undertaken, but for some people the discipline of keeping a journal can create space for the learning which has occurred as we parti-cipate with others in training events, in committee work, as facilitators, and in the variety of activities we may undertake as part of our personal development.

### Extracts from a reflective journal

*18 April*—Participated in a training day set up by Norfolk Trauma Counselling Network. Aware it was a group which included several ex-clients and supervisees (such is the nature of a training group when you live in a provincial city!). Role-play as members of a group of workers in a major industrial accident. I really got into the feelings— aware again how powerful role-play can be, and the importance of debriefing. (Remember this when we are asking people to role-play in bereavement training course next week.) Key learning was that debriefing is not a therapeutic process, but diagnostic—an opportu-nity to identify those who would need individual work at a later stage (for bereavement counselling or for post-traumatic stress) and those who are likely to be able to use normal coping strategies to work through the impact of the trauma. Good to be part of an excellently designed workshop. Trainers should become participants on a regular basis!

*29 April*—Conference on 'The Impact of Suicide' at UEA. I facilitated a workshop on 'Supporting the Professionals' (a) when clients unexpectedly start talking about suicidal feelings and (b) when the worst happens and there is a suicide. How do we acknowledge and care for ourselves? Seven people in group. I offered a simple structure: talk in pairs for 10 minutes, then a tough case study. People came from different disciplines (church, counselling, youth work)—their reactions to the case study were interestingly different. Good mutual learning process which I did not foresee. Did I move them too fast through (b) caring for ourselves? (1 1/2 hours too short for this theme!). Used handouts for recognising secondary traumatic stress, which for the professional worker is likely to follow suicide of a client. (I do tend to trust that people will be sufficiently engaged in the session to continue exploring the issues, and will use material in handouts.) Reflecting later, I felt it had been right to create a clear structure to hold participants when we were working for a short time with such a theme as suicide. It could easily have turned into a therapy group.

*May, over several days*—Reading *After Silence*, an extraordinary, courageous and self-aware true story by a writer who at age 39 was raped by a stranger in her own home, and her search for therapeutic help. I have worked over the years with several clients who suffered rape and its aftermath. This book has given me a much deeper insight into the long complex journey of recovery. Her painful acceptance of the fact that the person who suffers the trauma of rape can never be the person they would have been parallels the difficult recognition made by several of my clients. I shall recommend it to some colleagues and supervisees.

## A developmental model

I have deliberately entitled this chapter 'Personal and professional development', rather than 'Continuing professional development', for I want to be clear that, for me, ongoing development as a counsellor and psychotherapist encompasses far more than a required number of hours each year. In these times of increasing demand for proof of professional development, bringing counselling and psychotherapy into line with other caring professions, it feels even more important that we see CPD in terms of our own unique journey of learning, of discovery, of dialogue, of reflection, of creative expression, of self-nurture, rather than as a series of hoops to jump through, to fulfil criteria.

I have found the clarification of BACP categories of CPD to be very helpful and have used them in this chapter. However, it is to be hoped that the requirement for an Annual Development Plan will not limit or inhibit the creativity and spontaneity which I believe is a necessary part of personal and professional development, and cannot always be pre-planned a year ahead. I trust that those who are asked to take on a role of mentor will encourage counsellors to broaden their vision before they begin to focus down on the developmental needs they will seek to meet in the coming year. A developmental need might be to undertake a creative activity, to find a course to develop awareness of difference, to read several books around a particular issue, to plan and offer a workshop or lecture on a theme of their choice, or to take a more active role in an organisation connected with counselling/psychotherapy.

There can be a healthy tension between the limitations of meeting criteria and the creativity inherent in the opportunities to learn through writing down reflections upon practice. The maintenance of a log of all our developmental activities, together with a personal reflective journal, will provide an *aide mémoire* and perhaps challenge us to explore other aspects of ourselves in our personal and professional life.

I have tried to describe a journey through stages of learning, discussing, researching, integrating and sharing what we discover, together with periods of reflection and relaxation. We will circle back through these stages from time to time, for there are always opportunities and challenges to learn new concepts, new approaches, and above all to widen our awareness of difference, of the other, of what is going on in society, and the impact on our clients and ourselves. It can be an exciting journey.

## References

BACP (2000) *Criteria for Accreditation*. Rugby: British Association for Counselling and Psychotherapy.

Goleman, D. (1996) *Working with Emotional Intelligence*. London: Bloomsbury.

Johns, H. (1997) Self-development: lifelong learning. In I. Horton and V. Varma (eds), *The Needs of Counsellors and Psychotherapists*. London: Sage.

Raine, N. V. (1999) *After Silence*. London: Virago.

Schon, D. A. (1983) *The Reflective Practitioner*. Aldershot: Arena.

UKCP (1999) *Continuing Professional Development: Principles and Requirements for Member Organisations*. London: UK Council for Psychotherapy.

Whyte, D. (1997) *The Heart Aroused: Poetry and the Preservation of the Soul at Work*. London: The Industrial Society.

Wilkins, P. (1997) *Personal and Professional Development for Counsellors*. London: Sage.

## Appendix: British Association for Counselling and Psychotherapy Annual Renewal of Accreditation/ Registration

### Section 4: Continuing Professional Development (CPD)

Categories and examples:

#### Category 1: Short courses on professional issues

Examples:   Courses undertaken in areas of special interest or concern which are relevant to counselling practice, e.g. working with abuse, working with trauma, bereavement, brief therapy.
These may be offered by training agencies or 'in-house'.

#### Category 2: Seminars and conferences

Examples:   BACP and divisional conferences.
Seminars/conferences on topics relevant to professional practice, which may be organised locally, nationally or internationally, by individuals or organisations.

#### Category 3: Study for further qualifications

Examples:   Further award-bearing training in relevant professional field, e.g. certificate or diploma in supervision, or brief therapy, or trauma work.
Higher degree in counselling.

#### Category 4: Encouraging the development of others

Examples:   Designing and facilitating workshops.
Offering a training session or giving a talk at a conference.
Writing, e.g. articles, book reviews, books (relevant to professional practice).
Published research.

Initiatives taken alone and in consultation with peers to create and develop. New ideas relevant to counselling and making these available to others.

## Category 5: Committee work/meetings

Examples:  Counselling-related committee work, local or national.
Consultation with counselling colleagues leading to initiatives.
Membership of committees where counselling may be represented to others.

## Category 6: Personal development

Examples:  Participation in groups.
Personal therapy.
Learning new skills.
Acquiring knowledge and new insight from reading, films, plays.
Time and space for reflection.

Those applying for BACP re-accreditation are required to undertake at least 30 hours of activities which have contributed to their professional development from three or more of the above categories. At least one activity must be from Categories 1–3.

# Part IV

# Survival in practice

In professions such as social work or nursing or teaching, training is likely to have enabled the student to focus on areas of particular interest, so that after qualifying they will be able to apply for a salaried post where this can be developed. Counselling and psychotherapy do not have this kind of structure and there is no guarantee that there will be work after training; in fact it is very unlikely that practitioners will find a salaried post at this stage. It is for each person to find their own path, to sell themselves and to build a portfolio of clients. There are many uncertainties and insecurities.

The eight people who have contributed to this section of the book all write directly out of their experiences in different sectors of freelance practice. Chapter 10 very specifically tells the stories of four counsellors who had qualified within the previous five years. Their experiences and choices are very different and yet are representative of the various ways in which people work to 'survive in practice'.

Two areas where counsellors may find work on a freelance basis are in NHS primary care working with clients in general practice, and in Employee Assistance Programmes, which offer a range of counselling and consultancy services to national and local organisations. There is likely to be some guarantee of work, though not necessarily on a regular basis, and many counsellors have chosen to put their energies into working in one or both of these sectors. For the experienced and established counsellor or psychotherapist there is the possibility of working with long-term clients on a regular basis; this way of working has its own demands and satisfactions.

# Chapter 10

# The early years

*Joe Daggers, Jacky Moss, Leebert Hughes and Gerry Virgo*

Four counsellors who qualified about five years ago were invited to reflect upon their experiences. Their paths are very different and have been, sometimes still are, demanding, insecure, stressful and yet satisfying. Perhaps it is not surprising that during the period in which they were each writing their 'story' for this chapter three of them faced major challenges and their work took off in new directions. It is in the nature of freelance that we do not know what will be round the next corner and whether or not we shall decide to say 'yes' to opportunities when they come.

## COUNSELLING PEOPLE: A COUNSELLING PARTNERSHIP

*Joe Daggers*

This is the story of how I and two friends and fellow students, whom I met on a counselling diploma course, set up a new counselling partnership and, very stumblingly at first, learned to run it. To our surprise, we encountered considerable hostility to our entrepreneurial effrontery from some other counsellors. How dare we set up on our own without the tutelage of a voluntary agency or the patronage of some other well-established counselling service?

But, having worked for over 20 years as a librarian for local government, and having experienced the frustrations of a rigid hierarchy and a plethora of red tape, I felt strongly that it was important for me to encounter the opportunities, the risks, the freedoms and the self-discipline of self-employment for a while. And I have indeed found it to be an invaluable source of self-empowerment, which I do not believe that I would have been able to experience to the same extent working for a voluntary agency or in a salaried post (which is not to say that others may not find working in those other environments a preferable and more fulfilling alternative).

In spite of the apparently daunting odds, *Counselling People* is still here two and a half years on. I am still in it, although for differing reasons my two partners have recently left. Even if the business fails now, I for one will have found it an extremely valuable and exciting experience and one which I would not willingly have foregone.

When I look back on the year in which I completed my counselling diploma, the image which most frequently comes to mind is that of a cocoon. All the participants on the course seemed cocooned in our private world and for long stretches of time seemed to be able to forget or ignore the harsher outside realities. As the course drew to a close there was a slow and painful awakening to the fact that most of us had to re-enter the world and earn a living. Excellent as the course had been in acquainting us with the theory and practice of counselling, it had done very little to equip us with the knowledge of how to set up in private practice.

Only one nod was made towards that possible aspect of our future in the very last week of the course; this entailed informing us about further training courses which would require another outlay of cash that very few of us had!

As a newly formed partnership, our first task was to find some suitable premises from where we could counsel. This is generally the largest fixed overhead of any counselling enterprise and anyone who counsels from home is at a considerable financial advantage. However, there are other well-documented disadvantages to counselling from home. The most serious to my mind is that, unless one already has an established reputation, it may present a lack of professionalism.

We were fortunate in finding suitable premises quickly. They were in a large office building quite near the city centre. It was a single furnished room which cost us £200 a month to rent. That included all bills except the telephone. While the business built up, we proposed to cover this and other costs by contributing £80 a month each. We were able to discontinue this subsidy after eight months and indeed, after 15 months, felt we were doing well enough to move into two adjoining rooms at a total cost of £340 a month.

The most daunting struggle in the early stages of a new business is to become noticed. It is extremely difficult to gauge the most effective ways to advertise. In retrospect I have to say that I think we misdirected much of our energy in those early days of *Counselling People*. We had several thousand leaflets printed and, systematically targeting different areas of the city, delivered them by hand. We advertised in the local paper. But, because we started up in July, we would have to wait seven months to take advantage of what seems to be one of the most effective advertisement for counsellors—the *Yellow Pages*. However, at least we had the psychological boost of focusing our initial enthusiasm and energy onto *something*. And one or two clients did begin to trickle in. A few of the laboriously delivered leaflets must have struck a chord. Or maybe someone *had* noticed our newspaper advertisement after all.

The other type of promotion which we began to practise was offering a service to local businesses. This involved trawling through the *Yellow Pages* and telephoning larger businesses to find out, firstly, whether they had an existing counselling service and, if not, whether they might be interested in anything we had to offer. This is a time-consuming but potentially very valuable way of promoting a counselling service. The most frustrating aspect of it is the time wasted in speaking to the wrong people, for it is by no means always clear whose area of responsibility in a company the establishment of a counselling service might be.

However, dogged persistence won its just reward. By means of repeated enquiries by telephone and letter we had after 18 months succeeded in getting contracts with two large companies. We had also come within a whisker of securing what might well have been a profitable contract with another, but unforeseen circumstances intervened to deprive us of that, in what appeared to be the final stages of the negotiations. You win some, you lose some!

The advantage for the private counselling practice of corporate work is that it provides a bedrock of financial security and is less subject to the vagaries that affect the flow of individual clients. But the difficulty of securing even one corporate client should not be underestimated. It would have been easy to be terminally discouraged by the large number of rejections, a number of them quite offhand and bruising. On the whole, though, I was impressed and gratified by the level of courtesy and interest shown by our potential corporate clients.

I remain firmly convinced that, despite the greater degree of boldness required by the telephone, it is the most effective method of approaching firms in the first instance. It establishes a more immediate and intimate personal contact than a letter, although it is always worth following up this first call with a letter and information pack, unless specifically requested not to do so. If contact has already been made by telephone, such correspondence is much less likely to find its way straight into the rubbish bin and may indeed be put on file, as promised.

Another valuable outlet for publicising our services has been doctors' surgeries. A surprisingly large number of doctors have proved perfectly amenable to displaying our leaflets. With increasing pressure on surgery budgets for counselling, many doctors are pleased to be able to recommend private counselling to those patients who do not want to join a waiting list and can afford to pay.

In order to be able to advertise more effectively in the future, it is important to determine which advertising is working and which is not. This can only be done by carrying out some home-grown market research—by asking all new clients where they came across our name. On certain occasions this may not be possible (when clients are very distressed, for instance) but in most cases clients are willing to oblige.

We found that the majority of new clients had seen our advertisement in *Yellow Pages*. But to have the best chance of ensuring that any initial enquiries were transformed into paying clients, it was necessary to try to see that *someone* was on the end of the telephone for as many hours of the day and evening as possible. Although better than nothing, an answerphone is an inferior alternative to a live response.

It appears that what many people seeking counselling, or indeed other services via the *Yellow Pages*, do is to ring a series of numbers until they actually speak to someone. Thus those companies that can arrange to have the phone answered personally give themselves a huge advantage. This is more true of counselling, compared with services such as plumbing or removals, where people are more willing to leave a message. Many people seeking counselling are troubled and uncertain and need the balm of a sympathetic response, not the cold comfort of a disembodied voice, however expertly recorded.

Our group evolved a rota whereby the office phone would be redirected to one of the partners at their home, or to a mobile phone when no one was in the office. This was particularly valuable in the evenings and at weekends and brought us clients who, had we not had this system, would almost certainly have gone elsewhere.

Another problem which has to be faced at the outset when setting up a private counselling practice is what to charge. Money and counselling have traditionally had a rather uneasy relationship. The low-cost counselling offered by voluntary or quasi-voluntary counsellors can sometimes make the private practitioner feel somewhat grasping and mercenary. And yet businesses have overheads which have to be paid. It is not ignoble to wish to recoup the costs of a fairly expensive training by charging others for benefiting from that skill. It is not ignoble to wish to earn a living from practising a vocation. What is more often crushing and depressing for counsellors is *not* to be able to do this.

Initially we thought to compete with other counselling practices and pay deference to our own inexperience by charging only £18 a session. But because we had a sliding scale according to need, our average take per session was considerably less than this. After nine months we realised that our charges were not really competitive and may well have reflected badly on our perceived professionalism. We duly raised our top rate to £30 and immediately saw a quite large increase in income.

As for negotiating with clients over fees, many counsellors initially balk at the prospect of this. They may see it as sullying the purity of the process (rather than being an integral part of the process). But in my experience most members of the public are surprisingly sympathetic and understanding about money. They pay for other services and most of them expect to pay for counselling. And, even though we do still have a sliding scale, an unexpectedly large number of clients pay the full rate without demur.

What strikes me forcibly after two and a half years working in a private counselling practice is the necessity of running it as an efficient small business. Without making use of such practices, private counselling partnerships cannot hope to succeed. With an ever-increasing number of counsellors jostling one another for clients, advertising needs to be carefully planned, astutely directed and minutely monitored. With limited funds available, such forethought and discrimination are imperative, especially as there are more and more companies trying to sell advertising space to unwary counsellors. Some of this may be worth having—such as a space on a hospital appointment card. But much of it will bring in very little, if any, extra business.

The foregoing may have painted a picture of a partnership almost wholly absorbed in trying to create a financially successful business and for the purposes of this chapter I have hitherto concentrated exclusively on this area of what we did. But I think that all the partners would agree that our joint supervision sessions and mutual support, in the face of emotional tribulations and often demanding and difficult clients, were an equally, or even more, important aspect of our association. They provided a spiritual grounding for the partnership without which any material success would have been meaningless.

## FROM THERE TO HERE

*Jacky Moss*

I am a person-centred practitioner who gained my counselling qualifications through a person-centred diploma course during 1994–97. I now earn my living as a self-employed freelance counsellor and group facilitator. I have worked in a variety of places, up to seven at any one time. I also offer workshops in one place I work. So how did I get here? This is a personal view, my own individual path 'from there to here'.

After qualifying I continued to work as a volunteer in the counselling centre that had offered me the opportunity to practise as a student. I was well supported in this place and I very much valued the long-term work with a wide variety of clients drawn to this charity, which offers counselling to all independent of ability to pay. This was an active choice. I decided to invest a large amount of my energy working with nine or ten clients each week for a considerable length of time. My confidence developed in proportion to the increasing hours of experience, with the opportunity to do long-term work and where some clients had concurrent mental health involvement. I met and worked with other people in the local counselling world, making network contacts with professionals from whom I knew I would hear of likely opportunities when they arose.

I did only intensive voluntary work for a year after qualifying, relying for family living expenses on a small pension from a previous professional job plus some capital. My partner was very supportive of the path I was taking, and I moved to a smaller house, which reduced the mortgage. Having funded my training and then a transition year, from capital to the tune of probably £25,000, it seems in retrospect a big risk, this re-evaluation of life and starting again.

The gains are both professional and, to a large extent, emotional and spiritual. I am now, more than two years on, making a living as a counsellor. To put that into context, I continue to receive my small pension and am part of a dual-income family. I take six weeks holiday a year, time which is, of course, non-earning. To summarise: first year post-qualification, no earnings; second year business profit £1262; and now by the end of this third year I am currently earning around £1400 per month, which is taxable. There is no security in what I do because funding can dry up at any time.

If I had seen these figures, if they had been there to look at, would I have done it? Well yes, but that is the person I am—I leap in and try and swim. I propelled myself into it because I believed in what I was selling. I was integrated in it—it was not a job, it was me. And I threw myself into a course of action because I wanted to do it—deeply wanted to do it. I filtered out what I didn't want to hear, like the dangers, the responsibility. I only heard what I wanted to hear, that it was possible and I could do it . . . and I have.

I knew there was other work. I took my courage in both hands and put myself out there in the market-place, lots of fingers in other pies. You get known and then one day the phone rings; sessions are offered here and there. It is wonderful to be recommended. The important thing though is not just getting work but keeping it and being asked again. You can get work by pushing for it, or by a fluke, or by recommendation, but being able to maintain the flow of work is the key. I was offered one job because I talked with someone I met in the opticians; another job followed an interaction with a person I met through my connections with the counselling agency. In both cases I made an impact. By being myself wholeheartedly and openly I was seen as potentially valuable in the client work. Then I found I was being asked back again and again.

There were anxieties in me: 'Can I offer this?' I learned to hear the feedback. It took me a long time to realise that there were people out there who thought I could—people who were recommending me as someone to talk to who might help. I had decided to try things that were offered to me to see if I could do them, and was prepared to travel, sometimes over long distances. I was prepared to work initially for very little money, because I wanted to do the work; in one instance for four hours I was paid £15. It got me known and trusted. Then I was able to be more selective and no longer do some of the early activities. I took a risk in not accepting a contract for work I had been doing, since the fee offered was reduced to a low level.

All this determination came from a place in me that never wanted to be part of a single institution again. I can get immersed in institutions and take on an organisational identity. I can get absorbed, sucked into a worthy cause and then become dysfunctional in it. My professional need is to be creative with myself, within different settings and with a variety of people, taking the freedom to develop and change, seeing life as a flowing river. I wanted to retain my own identity, I wanted to retain my 'isness'. It is this desire that leads me on.

I have worked with children and with adults, in the areas of addiction and mental health; I have worked in groups and with individuals. With this experience I am now able to identify where I function best, and where the cost of giving is too great. I like being involved, setting things up from scratch, and I have the energy to stick at things until they happen. Where my friend and colleague collects leaves and makes a pile, I shake the tree. Because I have a good relationship with my gut feeling, I know when I want to commit myself and so I do not get swept into things. Now I am tailoring my work into avenues for creative work with addiction, where there is the challenge of 'anything is possible', and I have also recently ended my voluntary work.

I much prefer to work in a team. There is safety in watching others and being watched by others; this gives me the limits and the freedoms to be creative. As a child I had to function on my own and became autonomous. But there was no mirroring, no feedback, no awareness of growth because I only had reference to myself. My life drama was only within myself. Only when I put my beliefs and my power out in the world did things change—when I valued something beyond myself.

Accreditation is still in the pipeline. I want to do this but am perhaps a little paperwork phobic so it has not yet come to the top of my list. I am proud to say that I have sold not a qualification but a training, and I have been employed for my demonstrable skills. However, I can feel vulnerable in a world of MA and PhD qualifications. I sometimes feel like a tree trunk, where qualifications are the twigs, and I am without twigs. I am person-centred and congruence is central, but yes, I feel unprotected sometimes and then I read Charles O'Leary and I don't feel so alone. Arrogance has served me well—arrogance as a positive investment in myself. I let people know I really believe in what I am saying. This is clearer in the context of a supervision relationship with the endless checking that I am on track. I like a quote from Narcotics Anonymous: 'Attitudes are contagious, are yours worth catching?'

The key thing is that I am out there doing it. I feel safe with clients because I know myself well. I feel I won't harm anyone if I put myself alongside them. In what ways I 'do good' is another question for another time. The development of myself is what has enabled me to go forward, using opportunities for continuing personal and professional development.

Then there are relationships with peers and friends. Do I say 'I have been offered this piece of work', knowing my companion could be my competitor? I am in competition with people with whom I have been through the fire during my training course. You have to work through fair means, being well informed and dispassionate, not sycophantic. It means competing in a fair market, not just feeling competent but being prepared to come out and say 'I am your equal and I can do this piece of work.' I had felt that competition with peers would be an issue for me, but it hasn't blocked my path.

I did feel fear. The fear that it wasn't simply a *profession* I was selling, I was putting *me* out there. The matter of success or failure was chilling; can I 'do' relationships or can I not? Failure would be failure of my relational self; acceptance meant acceptance of my relational self. This self has grown in a healthy way out of my early battle armour, as the youngest of four daughters, where I had learned to be special, specially strong, specially competent, specially fearless, specially having no needs. The way I am writing here now is the way I have grown to be in life, prepared to be me and accept feedback, to be open to people's responses to me. I can ask for myself what I do need and refuse what I don't need. This is me, a counsellor in action.


## MY JOURNEY

*Leebert Hughes*

What was I doing before I entered counselling? Well, I did an apprenticeship as a mechanical engineer for a local company, building power stations, and stayed with this firm for 17 years. My responsibilities included training apprentices and technicians in manufacturing techniques; but although I enjoyed the work I always had an interest in electronics. So I worked in the daytime and went to night school in the evenings to study electronics. After I gained the qualification I left mechanical engineering and became a self-employed electronics engineer, supplying and installing security alarm systems.

It was a big leap from engineering to counselling. I became interested in counselling through my voluntary work with the probation service and my local church and a friend suggested I might undertake a course. My journey started in 1993 when I enrolled on an 'introduction to counselling' course. I enjoyed it and continued through the levels, culminating in a diploma in 1996. I am person-centred trained, although I would not consider myself to be a purist, in that I sometimes use techniques from other orientations if it is appropriate for the client.

Person-centred theory has some common links with my Christian beliefs: to be respectful of others, the importance of being real in any relationship and showing understanding and caring for others. For me this theory is about meeting basic human needs in order to facilitate change. If I can create the right atmosphere and help someone to feel safe enough to explore their issues, they are empowered to become more self-sufficient. I enjoy working in a person-centred way and it works for me.

While I was studying for the counselling diploma I developed a problem in my shoulder which necessitated two operations, and because of this I could not continue to work as an engineer. Disappointed and angry to be told I could not continue to do the work I enjoyed, I somewhat reluctantly began to consider my career options. I came to the conclusion that I would make counselling my next career once I was qualified. It seemed to me at that time that I would be able to walk straight into a job or make a lot of money working privately!

After qualifying I was confident that I would quickly find work. There were jobs in the daily newspapers, but 'guess what?': they wanted people with three years' experience and/or BAC accreditation. Somewhat discouraged but determined that I would make counselling my career, I went back to the drawing board. One of the requirements of the diploma course was to have a placement, and while I was training my placement was in a GP practice. So I approached the GPs requesting them to now pay me for the service I was providing for their patients. To my delight they agreed to pay me for one afternoon a week; this was a start but not enough to survive financially.

My next step was to attempt to set up in private practice, working from home to keep my overheads down, even though my researches highlighted the difficulties. I had cards and flyers printed and wrote to various organisations, expecting a good response from the efforts I had made. But weeks and months went by and clients were not coming and I was not earning. I began to wonder if I had made the right decision. Yet colleagues and other professionals were telling me there was a demand for black counsellors. Yes, there was a demand if I wanted unpaid work.

The early years were difficult. There were times when I wanted to give up because my dream of being able to make a living from counselling was not being realised. Then I would get a couple of hours work, which gave me hope. Writing letters, filling in application forms, attending interviews, earning no money, all this was very frustrating, and it seemed I had a skill that no one wanted, except for free. When I did get an interview, I would often be told that they were looking for someone with more experience. I was conscious that I am male and black, and I do not know if this was a factor.

I continued to approach GPs, schools, hospitals and the health authority looking for part-time or sessional work, but it seemed the well was dry. I applied to employee assistance programmes, but they wanted three years' experience. Eventually I signed up with one EAP and received some referrals; then someone from that organisation came to visit and see where I was working, and from that day I have not received another referral. The fact that white colleagues in my area who had joined the same EAP were receiving referrals raised questions in my mind.

I soon realised that I could not make a living this way. If I were to continue I would need to supplement my income with other work. Having done a teaching course prior to my counselling training, I began looking for part-time teaching in counselling, and managed to secure work teaching counselling skills, levels 1 and 2; then I obtained some sessional work at a local university. Things were improving, but the summer months were hard financially. I needed to find work which would bring me an income through the year. This led to part-time work with a primary care group.

The first GP practice I worked in was in a predominantly white area. I would notice the shock of some clients when they first met me. Some would be polite enough to stay for the first session and then not come back. Others, but not many, would leave before we even had time to make a contract to work together. I have also had black clients who had expected to see a white counsellor, and seeing me is a shock to their system. One asked me 'What can I learn from you?' and went out through the door. This question and their behaviour left me feeling rejected and angry. To be rejected by anyone can be hurtful, but to be rejected by one of my own somehow intensified the hurt I felt when this happened.

It is hard work to keep the wheels turning. As I reflect, I have done well since I became qualified, despite the difficulties in getting started. While I have four different jobs, they are all counselling related. I am always on the move, teaching two 'level 2' counselling courses, some lecturing at a university, working for a primary care group and my private practice. The teaching keeps me in touch with current developments in the counselling world and the face-to-face work keeps me in touch with the issues which clients bring to counselling.

Working in this way is very demanding; I work harder than when I did a full-time job. I am just able to keep my head above water financially, so if any of these jobs ended I would need to replace them very quickly with something else in order to survive. As a trainer of potential counsellors I hear students talking about finishing their training and walking straight into a job; the difficulty sometimes is getting the message across to them that this is not the case, without crushing their enthusiasm. It is ironic that I am training my future competitors.

I have had to be determined, working through my disappointments and frustrations to get this far. The journey has not been all bad. I have met and worked with some lovely people, black and white. I am at a point where I am making a living. It is hard but the struggle goes on. Hopefully I will achieve my goal, where working as a counsellor will give me and my family a comfortable living.

## DON'T GIVE UP THE DAY JOB

*Gerry Virgo*

In a moment of synthesis, after listening and absorbing throughout a day conference in May 1999 entitled 'Collaboration, Competition and Collusion' my contribution to the plenary session was 'Don't give up the day job' (Clark, 1999). I had involved myself in the day, on the tide of my enthusiasm for this profession, on the threshold of my potential life as an independent practitioner and five years after beginning a part-time person-centred diploma course. Like the majority of trained counsellors referred to by one of the speakers, I actually earned my daily bread elsewhere, with a major public institution. I found it scary but a relief to be faced with some facts about the difficulty in earning a living in counselling, the number of hours of client work needed and the small proportion of qualified people who are full-time therapists. So it seemed simple, accept the status quo, carry on doing my best to do a good job where I was, and find better ways of managing my discomfort with that sense of personal disempowerment so often triggered in me by the system.

This led inexorably to facing loss, of some barely articulated hope of a future for myself that more closely matched the way I had found I could be. I knew that my training had enabled me to improve the quality of my attention to those customers of the service that I met in my daily work, and that it was not always the same as what I was asked to deliver. Like those people in the hopeful vision expressed by Brian Thorne in his 1998 Joseph Payne lecture, I had experienced myself as valued, and I did not fit easily into the dysfunctional system which threatened my newly won self-respect. He spoke in the context of seeing an education workplace obsessed by standards assessment and quality control in which a sense of worthlessness is reinforced for many.

At this point I faced the very real difficulty of providing for my family at the same time as wanting to work in a way that seemed ethically sound and respectful of people. As a single householder with two children in full-time education I was committed to maintaining a home and a degree of financial stability. The impact on me looked likely to be a delay in, or abandonment of, a career in counselling and probably restricting myself to volunteer work. This was a loss indeed. I found a sense of connection in an article in the *BAC Journal* by Peter Farrell (1999), where he talks of a conceptual step that he believes goes beyond the current four step theories around the loss of a situation or person and the changes that follow. He proposes that bereavement also flags up the impermanence of life, that it challenges the way we hold an image of permanence and solidity on our own lives and that of others. At this point I looked at the impact of choices and commitments made earlier in my life.

As ever in my openness to the person-centred experience, a position of apparent clarity in fact opened the door to a consideration of change, and thus the prospect of facing giving up my imagined security. Could counselling offer me a realistic alternative living?

I am sharing here my questions to myself that day, that perhaps freelance counselling may bring with it a day-by-day familiarity with the existential. That offering 'Who I am makes a difference' to the world involves risk; there is not a lot to hide behind if things get tough. I do not know if what I seek in the world of counselling is different from the safety I have pursued in working for institutions, but I can see that the particular hope of security through an unfulfilling job, like blue-tack on a wet surface, is not sticking very well any more.

I have long been struck by a sentence from Soren Kierkegaard quoted by Rogers and Stevens (1967: 167) 'Life can only be understood backwards; but it must be lived forwards.' So I will begin by looking back on the journey to here, still on the brink of the world of freelance counselling, and then flag up the direction of travel that is emerging.

## Training and costs

My log of courses and experiential activities begins in 1990 and between then and June 2000 runs to 33 separate activities, some of which are ongoing. Included in this are training opportunities in a variety of approaches, including gestalt and transactional analysis and a good many in the person-centred approach, which eventually became the orientation of choice for me. I have engaged in over 50 days of residential person-centred group work in addition to training situations and this has been an essential component in developing my awareness of self, and self in relation to others, which is so vital in the process of therapy. Then there have been additional trainings in brief work, couples counselling, focusing and many more.

It is tempting to regard personal development as an optional extra, a kind of indulgence, but I think differently. My work with one client led me inexorably to the conclusion that I was opaque in a significant area of my own personness, my acceptance of my own ordinary human sexuality. I did not shrink from the conclusion that I was not offering the best service I could here. So, with a sense of adventure I set off on a weekend entitled 'Love, Intimacy and Sexuality'. Getting there was easy, rather like the idea of choosing new soft furnishings, but facing the wobble factor in my own psyche took a new level of courage and commitment to my own process. Several residential weekends later, at not inconsiderable cost in time and money, I am happy to know that I operate with more ease in this aspect of the counselling relationship, where before there was only a vacuum in my ability to symbolise my experience. My personal relational life has changed as a result and so my ongoing experience of being a person is enhanced and growing.

In fact I have come to recognise a strength in me. I am prepared to accept my gaps, to recognise signs of avoidance or denial or just plain ignorance and I am then happy to search out and respond to learning opportunities. With my more recently learned skills of talking about the way I experience life events I can expand my universe, rather in the manner of a fractal, each new focus containing the seeds of the old and the experience of the new. I know that this is very much a theme of the person-centred approach, and one with which I am very much in tune. This is expressed well by Charles O'Leary, who offers in his model of the person-centred relational counsellor:

> One person seeks to become aware of, to symbolise accurately and to accept all parts of herself. . . . There is less and less difference between her concept of herself and what she thinks she should be; therefore, she has less and less she has to defend against. And therefore she has the freedom to see and hear another person actively and objectively.
>
> (Charles O'Leary, 1999: 9, 10)

So I look at the activities I have engaged with and know that they have all contributed to professional and personal development and in fact underpin all the learning and reflecting on my counselling practice. They have not been chosen because they look good on my CV, but because I aim always to be safe and empowering as a practitioner.

And the cost? In addition to the cost of my diploma course I estimate I have spent £1000+ on additional training; £3300+ on group work and personal development; therapy (£900) and a good deal of travel to various far-flung venues, say £1500. Although this represents my very personal choices, I give these figures for your consideration, and indeed my own; they add up to more than £9000 over six years and added to my diploma training (£3900 up to 1997) represent a considerable investment of at least £13,000. I made a personal choice to devote one day each week solely to unpaid counselling in the voluntary sector and the accompanying travel, so there is a figure for loss of earnings as well.

I used some capital and some earnings to do this and regard it as money very wisely spent in terms of being happy with the gains in personal and professional confidence. As for recouping the investment? I guess I see this more as a leap in integrity and a vote for voluntary austerity. I am pleased that I trusted myself to do the courses, attend the residential groups that I did, and I believe that this rather organic way of proceeding has enabled me to learn how to learn in this work. I am more often drawn now to participant-facilitated activities as I feel confident there, and also to trainings which target specific gaps. So the urgency to spend out has reduced, for the moment at any rate.

## One year on

Having dug in to make the best of my situation and be a responsible parent and member of society, what followed did not fit my imagined plan. Changes in my place of work led me into difficult times and a period of reflection. Slowly it dawned on me that the work I had done on my personal way of relating had in fact rendered me less able to pursue the party line when I was unhappy with developments at work. My commitment to the self-authority and self-determination of clients was now in conflict with an institution responding to demands made upon it. Having made many steps towards increasing my positive self-regard I found my tension increasing when I was unable to express my concerns within the structure. It was a kind of reverse of the process described in the earlier quote from Charles O'Leary (1999). In my counselling work my view of how I should be was more closely matching my experience, whereas in my employment the reverse was true as I tried to absorb an increasingly directive attitude. As the gap increased so did my anxiety and at this time in my life I was unable to deny the experience of my anxiety, a concept well explained by Jerold Bozarth (1998) in his chapter 'A reconceptualization of the necessary and sufficient conditions for therapeutic change'. My old defensive manoeuvres were thin and threadbare. I became, in effect, a guinea-pig for my own theoretical beliefs, an embodiment of a changed view of self.

This was not an easy time, experiencing the loss of my version of a cherished ambition to be a sensible and responsible person. However, the discomfort set me off in pursuit of paid counselling work in an exceedingly determined and ultimately productive way. In revising my CV I found I had marketable skills. I have now taken up a salaried part-time administrative role in a counselling agency in the voluntary sector and this leaves space to develop further as an independent practitioner. Less money, only as secure as the next funding bid, and I am inordinately pleased with myself. Voluntary austerity has never looked so attractive. I am meeting the existential head on. My security is in myself as a person, I find I do trust myself to roll with the vagaries of fortune and funding agencies, and to survive creatively whatever turns up next—a psychological version of expecting to land upright like a cat!

Time will tell, but this is the story of one counsellor—a career change yes, but so much more. I did it with financial resources from past times and I have yet to face the reality of resigning from what little pension I had begun to build up in the last few years. Retirement at 65? I think not. Perhaps having a history of being work-focused will stand me in good stead here as I now expect to work to support myself well into old age. Fortunately the acquisition of material things has never been terribly important to me. However, the financial impact of dealing with mechanical breakdowns in both house and car has been terrifyingly real in these first few months of my independent life. The pressure is on to expand the amount of freelance counselling that I already do, although equally urgent is the development and maintenance of balance in my life. One result of my hard-won self-awareness is an increase in respect for both my person and my needs so I cannot, in all conscience, drive myself to work beyond my limits. My new day job in the counselling agency is interesting and rewarding, and it takes a good deal of energy; I do not rush home to counsel clients at the end of a day in the office. So no easy answers to the money situation there. I find that a network of friends, family and colleagues is an essential part of my life, giving me support, laughter and sometimes a shoulder to cry on.

I have been helped so often by reading the stories of others, and the symbolisations of process in counselling that authors offer for us to think about. John McLeod is one; writing in the journal *Counselling* in 1999 he speaks of counsellors as *liminal* figures, who exist on the edge of social groups or institutions for the purpose of enabling individuals to re-enter the social world. His description is of a person who both embodies the values and beliefs of a culture but who is also comfortable with the chaos or despair of being at or beyond the edge of the social. McLeod's words evoke a powerful resonance in me, with my struggles over money, security and responsibility to others. I feel on the edge, and beyond, of a commercially oriented society.

## References

Bozarth, J. (1998) *Person-Centred Therapy: A Revolutionary Paradigm*. Ross-on-Wye: PCCS Books.

Clark, J. (1999) A conference: *Collaboration, Competition, Collusion: The Challenges, Dynamics and Politics of Freelance Counselling and Psychotherapy*. University of East Anglia.

Farrell, P. (1999) The limitations of current theories in understanding bereavement and grief. *Counselling, British Association for Counselling Journal*, 10(2): 143–146.

McLeod, J. (1999) Counselling as a social process. *Counselling, BAC Journal*, 10(3).

O'Leary, C. J. (1999) *Counselling Couples and Families*. London: Sage.

Rogers, C. and Stevens, B. (1967) *Person to Person: The Problem of Being Human*. Utah: Real People Press.

Thorne, B. (1998) Standards, stress and spiritual danger: reflections on contemporary education. *Education Today*, 48(3).

# Chapter 11

# Counselling in primary care

*Benita Cowen and Nigel White*

The National Health Service (NHS) is one of the largest employers in Europe, with over one million employees, and has a budget in excess of £40 billion. It endeavours to offer a wide range of services for illness, upset and disturbance. Reid (2001) describes general practice as 'a place where members of a community go to talk about their symptoms and feelings of distress. What they want is for someone to listen and understand, in a safe and non-stigmatising environment, and if possible help them understand their experiences and come to better terms with conflicts or uncertainties, thus alleviating at least some of their emotional or physical pain'. Counselling is now becoming a well-recognised intervention as part of patient care. NHS employment of counsellors is growing, leading to the possibility of it being one of the largest growth areas for counsellors.

Our experience of offering freelance counselling is within primary care settings where we work as practice counsellors. Our responses come from a personal and emotional, as well as a rational and intellectual level. We write at a time of ongoing change within the NHS and specifically in primary care, where the future for freelance work may be limited. However, it appears that the trend towards employed practice-based counsellors is increasing. This may also be true of hospital and hospice settings with counsellors working within oncology, HIV and pain clinics.

Counselling is held within differing structures such as psychology departments, community mental health teams and primary care services. This varies depending on regional preferences, and there is no national consistency. Counselling in the NHS has entered an enormous learning curve, as it grapples with limited resources, evidence-based practice, clinical governance, as well as patient and political preferences. Therefore, at the time of writing, counselling and the employment of counsellors within this setting face many challenges.

Central to these dilemmas is the status of our theories and the nature of our 'knowledge' as counsellors and psychotherapists. We struggle with how our counselling culture fits into an existing predominately medical culture— one that is very different from our own. Perhaps we will need to learn a transitional language to enable us to communicate effectively about these differences.

The patient visits their doctor because they recognise something is wrong with themselves or they bring concerns for those close to them. They may be seeking advice, diagnosis, reassurance, medication or referral on to an appropriate expert. The doctor is the gatekeeper for a variety of treatments available to patients.

Most counsellor training courses prepare counsellors to give a very different type of help from that which is appropriate in primary care. It seems that many counsellors are trained to help in a process of consciousness raising that might lead to the patient's distress being alleviated, but only via the scenic route of self-discovery, integration and self-actualisation. This might be appropriate for a patient who comes to the surgery and says, 'I want to discover who I am.' But in reality patients come to see a counsellor for help in relieving symptoms, or getting rid of difficult thoughts and feelings in relation to uncomfortable or confusing life transitions and events. It is important to have an understanding of this subtle expectation of the counsellor, who may be perceived as being in control of the 'getting rid'.

Working in primary care will inevitably mean being exposed to a variety of different perspectives on health and illness. Usually only specialised counselling training courses address such areas. As counsellors, we need to be aware of how our own perspectives, both personal and theoretical, influence our helping styles within this setting.

Most of us are born into the world with the help of the medical profession and many of us will die with their help too—the well-known 'cradle to the grave' NHS. We all have first-hand experiences of being a patient and we know of our family, friends' and colleagues' stories, both good and bad. We live in a world where illness and ageing have the ultimate power to end our lives, whether or not we wish to die. Working in primary care reminds us of our own medical history in relation to the surgery setting, the doctor and the 'helpless' patient and of our own mortality.

How are we to understand the power balance between the counsellor, the client/patient and the doctor, both within and outside of the therapeutic relationship? It is an area we are likely to struggle with for a long time, as each of us discovered in our early experiences of working in primary care.

### Nigel

I saw three clients a week. I was trying to be very respectful and Rogerian and I made open-ended contracts. In those days I was tuning my ear to the language register of the area and frequently made mistakes. When I said, 'You've told me the story of what's happening at work . . .' clients would be indignant, saying, 'It's not a story!'

At an early meeting with the doctors I was asked for some kind of feedback so they could know when clients were attending. Feeling the sacred tenets of confidentiality were under attack, I said I would let them have names, dates and whether clients attended or not, but that was *all* I was prepared to divulge. In response to this outburst, there was a mixture of surprise and puzzlement as I was reassured that this would be fine. (Traditionally confidentiality within this setting can be regarded as 'shared' within the team. Counsellors have often been labelled as 'precious' and withholding for not entering into this team approach.)

I joined a local group for counsellors in primary care. We met in the evening, once a month, at the house of someone who had been doing primary care work for years. She was a psychotherapist who saw patients long term in her GP surgery. The group was the only place I heard people talking about the kind of experiences I was having. It was here that I learned that counsellors in other surgeries were getting a lot of unsuitable referrals—people who were not ready to reflect on whatever was happening in their lives. I began to appreciate that my doctors were a bit special.

In the surgery I felt like a visitor, yet I felt it incumbent upon me to act like a member of staff. My pay came from health promotion clinic funding and I wasn't paid when clients didn't attend. The doctors wanted to see every client after their counselling so they could evaluate the outcome. I didn't know if I was a regular part of the team or if I was just passing through.

### Benita

I was quite nervous starting out as a practice counsellor. My previous counselling experience was mainly with students. It was quite a culture shock to enter the world of general practice.

I experienced working in nine different surgeries and each was unique in the way that my skills and professionalism were received. My first surgery experience was in a deprived inner city area, with a large ethnic minority population, Irish, Afro-Caribbean and Asian, of whose cultures I knew little. Most people were in need of better living conditions and employment. The idea of people using their own inner resources to improve their lives was a concept quite alien to the doctors and the patients. It can be unhelpful to counsel someone whose real immediate need is for a job or adequate housing.

The practice team and I had an unconscious mixed view of my role. I could be seen as 'the saviour' rescuing the practice from patients with difficult problems, or 'the slave' subservient to the doctor, or 'the dustbin' relieving the practice of anxiety-arousing patients, or 'the rival' in competition for improved patient outcomes with far more listening time available than the doctor.

The difference between patients', doctors' and counsellors' expectations of what makes us 'better' has many repercussions in a setting where human vulnerability, anxiety and distress are the daily diet of our work. Many doctors are in fact doing their best to treat patients as whole people in a social and political context rather than just as a 'disease' or a 'case'. Furthermore they are often doing so under intense pressure from patients to relieve their anxiety quickly and/or to prescribe something to make them feel better, as if the doctor has a 'magic wand'. This expectation can also be laid at the counsellor's door.

Given the ideological chasm between the origins of the two forms of helping—medical intervention and talking therapy—it is extraordinary that counselling began to be used in the NHS at all. It is a testimony to the persistence of the patient's need to be listened to, and also a testimony to the ways in which diversity can be permitted within the NHS.

The predominately male medical profession of a hundred years ago would not have conceived of using talking treatments for people with moderately severe disturbance. The fact that we do today is an indication of major shifts in the way we, as a society, deal with illness, upset and disturbance. It is linked with how we see ourselves as carers and what potential we feel there is for one human being to help with another's suffering.

Given the anxiety generated by these issues and the current climate of divesting the medical profession of its traditional paternalistic powers, how does the primary health care team relax its established systems to allow for the government's requirement for the development of 'patient-centred' care? Therapy has had a part to play in bringing these changes about. Our culture seems more able to recognise the psychological and emotional aspects of life and that we are much more complex than was once thought.

There seems to be a tension between the perceived scientific certainty about medicine and the uncertainty about which kind of talking treatments work for whom, and in what way. As talking treatments, including counselling, are seen as helpful we could assume that this shows that our human frailties and vulnerabilities are coming to be accepted and included within a scientific culture. This is beginning to heal the dysfunctional model of a mind and body split, which has been a historical blind spot for mainstream medicine within the Western world. Within this wider social debate, the tension around the amount of talking and listening time that can, or should, be given to each individual's human needs continues to be a feature of the NHS—for doctor, patient and counsellor.

Counselling plays a part in the cultural debate about what we are as human beings. Paradoxically, in primary care, this can sometimes cause the counsellor to fail to listen to what the client says they want. Counsellors can be so aware and concerned with insight into personal dynamics that they can sometimes dig deeper than necessary. When a client says 'I want to feel happy', this may be exactly what they want. Within the limitation of short-term working, a primary care counsellor has to start from the perspective of the client and the more they can work within the idiom chosen by the client, the faster they will be able to help.

We need to consider how the influence of a medical model, that traditionally has sought to define mind and body as separate entities, fits with a counselling model. The frequent use of prescribed drugs for depression has promoted the view that depression is a biological illness that can only be treated with drugs. This rigid attitude is now changing, mainly due to patients' unwillingness to rely on 'a pill' to solve their problems.

Quick help is what most patients want. They come to the surgery only when they feel that they cannot 'go on' and ask us to help them get back to a point where they can 'go on' once more. It is very rare to hear a patient say, 'I want to spend six months exploring my problems.' Six-session models, solution-focused therapy and brief dynamic therapy all offer ways in which we may conduct conversations that make the most use of the patient's own solutions and their own style of coping.

The speed of a mode of helping is also an ethical consideration in a setting where so many people are seeking help. The counsellor's responsibility, like the doctor's, is to the population served by the practice, and not simply to the one person who is in the room. This is quite different from working in private practice, which is far less pressured. Counsellors in primary care are required to share out their resources of time and skill as widely and as effectively as possible.

Within the primary care team, the role of counsellor can be complex and not always overtly apparent to the parties involved. Some of the doctor's skill involves helping patients tolerate the losses and uncertainties of difficult periods in their lives. It is sometimes to help patients such as these that the doctor refers them to a counsellor. Also the support of patients who repeatedly attend surgery can be shared with the counsellor, even where there is no great expectation of change. It is encouraging to note the popularity among doctors of having a counsellor in the team. This can be seen from the way surgeries advertise a doctor's post, saying 'counsellor in post'.

When a counselling and psychotherapy training has been completed, we are still very much apprentices in our craft and there is much to learn about our new work environment. So much time has been spent learning new skills, developing self-awareness and learning a new language that little thought is likely to have been given to how the languages, values and ways of thinking embodied in the culture of general practice will relate to and dialogue with the culture of counselling and psychotherapy.

## Nigel

I found I couldn't stay interested in the distinction between the words 'client' and 'patient'. I began to use the terms interchangeably.

I was on an advanced training course in cognitive analytic therapy (CAT). It felt appropriate to the primary care setting to be doing brief work. I was using a Mann-type psychodynamic model so everyone ended up working on loss in relation to the referring problem, at least as far as they would permit. I was interested in the underlying dynamics and whenever a client said anything, I thought, 'What's behind that?' Every patient ended up with six sessions, whatever the referral problem.

By this time I was running the 'counsellors in primary care' group, which expanded as counsellors were employed under fundholding. The original members retired or moved on and we found ourselves as the senior members. We felt in the forefront of something, of some kind of expansion. At the peak of this we set up a mentoring scheme to help new counsellors find their feet in primary care. We were invited, as a group, to give a presentation at a conference. For a heady moment we thought we might start a company. We never did.

Someone else did. A local counselling agency had contracts with several surgeries and I began working for the agency in two surgeries. I felt less involved as a subcontractor delivering someone else's model, but it was work. I was then in three surgeries for three hours a week each. On one day I drove, at lunchtime, from one side of Leeds to the other to get from one surgery to the next. With my higher education job, I was seeing 19 clients a week, plus one or two in private practice.

The agency pay was higher than the pay at 'my' surgery and this allowed me to bargain for a better deal. I was paid a flat rate, whether patients attended or not. When health promotion funding dried up I was kept on, with the doctors paying my wage out of their own pockets.

General practice is a place where time is perceived as a rare commodity. There is a 'busy', 'don't interrupt' or 'be quick' mentality. Opportunities to speak with one another in a relaxed and open manner can be few and far between. It is here that counsellors can begin to feel a sense of isolation and defensiveness, especially as they often work part time and in more than one surgery.

Communicating needs within a medical context can be fraught with tensions. Counselling training changes us in many ways. In particular we are most likely to have internalised the skills of unconditional positive regard and empathy. In contrast, doctors tend to communicate in a busy, direct and assertive manner. It is seldom appropriate to attempt to increase intimacy and openness when speaking with fellow professionals about roles or pay and conditions! Developing our assertiveness and negotiation skills is vital if we are to advocate our own needs. We learn to be quick and direct in our communications. Social events such as Christmas parties, summer barbecues or a 'leaving do' can add a welcome sense of relationship and humanness to what often feels like a dysfunctional communication system.

We have both had to continue to learn how to manage our professional loneliness, as we seek to offer a psychological perspective in a predominately 'fix it' culture. An extrovert personality can stand one in good stead for making quick, friendly connections with reception staff and fostering working alliances with those who refer clients to your service. For the more introverted personality it might be thought by the practice team that quietness is somehow 'withholding', playing more into the unspoken myths about what we do. Having a suitable room in which to work, where we will be uninterrupted and have comfortable chairs as well as clocks and tissues, can all be areas for potential disputes with the practice team.

### Benita

When I began work in general practice there was still considerable freedom to innovate. My training in humanistic approaches was about opening up possibilities. Creating my own service was about that. I found it very rewarding, a real sense of achievement. I was left to develop my own systems for assessment, referral criteria, forms for outcomes, audit and evaluations. The counselling service grew from my own experiences and developing knowledge base. I can remember having to carry chairs into the designated room for months before I found the assertive skills in which to negotiate for reasonable working conditions in which to offer counselling. Now it is all a more structured and focused experience.

A counsellor's sense of value can be deeply challenged working in primary care. Like our colleagues within other mental health services, demands and expectations are high. Inappropriate referrals can lead us to feel overwhelmed and unsatisfied. Finding a balance between what we can realistically offer and what we would like is a complex interplay requiring large amounts of patience. We have to be willing to educate the team about our different ways of working, giving the reasons behind why we need something to be a certain way. It would be useful if training courses could spend time preparing prospective counsellors to comprehend and manage the frustration and stresses of working in different work settings.

It can be helpful through our own personal therapy to become aware of some of our unconscious motivations for working in our chosen occupational setting. Insecurity and anxiety can lead us to familiar behaviour patterns when dealing with uncomfortable feelings. Possible strategies are to 'adapt', 'fit in', 'people please' and 'withdraw' or appear to 'offer something special'. When we first start out we are likely to lack confidence in our own authority as counsellors and the benefits we can offer to our clients.

### Benita

Working within a medical environment can produce large doses of anxiety, be it our own or that of the system. I went through a time when a family member was dying of leukaemia and a close friend was dying from ovarian cancer. I became very sensitive to my own mortality.

It was emotionally demanding working with clients who were also adjusting to their own losses or illness. I couldn't escape my own fear of becoming ill or dying. I would listen to people's symptoms and imagine that I had whatever they described. I was fortunate to have tremendous support networks. These enabled me to go through a very bleak period in my life while still practising. It was not so easy to obtain support at work from the practice team. There seemed to be an expectation that, as a counsellor, I could cope with all life events as if I were superhuman in some way.

This is also true with clients, where it is important to be aware of the perceived 'wellness' of the counsellor and the perceived 'illness' of the client. We can be seen as experts on normality and asked to judge the level of sanity of others. We are somehow invested with a psychological power, rather than power based on scientific knowledge. I personally have recognised how important it is to make a considered response to a client's questions on what I deem to be normal. This can be especially relevant when working with clients from different cultures whose norms around health and illness may be very different from our own cultural history.

In common with others who work in the NHS, there are many different ways that a counsellor can conceptualise the relationship between themselves and their employer. A brief survey of some relationship dynamics that we have observed will serve to illustrate what practitioners may encounter, either in themselves or in colleagues.

- *A misguided NHS in relation to a reforming counsellor.* This naïve position is one that some counsellors start from, seeing themselves as having answers where others have failed. This position is not maintained for long in the face of experience!
- *A benevolent NHS in relation to a nurtured counsellor.* It is common for employees of any kind to begin a new employment opportunity with this unrealistic hope. Early disappointments soon provide the disillusion that moves us on from this expectation.
- *A chaotic NHS in relation to an insecure counsellor.* This is a position that many employees in the NHS are struggling with, constant political change after political change sweeping through, seeing themselves as pawns in a game.
- *An omnipotent NHS in relation to a worthless counsellor.* We have all had experiences of feeling deskilled in response to particular authoritative stances taken by medical professionals, especially when expressed in language we do not share. The culture clash may push us into feeling helpless and useless. We need the resilience to overcome these moments.

- *A punitive NHS in relation to a defensive resentful counsellor.* This is an all too common position within a culture based on a pecking order. One has only to think of the dismissive way theatre nurses are treated by many surgeons and of the way the nursing profession is continually battling against low pay.
- *A critical NHS in relation to a striving counsellor.* Some of the efforts that counselling has made to be accepted as a new profession are full of the striving for approval that the 'new kid on the block' would exhibit. The sought-for approval has not been given, but counsellors continue to spend hours of their own time doing further training, accreditation and evaluation in anticipation of rewards that may never come.
- *An NHS that values counselling in relation to a counsellor who is an equal but different member of a team.* Perhaps, in the future, we may see this emerging. Until contracts and pay scales are laid down in such a way as to give a fair return for the training that counsellors undertake, then this dynamic cannot become stable. There are some counsellors who have reached this position in individual settings, but the majority continue to be insecure in their employment status.

Many counsellors would like to see a coming of age both of their own profession and in the attitudes towards it by other professions within the NHS. How this might come about is complicated. There appears to be an atmosphere of defensiveness and competition from some other health professionals towards those they see offering talking therapies or counselling skills. Even within our own profession we have different competing organisations representing counselling and counsellors. We have organisations to represent our interests, such as Counsellors in Primary Care (CPC), the British Association for Counselling and Psychotherapy (BACP), the Faculty of Health for Counsellors and Psychotherapists (FHCP) and Counselling in Primary Care Trust (CPCT). Perhaps their presence offers hope to those of us who strive for better pay and conditions.

Counselling has prospered in general practice because it has been seen by practice teams as accessible and cost-effective. When doctors were given financial control over their budgets in what was then called 'fundholding', the employment of part-time practice-based counsellors became an option. Doctors were feeling frustration at being unable to offer appropriate help to their patients, due to long waiting lists for psychology or secondary care services. In-house counsellors were seeing similar patients to clinical psychologists at a fraction of the cost and with shorter waiting lists. Psychology departments can be over-subscribed, under-resourced and sometimes presented with inappropriate referrals. This all generates long waiting lists. There are many examples of psychology and counselling respectfully working alongside each other. There is also evidence of rivalries and competition in the two professions for status and recognition.

In this harsh environment, if counselling were ever to become one of the NHS's 'core professions', it would be by the force of two irresistible arguments: firstly quality of outcome, and secondly value for money in relation to the alternatives. Current research is now focusing on these issues (King *et al.*, 2000). It remains to be seen whether counselling manages to establish itself as a discrete profession, with its own identity, or if counselling will be added to the skills base of nurses, occupational therapists, doctors, health visitors and community psychiatric nurses.

The counsellor who chooses to work in primary care will be embarking on a journey to find a way through complex personal and organisational dynamics within the practice team. Both authors have found it helpful to belong to a local group of counsellors working in primary care. Such a group can be an oasis in what can seem like a desert, and can be an important part of continuing professional development. It can be a place where people are free to talk about experiences, concerns and achievements, which are common to working in general practice. There can also be challenging times, when there may be competition with others for the same job.

The NHS is often accused, by those who work in it, of not valuing the work they do. Counsellors are no exception, yet we *are* presented with an ongoing learning opportunity to protect and nourish our sense of worth within this greatly consuming place where little positive feedback is freely given. But it can be dispiriting at times.

### Nigel

My work with clients continues—a flow of human perplexity and suffering, unchanging in its ability to throw up new challenges, and to go on and on.

I am now working in a room I like to call the doctor's library. In fact it is the store for all the journals and text books as well as housing the noisy computer server for the surgery network. I am the only member of staff who uses it for my three hours a week.

I have my own filing cabinet where I can lock away patients' notes. I have two clocks—both with drug company logos. When I asked the practice manager for the second one, explaining that I wanted to put it in the patient's line of sight so they also could be aware of the elapsing of time and take their part in the management of it, she said, laughing, 'Oh it's highly technical, this counselling!' I laughed too (my standard way of dealing with surgery banter) and went away with the impression that counselling, to the practice manager, after 10 years, is tea and sympathy without the tea. I know that when it comes to the resilient human kindness that is the most important ingredient of all, there's nothing I have to offer that the reception staff don't have and more.

Of course there are other aspects to counselling, but these are invisible to reception staff and even, when done well, to patients. By this time I have completed the CAT course and have additional training in solution-focused therapy (SFT). When I received BACP accreditation I didn't try explaining to anyone in the surgery what it was. I use SFT when it seems to help and CAT when it doesn't, as well as person-centred in some cases. My average contact length is around three to four sessions with clients, getting a wide variety of responses to their situation between one and six sessions, very occasionally up to ten.

I still work in one surgery for the agency, but I gave one up. Sixteen clients a week are enough. I kept 'my' surgery even though it is less well paid, since it is more satisfying to run my own service. After many years the counsellors' group has dissolved. I have stopped being active in the future of counselling in the NHS: there's no point—the bodies we tried to negotiate with have themselves disappeared. I still have no contract of employment for my three hours a week and I still feel like a visitor, but when fundholding disappeared I was not affected, as the surgery never went fundholding in the first place. I don't know how the new changes will affect my existing contract.

Next week there's a review of counselling with the doctors. We manage to meet formally like this once every 18 months. I have prepared an agenda and, for the first time, have put 'Counsellors' pay situation' as one of the items. I am still being paid more by the agency than in 'my' surgery. A while ago, while doing my accounts, I discovered that, by oversight, I had not been paid for several months. When I told the staff there was much teasing. Surely I must be very rich not to notice that my monthly cheque had not been paid? The pay from three hours a week doesn't make a lot of difference one way or the other.

My use of CORE[1] has made counselling the most evaluated of all activities in the surgery. We will discuss the findings at the meeting next week, which will be too short to do more than skim over the

---

1 Clinical Outcomes in Routine Evaluation; CORE Information Management Systems Ltd, 47 Windsor Street, Rugby CV21 3NZ, UK.

surface. I am relieved to find the results look good, even though we don't yet know how to understand them.

I thought of putting the future of counselling in the surgery on the agenda for the review. But it's pointless spending time on it as nobody knows where counselling stands or will stand. Nobody knows if I am just passing through.

It is important to consider the amount of uncertainty and loneliness that we might need to tolerate, in order to be a counsellor working in primary care. This sense of isolation partly arises from differing expectations about degrees of participation and mechanisms to achieve it. Close interaction between counsellor and doctor can contribute to the quality of treatment. Both can learn to appreciate the opportunity to discuss emotional issues in patient care and patient relationships, and to review referrals. In general, medical working practices do not readily accommodate the amount or quality of dialogue required to support counselling. It takes time to build this degree of understanding. Nelson Mandela has wisely said 'I have discovered the secret that after climbing a great hill, one only finds that there are many more hills to climb.' Nowhere is this truer than when working in the general practice setting.

### Benita

I am coming to the end of my contract with two practices where I offer a managed counselling service for approximately 14 hours a week. It has been a substantial part of my income as a freelance practitioner. I have very mixed feelings. The primary care group is looking to have a managed counselling service providing equity throughout the whole district. I really support the idea of counselling being integrated within the NHS with all the terms and conditions that go with employment and the standardisation of services across the patch. On the other hand, I am losing a much-prized contract that enabled me to develop a high-standard counselling service with many freedoms and insecurities. This experience I have greatly valued. I feel that I am about to lose some of my own personal autonomy within this setting. I hope to continue working in general practice, providing the terms and conditions are favourable. I can still keep my freelance status working with my private clients and supervisees.

For those considering working in primary care it can be helpful to find a voluntary post with an existing counsellor already in practice. Some areas have well-managed schemes for trainee counsellors but such placements are usually unpaid. In the past, trainees were able to offer their services to sympathetic practices on an *ad hoc* basis. It is more difficult now, as evidence-based practice and clinical governance affect the way services are delivered.

In the future it will be important for trainees to have some understanding of the mental health field. The more we are aware of the issues relating to a medical setting such as medication, risk assessment and models of health and illness, the greater the chance of finding work.

Hard work by mostly freelance counsellors has paved the way for counselling to be offered as an integral part of the services available to patients. Primary care is both a fascinating and demanding place to work. One needs plenty of emotional and physical stamina, a broad range of therapeutic skills, good supervision and a willingness to engage assertively in the complex dynamics that affect our work on a daily basis.

Counsellors need to be able to communicate to the practice team the kind of service they offer and how it meets the needs of the practice and its patients. We need to be prepared for challenges and respond with reasoned argument and evidence. Lastly, it is important to recognise and deal with our own anxieties through peer support and supervision. The stress aroused can be used to understand our clients and the organisational context in which we work. We need to recognise that our emotional responses will wither if our encounters within the practice team are not respected and affirmed.

Working as a counsellor in this diverse setting can be rewarding. Helping clients find their way through often uncharted waters can be very moving. Counsellors can celebrate the fact that their strengths are acknowledged and valued, judging by the popularity of counselling with patients and practice teams. Counselling in primary care is still in its infancy. As it grows, there will be a need for more collaborative styles of working to be developed, together with the ability to tackle differences in ways that enhance our professional standing.

## References

King, et al. (2000) Randomised controlled trial of non-directive counselling, cognitive-behaviour therapy, and usual general practitioner in the management of depression as well as mixed anxiety and depression in primary care. *British Medical Journal*, 321: 1383–1392.

Reid, M. (2001) Evaluating the effectiveness of counselling in primary care: taking a fresh look. *Counselling and Psychotherapy Research*, 1(1): 24.

Chapter 12

# Working with Employee Assistance Programmes

*Charlotte Johnson*

Workplace and employee counselling has become a growth area as more employers see the benefits of providing support for their employees; thus more opportunities have arisen for organisations to provide counselling and related employee support. Employee Assistance Programmes (EAPs) originated in the USA and the number of providers in the UK has steadily grown over the past 15 years. EAPs offer their services across all sectors of the market-place and in all geographical areas where their client organisations have employees and this represents a huge number of individuals able to access counselling support. EAPs depend on independent counsellors (affiliates) to offer individual and couples counselling to their client organisations. They would actually find it difficult to maintain the quality and scope of their services without access to a wide range of experienced and professional counsellors and therapists, many of whom are working freelance.

This chapter is written with the following groups of counsellors in mind: trainee counsellors, newly qualified counsellors who may be exploring their options for freelance working, and experienced counsellors looking to expand their practice or experience into the context of EAP counselling. I have taken a pragmatic approach in addressing the following questions:

- What are EAPs?
- How do they differ from other workplace counselling?
- What range of services do they generally offer?
- What is the nature of face-to-face counselling in an EAP?
- What do EAPs generally look for from their affiliate counsellors?
- What are some of the professional issues counsellors face in EAP counselling?

These questions will hopefully lead readers to consider if this is an area of counselling practice which interests them and what they would want from working with an EAP. There are practical considerations that freelance counsellors will need to address, as well as questions about their own philosophy and therapeutic approach, and whether these are compatible with the ways in which EAPs work.

Some of the terms that will be used throughout the chapter are:

- *EAP*—the organisation providing the employee support and counselling services.
- *Affiliate counsellor*—the freelance counsellor contracted by the EAP to provide face-to-face counselling.
- *Client organisation/employer*—the employing organisation that contracts with the EAP for services for their workforce.
- *Client/employee*—the individual employee using the EAP for support.
- *Case manager*—the person in the EAP who manages the case and is the point of contact for the affiliate counsellor.

I have written this chapter from my own experience of building up my freelance practice over a number of years. I am an affiliate counsellor with a number of EAPs and thus have experienced the different ways in which they approach their work with their client organisations, their individual clients and their affiliate counsellors. Through my contact with various providers I have learned what suits me, my preferred way of working and how this relates to my personal and professional values. I hope this will offer some useful insights to counsellors interested in engaging in what can be demanding and interesting work.

## Employee Assistance Programmes and workplace counselling

Basically, an EAP is a range of employee support services. These are provided by commercial organisations offering an independent and confidential range of services designed to support employees in resolving personal and work problems, which may be affecting their work performance.

An organisation buying in EAP services is doing so because there are benefits to their employees and their business. Access to the EAP for the employee (and usually their immediate family members) is promoted as an employee benefit, alongside other benefits like private medical insurance and staff discount schemes. It will be advertised through posters, leaflets, company intranet (the company's in-house website), briefings in induction programmes and, sometimes, specific briefings in the organisation.

The reasons why organisations choose to introduce EAP services vary. In an in-depth study Highley-Marchington and Cooper (1997) found that the majority of companies introduced EAPs without conducting any analysis or audit to identify the need for such an intervention. They further identified that the key reasons for doing so were to demonstrate that they 'cared' for employees, to help their staff adapt to change, and to respond to increasing levels of stress within the organisation. Some organisations will have a strong 'investment in people' culture where employee counselling, support and development are seen as an integral part of their 'people are our most important resource' values.

Organisations also have strong commercial and legal reasons for buying in an EAP service. Competitive organisations want employees to perform at maximum capacity, deal with rapid changes in technology and systems and, generally, hold their own in the business world. Most managers are aware that employees dealing with personal problems will be less effective in their job. In addition, organisations have a formal 'duty of care' to their work-force, which is enshrined in health and safety legislation. Support through counselling is seen as a valid way to show duty of care, and with the increasing threat of litigation for workplace stress it is also seen as a valid way for an organisation to protect themselves from liability. This issue is explored in a recent article by Jenkins and Pollecoff (2000).

EAP providers adhere to the codes of Standards and Practice of the International Employee Assistance Providers Association (EAPA), which has a UK branch to serve and promote the interests of UK providers. Arthur (2001) states there are 14 major EAP providers offering counselling to at least one and three-quarter million employees across the UK. This figure will be higher when those employees' dependants eligible to use the EAP services are also included. A full list of EAP providers is available from the UK EAPA.

EAPs provide a comprehensive menu of services for their client organisation. Typically these might be:

- 24-hour telephone counselling.
- An information and advice service (based on a Citizen's Advice Bureau model).
- Short-term face-to-face counselling (individual and couples).
- Managerial consultancy (by telephone).
- Trauma and critical incident debriefing.
- Organisational consultancy and training, e.g. stress audits, personal development training.
- Support and specialist human resources advice on policy development, e.g. harassment policies, alcohol and drug policies.

This range of services will be tailored to suit the particular needs of the organisation and an element of this will be based on what the organisation can afford. For example:

A local authority, with a workforce of 3000, might buy a package of 24-hour telephone counselling and information and advice services.

The information and advice are comprehensive, covering consumer and legal affairs, money management, family matters and employment issues. If face-to-face counselling support is necessary, the EAP might suggest possible options, e.g. counselling through a GP, NHS services or voluntary services.

A multinational corporation, with a workforce of 12,000, engaged in safety-sensitive businesses, might invest in a more comprehensive provision. The range of services includes 24-hour telephone counselling, information and advice, face-to-face counselling sessions (six per client issue), managerial consultancy and critical incident debriefing in the event of an on-site incident. The safety-sensitive nature of the business means that there is a need for drug and alcohol assessment for those staff responsible for managing complex and potentially dangerous processes, e.g. chemical manufacturing.

### Other models of workplace counselling

The EAP model of workplace counselling is only one of a number of options for those wishing to develop counselling experience/practice in this area. Other possibilities include on-site counselling services provided by and paid for by the employer. This might be through a human resources or personnel department, or through an occupational health department. For example, some financial institutions provide in-house counselling, as do some of the larger retailing companies. For a history of the development of workplace counselling and models of counselling in organisations, see Carroll (1996).

However, other kinds of organisations are seeking to contract out counselling services to external providers, and although EAPs will bid for these contracts a number of newer 'players' (to use business jargon) are becoming competitors. These include insurance companies, independent providers of occupational health services and umbrella groups of independent counselling practitioners. These practitioner associations provide an alternative entry point into workplace counselling. For those who are interested in setting up such a group, it is important to consider the business implications in terms of the running costs, marketing and maintenance of contracts and these are some of the questions which need to be considered:

- How much time can you give in the initial stages of setting up?
- Will you work from home or look for premises? What will the financial or emotional costs of these options be?

- Where will you get your business from? Have you contacts interested and willing to offer you work?
- What services are you selling?
- If you are a group, how will you work together? Will you become a partnership or legalise your agreement in some way?
- How will you share the start-up costs, or share the money generated through your work?
- How will you market yourselves—leaflets, press releases, websites, radio interviews?
- How will you introduce yourself to potential customers?
- You may need to develop business and administrative skills—where can you do this?

These and other business-related issues may require relevant experience in administration, financial planning and management, and personnel/human resource matters.

A major benefit of working as an EAP affiliate is having time to concentrate on client work, with its associated administration/casework taking up a limited amount of time.

## The nature of face-to-face counselling in an EAP

The range of services offered means there are interesting opportunities for freelance working within an EAP context. The main area is client counselling, whether by telephone or face to face. Opportunities may also exist for those with relevant experience in training and consultancy, e.g. stress management, counselling skills courses and assertiveness training. A rapidly growing area of work is critical incident debriefing, which will require appropriate training in a model for individual and group debriefing. However, the focus of this chapter is on face-to-face counselling as this is the key area of work for freelance counsellors.

The usual model of counselling adopted is an assessment and short-term model. The contract details vary from EAP to EAP and from company to company. I have worked to contracts of an assessment session plus two counselling sessions, to contracts of up to eight sessions. The norm seems to be between four and six sessions. What all EAPs have in common is that the counselling model is time-limited, short-term counselling.

An early question to consider is whether short-term counselling fits with your model of counselling. If you want to work long term with clients, EAP counselling will not provide you with this opportunity. It is important to realise at the outset that EAPs are unlikely to agree to extra sessions unless there is a sound clinical reason to justify it and then only for a limited number of sessions. This is for a number of reasons.

Primarily, EAPs are set up specifically to provide short-term counselling; the purpose is not to offer long-term work but short-term problem resolution. This is clearly defined in the UK EAPA *Standards and Professional Guidelines*, although there is acknowledgement that some flexibility in determining the number of sessions is needed as rigidity can prejudice the quality of the service provided to the client.

Secondly, EAPs are businesses and have contracts with their clients; they have boundaries to keep and profits to make. Having said this, I have not (yet) worked with an EAP which has not sympathetically considered the clients' needs and been creative in responding to a bridging period of support while a client is referred on. This might mean the EAP liaising with a personnel/human resources (HR) or an occupational health department; writing to a GP on the client's behalf and with their permission; or offering telephone support in place of face-to-face contact while a referral is being made. I would find it hard to work with an EAP, which insisted on strict adherence to the 'letter' of the contract, and which was not prepared to support a client in real distress.

So, what does this mean for face-to-face working? Questions to consider include:

- Can the client make use of short-term work? Are they able to talk about their problem? Are they motivated to attend sessions? Are they in touch with reality? Can they use feedback to help them explore the issue they are bringing and their responses to it?
- Is the presenting problem suitable for a short-term intervention? The counsellor needs to complete a thorough assessment, as they will make a decision based on information obtained from the client, which they are willing to disclose during this initial stage. However, we need to be sensitive to, and consider that, the presenting problem may mask an underlying problem, which needs more than the agreed number of sessions. This is not always apparent in the first session.
- Are there contraindications to suggest longer-term work or that another intervention may be more suitable?

These issues are discussed by Feltham (1997) and Jacobs (1988). It is important to remember that not all clients or the issues they present will benefit from long-term, short-term or indeed any other kind of counselling. There may be clinical reasons; or sometimes clients need straightforward, practical information. For example, a client who is experiencing anxiety about their financial difficulties may need financial advice to sort this out, rather than five sessions of counselling to learn anxiety management strategies. This is one of the areas where collaboration with another strand of the EAP services (the information and advice service) can be productive in appropriately supporting the client.

One thing in all of this is clear: if you are interested in working long term with clients, you need to look for these opportunities elsewhere. They do not exist in EAP counselling.

## What do EAPs look for when choosing a counsellor?

### Qualifications and training

It is important to be aware of the qualifications and experience that EAPs are looking for in their affiliate counsellors. Most EAPs are looking for counsellors who have completed professional counselling/psychotherapy training and are either accredited through a recognised professional body (British Association of Counselling and Psychotherapy, British Psychological Society, UKCP), or are eligible for accreditation with a number of years of supervised counselling practice. The number of years of counselling experience required varies, but generally EAPs are looking for a period of post-qualification/training experience; some stipulate four or five years, which links into their need to provide a professional service to their clients, thus protecting their business interests.

EAPs will also be looking for a particular blend of personal attributes and experience. Having spoken to a number of EAP clinical managers a composite picture of their 'ideal affiliate' would be:

- A professional approach to all aspects of their work—this would include reliability, consistency, high standards, and an ethical approach to clients and to the EAP.
- Personal attributes of warmth, approachability, assertiveness and professionalism which are reflected in their personal contact with clients, the premises they work in and their self-presentation.
- The model of their counselling approach is compatible with short-term, focused counselling.
- Assessment skills, including assessment of substance use/misuse, psychiatric conditions, and risk assessment, are well developed.
- Ability and experience of working with a wide range of presenting issues. Issues can range from work performance issues or workplace stress to alcohol abuse, bereavement, relationship difficulties, sexual abuse, anxiety and depression.
- Crisis intervention skills including the ability to contain very distressed clients with suicidal intentions are welcomed.
- And, finally, that the counsellor shows understanding of the organisational context of EAP counselling.

While this is an ideal, realistic EAPs also respect a counsellor who knows the limitations of their expertise and experience and will refuse a referral because they are unable to offer the client appropriate support.

### Organisational awareness

Organisational awareness is a key attribute for a counsellor working with employees. First of all, this means understanding the work context of the problems that employees bring to counselling. Secondly, it means having a balanced view between the personal needs of the individual and the business needs of the organisation.

A counsellor with good organisational awareness will ask their client how they are coping at work. Is the issue they are coming with work related or is it a personal difficulty that is affecting their work performance and thus compounding their anxiety?

> A depressed client takes off *ad hoc* days because they can't face going in to work. This adds to their problem because their manager, not knowing they are depressed, thinks they are becoming unreliable in their attendance. The relationship between the employee and their manager becomes strained and another reason why the employee takes more time off. The counsellor might facilitate the client's awareness of this, leading the client to discuss their personal situation with their manager. This may lift some of the anxiety and free energy to address the depression. The manager may also be more sympathetic if they know what the employee's problem is.

This interaction between the problem and the work context may form the basis of a counselling contract.

> A client presenting with depression identifies that the root of their unhappiness is that they don't like their job. This is because their shift pattern has changed and they see much less of their partner than they did. Further exploration reveals that they feel they had little choice in accepting the changes the organisation has made—the unspoken message heard by the client was 'If you don't like it, go somewhere else.' The counselling contract here may focus on developing their confidence to approach the human resources department to discuss the impact of the shift pattern and what possibilities exist for changing it.

It is also important that the counsellor remains objective in these situations. In the example above, the counsellor must keep in mind that the client's perception of 'like it or lump it' is only one side of the story. The counsellor may not know that the company has carried out an extensive consultation before any changes were made, or that the changes are being piloted and open to review. Many EAPs provide the counsellor with an overview of the client organisation, including challenges from the market-place and impending changes that might affect staff.

Balancing the needs of the organisation with the needs of the individual is not always easy for counsellors to come to terms with and can represent an area of internal conflict for the counsellor and, sometimes, external conflict with the EAP. In my early experience of counselling EAP clients, I found it hard to acknowledge that sometimes the organisation had 'rights' as well as the employee. This is one of the fundamental differences between EAP counselling and private practice. A good example of this is the need of the organisation for workplace safety taking priority over the needs of the individual.

An employee comes in to manage a safety-sensitive process under the influence of alcohol and refuses to acknowledge that there is a problem. They are referred to counselling by occupational health, who are not aware of the extent of the client's alcohol problem. The organisation has a very clear drug and alcohol policy as part of its terms and conditions and obviously this behaviour can put many people at risk. Throughout the counselling process, the counsellor is aware that the needs of the client are in conflict with the requirements of the safety-sensitive context. The counsellor does not want to breach confidentiality as they are working with the client to take responsibility for their problem; the client has told the counsellor they have reduced their drinking. However, they attend the counselling session smelling of alcohol, their speech is slurred and their behaviour agitated. They tell the counsellor they have been at work earlier in the day. The counsellor feels conflicted but recognises that if the client is attending work in this state they are a risk to themselves and others. They contact the EAP case manager to discuss how best to support the client.

In situations like this an EAP will seek a solution which maintains the confidentiality of the individual and meets the requirements of the organisation. This is not always straightforward and sometimes confidentiality will be breached in the last resort. Where possible the EAP will seek to maintain the client's confidentiality within the organisation, suggesting the client sees their GP for support. In rare incidents where the client continues to discount the existence of the problem, the organisation may have to be told.

Another example of conflict is where the counsellor believes that the organisation has a responsibility to the employee to support and help them keep their job. In some cases the organisation will limit this responsibility.

A client is referred by the HR department for personal support while going through the disciplinary procedure. They have been accused of harassing another employee. The client claims they are being victimised on this issue. The briefing from the EAP case manager describes an individual who appears to be 'impossible to manage', who causes problems for other employees and who apparently refuses to take any responsibility for changing their behaviour. The HR department views the counselling as the last opportunity for the employee to show willingness to resolve the issue. The counsellor is concerned that the counselling process is being used to put pressure on the employee and to deliver a message about the client's behaviour that the organisation is unwilling or unable to deliver itself. The dilemma facing the counsellor is 'Whose needs are you there to meet?'

There are no easy answers to this kind of dilemma, so having a supervisor who can help you think about and hold the client's interests at the heart of the process is important. Being able to talk to an experienced and sensitive case manager can also be helpful in untangling your own process and separating out the boundaries, which can be complex in organisational work.

It is also the case that an organisation can make good use of feedback from a counsellor who is organisationally aware. The EAP can collect such information and feed it back into the company at a review. Thus, companies can be encouraged to look at the impact of their working practices on their staff. Useful feedback to a company may be around themes of bullying and harassment, drug and alcohol use, that some employees feel devalued or unmotivated because of continual changes in working practices or procedural changes and this is adding to workplace stress. Such feedback can be used to educate the organisation about the well-being of their employees and encourage them to establish 'good' working practices.

### Counselling premises

Freelance counsellors need to have suitable premises to work from which are comfortable, offer privacy to the client and are accessible. If they practise from their home, they need to ensure that the boundaries are clearly defined so that family activities do not interfere with the counselling. They will also want to ensure that the family is inconvenienced as little as possible by their work. I have vivid and embarrassing memories from my early days of counselling at home, of one of my daughters throwing marbles down a flight of stairs onto the wooden floor outside my counselling room. At the time, I did my best to incorporate the disturbance into the therapeutic process! However, this was uncomfortable for everyone, particularly my client, and prompted me to make alternative arrangements for seeing clients in my private practice.

EAPs are offering a business service and most expect their counsellors to maintain standards consistent with business requirements. Some organisations now insist that employees be seen in consulting rooms in premises outside the counsellor's home. Most EAPs contract to offer counselling within a reasonable distance from the employee's home and workplace, generally within 15 miles.

### The 'business' contract

Counsellors are required to have their own public liability and professional indemnity insurance (usually to a minimum of £500,000, though it can be up to a value of £2,500,000). They need to comply with the supervision requirements of their professional bodies and EAPs are likely to ask for a reference from their supervisor before accepting them as an affiliate. They may also need to provide evidence that they are self-employed or are responsible for their own tax and National Insurance contributions, by providing the EAP with a signed statement to that effect, or their self-assessment reference number.

Before being placed on the list of counsellors, you may be required to sign an agreement (a binding legal document) laying out the terms of your role as an affiliate with the EAP. Essentially, you are entering into a business agreement or contract to follow the policies and procedures of the EAP. These will include acceptance of:

- The EAP's fee structure, including when you will be paid for your work, i.e. monthly or at the end of your counselling contract with the client.
- The procedures relating to accepting the referral, setting up appointments, completing paperwork (which varies from provider to provider),

contact with case managers to give post-assessment feedback or to liaise if a client needs additional support or referring on.

- Confidentiality policies and procedures relating to working with clients, and disclosure of information about the EAP's customers and procedures. There is also a clause about not soliciting private work from customer organisations while you are an affiliate with the EAP.
- The 'flagging' systems of the EAP, i.e. the procedure for supporting and monitoring clients who may be 'at risk'.
- Policies regarding the process of referring clients on for longer-term work.

Some EAPs state categorically that it is a condition of working with them that you do not continue to see the client privately. Reasons given for this include that it reinforces the ending of that specific counselling contract, and therapeutically sets a boundary between what is provided by the employer and what responsibility the employee has for themselves.

Another reason is that EAPs are concerned that self-employed counsellors do not exploit clients to boost their income. Obviously, this is unethical, but it is possible and probably does happen. I was aware of my own desire, in the early stages of setting up my practice, to have clients who wanted to work longer term with me as this would help me deal with my fears about the insecurities of freelance working. I used supervision to ensure that I did not exploit any client because of my own needs. However, I am also aware that my own experience does illustrate the need for EAPs to have policies that protect clients from exploitation. Freelance counsellors must also have mechanisms to rigorously monitor their own process and ethical practice.

Other EAPs accept that clients may choose to continue working with the counsellor on a private basis once the EAP counselling contract is completed. As an affiliate, I work with EAPs who have both policies and have found that the number of clients with longer-term issues who want to continue counselling is a small proportion of the total number of clients I see. I have also found that if the reasons for short-term counselling are clearly explained to clients, they understand and generally accept the rationale informing the policy.

Clinically, affiliates need well-honed assessment skills. This is particularly important as they will be assessing for suitability for short-term work, possible psychiatric conditions and substance abuse. In cases where continuing counselling or longer-term support is identified they also need a good working knowledge of local counselling, and of psychological and psychiatric resources in the public, private and voluntary sectors.

On a final point, a key aspect of the business contract is confidentiality. The confidentiality of the client is paramount, to be respected and it cannot be breached, unless there is an ethical reason for doing so. EAPs adhere to the codes of ethics and practice of BACP, BPS and UKCP, as will individual counsellors belonging to these (and other) professional bodies. As mentioned earlier in the chapter, this area can sometimes represent a conflict when issues around risk management are a factor in the counselling. As in other areas of counselling practice, when faced with the choice to breach confidentiality, the counsellor has a responsibility to consider if this is an appropriate and necessary response. Most counsellors will want to discuss such a course of action with their supervisor. In the context of EAP working, counsellors will also have to discuss their concerns with the designated case manager. This is the point at which a counsellor can feel very well supported by an EAP in managing a sensitive situation; or alternatively they may feel edged out of the process as the wheels of EAP policy begin to move.

## Case management studies

Case management is the mechanism by which EAPs manage the volume of referrals from their client organisations and the quality of the service they provide. A case manager is responsible for ensuring that the client is referred to an affiliate and then monitors the client's progress over the course of the counselling. A case manager can be managing a large number of clients from a range of organisations. But normally, large organisations have a dedicated case manager who gets to know the customer and understands the culture of the organisation and the range of issues and demands they are facing. The case manager forms the point of contact between the counsellor and the organisation; there is no direct communication between an affiliate and an employer.

While there is no standardised system of case management, there are some general similarities in procedures which the counsellor agrees to when they become an affiliate with the EAP. These are likely to include:

- Referral call to the counsellor and briefing by the EAP.
- Confirmation of the assessment appointment by the counsellor.
- Post-assessment feedback with the case manager, which includes your assessment of the presenting problem and the client's presentation, your view on how the sessions may be used and if the client will benefit from time-limited work.
- If there are no concerns about the client, you will have no further contact with the case manager until the counselling is due to finish or has finished. (If there are concerns, see 'Flagging' below.)
- Final feedback may mean another call to the case manager to say how the counselling went and will also mean the completion of the paperwork system the EAP uses. This will normally include your invoice for the work. (Some EAPs require you to invoice monthly.)

A major benefit to the freelance counsellor of EAP working is that case management can provide a safety net for the client who is in great personal distress. I have felt well supported as a counsellor on a number of occasions when a case manager has been able to offer support to a client while I have been on holiday. Case management can also offer support to the counsellor when an emergency arises. At the point of writing this chapter, I was admitted to hospital for an emergency operation; one telephone call to the EAPs meant that all my clients were informed and offered support during the time I was off work. This was a huge relief to me as I knew my clients were given the option of telephone counselling support or the possibility of seeing another counsellor if they felt they needed this before I returned to work.

A good working relationship with a case manager can provide the counsellor with professional support and lessen the sense of isolation of freelance working. The other side of this can be the feeling that a case manager wants to be too involved in the case, perhaps asking for feedback at each step of the way when the case is uncomplicated and there is no suggestion of risk. This can prove time consuming and occasionally undermining for the counsellor.

### Flagging

Each EAP has its own system for monitoring the clients they feel concerned about. This is usually called 'flagging'. A flag can be set at any point of the client's contact with the EAP and affiliate counsellor. There are a number of reasons why a client can be flagged, the predominant one being risk to self or others. Examples include the client being actively suicidal, a child being at risk, possible or actual violence directed at the client or from the client to others. A case can be flagged at any point; it may have already been flagged before the counsellor is briefed, concerns about the client's safety may come to light during the assessment session, or as the counsellor is working towards ending with the client. EAPs use different coloured flags to denote the level of risk; generally, a pink or yellow flag indicates moderate risk and a red flag is high risk.

If a case becomes flagged, you will receive a greater level of support from the EAP case manager. You may be asked to ring in after each session to discuss how the client is and how the counselling is going. If there is any deterioration in the client's presentation you can discuss with the case manager what action might be taken to support the client. This could include the client using the 24-hour telephone line for support; it may mean the client seeing their GP or in urgent cases the EAP making contact with the GP or other appropriate services. Where possible this is done without involving the client's workplace, thus protecting their confidentiality.

Some counsellors may feel that the EAP case management system is controlling and that decisions about liaising with other agencies or involving other agencies (e.g. GPs) can be taken out of the counsellor's and client's control. There is a tension that the EAP may put their needs for containing a potentially difficult situation first and the client's needs second. This raises the question of who has the contract with the client in the consulting room. The answer is not straightforward, but I think ultimately the EAP does, as the provider of the service to the organisation where the client works. The counsellor would not be offering the client sessions if this contract were not in place. So, in a situation where an EAP and counsellor disagree about action to be taken with a client, the EAP would have the right to terminate the contract with the counsellor and take whatever action they thought appropriate in support of the client.

An alternative way of viewing this is that the counsellor 'out there' is being supported in working with the client at a point when the client is vulnerable and probably most in need of support. I know there have been a number of occasions where a case manager or senior clinician has been involved in making contact with a GP or hospital and I have felt relief to be able to hand this responsibility over. It has freed me to concentrate on getting my client the support they need and want at a time of great distress. This is an instance of collaboration and cooperation where the case manager supports both client and counsellor. One of the issues for freelance working is that you can become isolated and have limited opportunities for working with colleagues. This can be very draining on your own resources when carrying clinical responsibility for vulnerable clients.

## Getting started with an EAP

Making contact with an EAP is straightforward. A list of member organisations can be obtained from the UK EAPA. You may choose to make initial contact by phone, probably with the affiliate coordinator or manager, but this may take time—people in these roles are usually very busy.

Initially, I sent a standard letter explaining that I was interested in extending my experience into this area of work and received a response from every EAP approached. I then determined which to follow up. This decision was made on the basis of the description of services the EAP provided, their selection process and where their client work was located. For example, it would not have been useful to go through a selection process with an EAP whose main client base is in the south-east of England when I am based in the north-east!

The selection processes of EAPs vary. In my experience, some were rigorous and wanted case studies completed, or to visit my premises. Others interviewed me over the phone; some asked me to complete application forms and did not ask for references or evidence of qualifications or insurance cover. You need to consider what the selection process tells you about the EAP. If there is a rigorous selection process, is the EAP being overly controlling, or highly professional? If the selection process is less rigorous, is the EAP lacking in professionalism and what might this mean in terms of support for you and your clients?

You will need to find out if the EAP has clients in your area. Consider if you want to put energy into applying to an EAP only to find they don't contact you because they have no clients in your locality. Also be aware that you are likely to be only one of a number of affiliates in the area. Work may be sporadic and even non-existent; I had been an affiliate with one large provider for two years before receiving a referral from them.

## Conclusions

So what does this mean for the freelance counsellor? Here are some key points:

1   EAPs are commercial organisations that sell a range of services to employers to support their employees. Employers buy these services for both moral and commercial reasons. EAPs operate within professional and ethical frameworks. They also aim to make a profit. Consider if your values fit with the values inherent in these positions.
2   If your prime motivation is to develop your career and professional practice, EAPs are not the only way to get experience of workplace counselling.
3   EAPs generally use an assessment and short-term counselling model. If that is not your favoured mode of working, then EAPs are not for you.
4   EAPs generally look for counsellors who have completed their training and are accredited (or at least eligible for accreditation). They want associates who will be credible in an organisational setting.
5   A key requirement for counsellors working with an EAP is organisational awareness. This means understanding the nature of organisations and how they impact upon clients. It also means appreciating that organisations have legitimate concerns that can impact on the client–counsellor relationship. These issues can present complex dilemmas for the counsellor.
6   EAPs have clear expectations of their associates that form the business contract. These expectations include the use of premises of a particular standard, confidentiality agreement, and strict adherence to administrative and operating procedures.
7   The selection process is two-way. Be clear about what you want.
8   EAPs vary in their approaches to counsellors and clients. You need to choose if you want to subject yourself to the discipline of the EAP's operating procedures. As the world of employee counselling grows and

competition for contracts increases, EAPs become more rigorous in their policies and this can lead to more controls being placed on affiliate counsellors.

To summarise, the main message of this chapter is that counselling in the workplace and, more particularly, freelance counselling for EAPs is a major growth area. Counsellors looking to work in this area need to consider their responses to the various issues raised above. The complexities of EAP counselling represent interesting opportunities and challenges for most counsellors. The debate about the role of affiliate counsellors in EAPs has gained momentum as counsellors and EAPs face the complexities and dilemmas of counselling in this context. This debate will continue as counselling develops as a mechanism to support both employees and employers.

## References and suggested reading

Arthur, A. (2001) The EAP debate. *Counselling and Psychotherapy Journal, British Association for Counselling and Psychotherapy*, 12(1): 7–10.

Carroll, M. (1996) *Workplace Counselling*. London: Sage.

Fader, J. (2000) Speaking out for EAPs. *Counselling, BAC Journal*, 11(9): 574–576.

Feltham, C. (1997) *Time-Limited Counselling*. London: Sage.

Highley-Marchington, J. C. and Cooper, C. L. (1997) An evaluation of employee assistance and workplace counselling programmes in the UK. In M. Carroll and M. Walton (eds), *Handbook of Counselling in Organizations*. London: Sage.

Jacobs, M. (1988) *Psychodynamic Counselling in Action*. London: Sage.

Jenkins, P. and Pollecoff, P. (2000) Opportunities for workplace counselling to minimize the threat of litigation. *Counselling at Work, Association for Counselling at Work Journal*, Issue 30: 4–6.

Munt, S. (2000) The EAP trap. *Counselling, BAC Journal*, 11(7): 419–420.

## Useful addresses

*UK Employee Assistance Professionals Association (UK EAPA)*
Premier House, 85 High Street, Witney, Oxfordshire OX8 6LY
Freephone: 0800 783 7616
Website: http://www.eapa.org.uk/

This association can provide you with a list of their member providers. The website has a section on 'What is an EAP?', details of publications and a list of providers.

*Association for Counselling at Work (ACW)*
Eastlands Court, St Peter's Road, Rugby, Warwickshire CV21 3QP
Tel: 01316 670110
Website: http://www.counselling.co.uk/ (this is the BACP website; click on 'Expert Areas' to access the ACW information)

ACW membership is open to anyone with an interest in workplace counselling. The association produces a quarterly journal, *Counselling at Work*. Details of back copies/articles can be found on the website.

# Chapter 13

# Working from home: a psychotherapist with long-term clients

*Gabrielle Syme*

## Introduction

Many psychotherapists and counsellors work from their homes although this is not necessarily the best environment, particularly if standards of privacy and confidentiality are compromised to make this possible. The major reason for working from home is probably financial, particularly when starting out. Thistle (1998) suggests that the costs of renting a consulting room will increase one's overall expenses by some two-and-a-half-fold (from £700 to £1850 in 1998). This difference is largely due to rental and travelling costs.

Other reasons for working from home, apart from financial, may be the pleasure one's own home gives and the possibility of being able to relax with one's own hobbies and pastimes if a client does not appear, cancels or is late. For some there is no better stress management than such activities as gardening, sewing or music making—none of which is likely to be easy in rented rooms.

Chapter 3 looked at the issues of setting up in private practice in general. This chapter looks specifically at the issues arising from working from home. All the problems focus round running a business involving vulnerable people, who must have their privacy, confidentiality and security maintained, in a private house, which is the home of the therapist and her/his family.

## Accommodation

The ideal house would have three rooms available for work: a counselling room (used solely for counselling), a lavatory and a waiting room. In addition it would have easy access for the disabled and be on a bus route. In reality most counsellors have to adapt the house they are living in and will not be able to buy a house suitable for private practice.

The actual location of a house may affect the type of client one sees as well as the client load. If it is not on a bus route and/or is in an isolated place clients will need to have a car, take a taxi or be driven there. This will impose a severe limitation on some clients and is likely to mean that clients will not come from all strata of society even if one has a sliding scale or concessionary fees to attract and accommodate the less well-off. Where a house is difficult to reach it is important that potential clients are informed of this in the pre-counselling leaflet if this is used and in the initial phone call or letter.

The ideal house might be one previously owned by a doctor or clergy-person with a study or consulting room. However, such houses are frequently large and probably expensive to buy and maintain and therefore beyond the means of many people. In addition, a large house may convey a message of considerable wealth that may or may not be true. There may be a large mortgage and possibly two incomes to sustain such a property. The large house and therefore an apparent differential in wealth could be very off-putting or even intimidating for some potential clients, possibly those on a low income. The fact that the counsellor has a sliding scale or con-cessionary fees so that they are able to work with low income clients would then be to no avail. However, other clients might be attracted by such a property, believing the counsellor to be 'just like them'. This would mean attracting more middle-class, wealthy clients. The large house might also stimulate envy or resentment, which could be an important feature of the work. If envy is to be a theme during the therapy, and it frequently is, then something will always arouse it regardless of the size of the house.

As indicated earlier, the ideal arrangement is a room dedicated solely to the counselling work, with a lavatory and waiting area close by. The latter needs to be sited so that the privacy of the 'next' client is not compromised when the 'present' client leaves. All three rooms need to be in a part of the house not used by other people living in the house, possibly with a separate entrance, which is not overlooked. Clearly this is rarely possible unless the therapist has been able to design their own premises, and compromises need to be made.

Some counsellors use a bedroom as a counselling room, which may be misconstrued by a client and make both the counsellor and client very vulnerable to abuse with either the implication that the counsellor expects to have a sexual relationship with the client or that the client may take the bed as an invitation or even permission to make sexual advances to the counsellor. It is of course unethical to have sex with one's client. It may be advisable not to have a bed in the room or to find a way to disguise the bed with a throw.

Paramount is the privacy of both the clients and the therapist's family. There are three aspects to this privacy. One is that both parties can come and go without meeting each other. Yet how realistic is it to stop one's partner from gardening, or one's children leaving the house to catch a bus just as a client leaves? I well remember being somewhat too firm in stressing to my family that they should avoid meeting clients—only to hear from a client that he had seen someone scuttle off and hide as he arrived. This episode left the client feeling that they had some dreaded disease and the member of my family unable to act normally and feeling she had committed a major crime! Many of the issues in this chapter need to be attended to without being too heavy handed or precious.

The second aspect of privacy is that if any or all of the three required rooms are also used by the family then how much about your life do you wish a client to know? This is particularly important if you are working psychodynamically, focusing on transference and projection. Do you try to erase evidence of young children by removing toys from the counselling room and entrance area or children's clothing from the lavatory? Do you remove family photographs? There are endless examples. A psychodynamic counsellor may well choose to have as little evidence of their private life as possible. Regardless of one's theoretical approach it is sensible to check the room before working. Again one needs to strike a balance and recognise, as I have already stated, that anything that happens can be used by the client and then in turn by the therapist to understand more about the client's internal world.

The third aspect of privacy is ensuring that clients do not meet each other as they come and go. One way of managing this is to leave sufficient time between appointments to make it unlikely. However, clients do arrive early, and aware that the counsellor has no waiting room wait in their car and consequently watch the previous client leave, thus removing the privacy of that person. If one has a property where this is likely to happen it is wise to mention in the initial conversation with clients that their privacy as well as that of others is a concern, and that to maintain this privacy they should arrive on time and not sit outside the house.

Many houses are not large enough to have a waiting room as well as a counselling room. I do not think a waiting room is essential, but if there is not one then clients need to know this. As mentioned earlier, clients often arrive early, particularly for the first meeting. This is probably due to anxiety about finding the place and being on time. Not unreasonably, by extrapolation from visits to doctors, solicitors, etc., clients would expect there to be a waiting room and may well be embarrassed and upset if they are turned away and asked to return later. This could even be sufficiently upsetting to inhibit the formation of a therapeutic alliance. It could be prevented by explaining that there is no waiting room and asking the client to arrive on time. This is also important if there is no receptionist, which is likely for few private practitioners can afford one. Without a receptionist the counsellor will have to answer the door to a new client who arrives early and leave a client in so doing. There would be times in a session when a therapist would not want to answer the door, which is all right if it is a casual caller or a sales or delivery person but not if it is a new client.

Apart from privacy, confidentiality is important, which means that what is being said in the room cannot be overheard by anyone else. This must be checked. In many houses there is very little sound insulation; if so, it is important to see if the room can be sound-proofed; if not, the counsellor must ensure that no one is in a neighbouring room. Other aspects of confidentiality such as keeping and storing records are common to any counsellor regardless of setting and are also discussed in Chapter 3.

## Telephone

Nowadays it would be almost impossible to work without a telephone. It is extremely rare in my experience for a potential client to make contact by letter. The time is fast arriving when a modem and computer will also be essential since communication by email is becoming very common and there are Internet registers of therapists and counsellors. It is sensible to have a separate line for clients (Syme, 1994; Thistle, 1998) then any phone call on that line will be from clients or related to business matters. This has two advantages. First, the counsellor knows what type of call to expect and is not thrown by thinking the person calling is a friend. If one knows a number of people with the same name it would be hard sometimes to be sure whether the 'Mary' on the phone is a member of the family, a friend or a client. Second, one does not have to teach members of the family and particularly any children how to handle the phone in case a client phones, nor have members of the family trying to handle very distressed people.

As we have seen, few private practitioners can afford to employ a secretary or receptionist. One should not answer the phone when counselling and therefore it is sensible to have an answerphone. Often there may be only a short gap between clients, so this time is needed to write up notes, attend to creature comforts, to relax if possible and to focus on the client who is about to arrive. With a short gap one may not want to be distracted by a phone call, whereas an answerphone enables one to choose when to respond. It is important that the recorded message indicates when there is likely to be a response. Some people do not like answerphones and are somewhat flustered by them, so it may help to give clear instructions on what information to leave. For instance: name, means of contact, time of the phone call, and whether the message should be short (some phones are programmed only to take a short message). Care should be taken that only the counsellor takes messages off the answerphone or else confidentiality could be broken. This leaves a dilemma when one is away. Is it acceptable for someone else to check the phone if one cannot monitor one's phone from afar? The technology exists to do this, but if it is not possible the telephone message should indicate that the call will not be confidential. For my own convenience I leave my client line answerphone on all the time. It is important that clients know this and that I will definitely ring them back to find a time that is mutually convenient to talk.

It is wise to listen oneself to one's own answerphone message to check that the message is audible, the instructions clear and the tone kindly. This should be checked regularly since tapes do fade or get muffled. Sometimes power interruptions can cause problems.

## Safety

Counsellors always take some risk when they arrange to meet a new client but clearly this is less in an institution where there are other people in the building. It should be appreciated that clients also take a risk and for them also it is greater when going to a private house. It may be for this reason that an EAP has recently negotiated a contract with a large company in which it has been agreed that counsellors only see their staff in an office in the centre of the city and not in private homes.

The risks clients take are that the counsellor is unscrupulous, violent (emotionally or sexually), abusive (mentally, physically, emotionally or sexually), mentally ill or incompetent. Obviously this is less likely, though not impossible, when a counsellor is employed or works for a voluntary agency. It is therefore important that clients coming to a counsellor in a private house are made aware of any professional association that their counsellor belongs to and how to make a complaint if there is malpractice. This information should be in the pre-counselling leaflet, if there is one. If not, the onus is on the counsellor to ensure that clients are made aware of their professional association in the initial conversation or by letter.

Clearly no abuse of clients is acceptable, but perhaps the worse form of abuse is sexual: clients are clearly vulnerable to seduction by unscrupulous therapists. Figures from the USA suggest that 9–12% of male and 2–3% of female therapists sexually abuse their clients. Organisations such as POPAN (Prevention of Professional Abuse Network) are immensely important because they raise the public's awareness of the danger and assist clients in lodging complaints.

Clients also risk having an accident while on a counsellor's property. The counsellor should look carefully round their house for any hazards and remove them. Obviously, by their very nature accidents are unpredictable, so counsellors working from home must ensure that they have public liability insurance. This may be on an ordinary household insurance policy but it should be checked because not all such policies cover part of the house being used for business purposes. Thistle (1998) suggests counsellors working from home should also have a first aid kit to hand, be able to administer simple first aid and know how to deal with sudden emergencies such as an epileptic fit, a diabetic coma, a heart attack or a stroke. I have had one client collapse on my drive and needed to call an ambulance.

Clients can become ill suddenly; so can the counsellor. This latter situation is obviously very difficult for a client if there is no one else on the premises.

A risk that counsellors take when working without another person on the premises is their increased vulnerability if a client becomes violent (sexually or physically) and abusive (sexually or emotionally). There are sensible precautions that can be taken to minimise the likelihood of a client being violent. However, no matter how cautious one is some people can become extremely angry and violent out of the blue. Thistle (1998) suggests that ideally one should only take referrals from known sources, such as a GP, a training institution or a reputable organisation. I have very rarely had referrals from such sources and many more come to me by word of mouth. Perhaps a sensible precaution when one has no knowledge of a potential client is to ask permission to write to the person's GP. If permission is given by the client one can then enquire of the GP if there is any contraindication, which might make counselling inappropriate. But even with this safeguard GPs can only inform one about the past and only then without disclosure of specific details—even if they are known to that GP. They cannot predict whether there will be violence in the future. One may·be taking more risks when advertising counselling in a public place such as a shop window. Should one acquire clients this way it is even more important *never* to be alone with them in the house at the first meeting and to have a personal alarm to hand. In conclusion, the assessment procedure needs to be very thorough, for the benefit of both client and counsellor.

It is wise to make a careful risk assessment before starting work. First, is there anything in the counselling room that could be easily used as a weapon? Second, how is the room arranged should you need to make a quick getaway? Third, are there objects in the counselling room that are of such value, whether financially or personally, that you would be very upset if they were broken? Fourth, are you prepared to work with a violent client or do you make a rule that if a client is violent you will terminate the work? It is important to have thought this out rather than be caught unawares. Another, almost essential, security measure is to have some sort of concealed personal alarm to hand or a panic button somewhere in the room. The former is more versatile as it can be activated immediately, whereas you would have to move to where the panic button might be discreetly attached to a piece of furniture, to a door lintel or windowsill. Some home security systems supply personal alarms or panic buttons linked to the burglar alarm. While none of these measures prevent an attack, the sudden noise may distract the attacker and will summon help if someone is nearby. Clearly, working from home without this precaution is more risky.

However, having someone in the house is not always possible for a counsellor who lives alone, nor might it be realistic financially to hire counselling rooms in a building used by other people. Counsellors in this situation need to pay special attention to their own safety, which may involve some restrictions and additional expenditure and even reduce one's earning capacity. They must take great care about whom they take on as clients and wherever possible only accept referrals from someone known to them. Should this not be possible it might be wise to hire a room, possibly in a local counselling centre or a GP's surgery, for the assessment session. This would be particularly important for female counsellors seeing a male client for the first time, presuming that a man would be stronger than a woman. Another safeguard would be to use a room in the front of the house as the counselling room so that it is easier to attract a passer-by's attention if necessary. Obviously it would be impossible to do this if the house were isolated and therefore the house needs to be close to others. A counsellor living alone might be wise to restrict their work to daytime hours only.

Therapists, particularly men, are vulnerable to false accusations of sexual abuse. One safeguard is, with the agreement of the client, to tape record all sessions, but this is not acceptable to counsellors from some theoretical orientations. Another safeguard that is feasible for all, since one cannot have someone in the room as a doctor does when making an examination, is to keep very careful notes and beware if a client becomes seductive. It is often when a client's sexual advances are rebuffed that revenge takes the form of a false accusation. If there is any threat of this it is essential to keep one's supervisor informed so one has a record of the concern in advance of any accusation and has some support.

This section might suggest that counselling from home is very dangerous and the general public violent and unscrupulous. This is not the intention, neither is it common but the aim is simply to encourage caution. In 25 years I have never been attacked nor had sexual advances made and have only once worried about someone's potential to be violent and once about something being broken in my counselling room. Most people coming for therapy are vulnerable and hurt and I am privileged to be so trusted and to share in part of their lives.

## Long-term work

There is some evidence that counsellors working from home do considerably more long-term work if they choose to do so. There may be several reasons for this. First, it is extremely difficult to get long-term counselling or psychotherapy from any public service (e.g. the NHS), voluntary agency (e.g. Relate), work-based counselling services or EAPs or counselling services in colleges of further education, higher education or universities. There are people who need long-term work and may be left with no alternative but to seek it in the private sector. While this can be very costly, many counsellors do offer reduced or concessionary fees to enable the poorly paid or unemployed to receive therapy. Second, working in the therapist's home may attract some clients because it gives the illusion of belonging to a family and may offer a feeling of greater intimacy, particularly if the counselling room doubles as a family room. Each time the client arrives he or she is being welcomed into a family home: a therapy in itself.

It is not surprising that this can result in considerable dependency and for some clients there is no doubt that this is the route to healing. The necessary or inevitable dependency brings with it special problems that the private practitioner has to handle and though they are not exclusive to private practice it is essential that they have been thought about and plans made proactively rather than reactively. The areas that need to be thought through are maintaining the boundary of the session and the relationship, managing letters and phone calls and managing breaks caused by illness, holidays and other breaks for professional reasons.

## *Boundaries*

For some clients dependency results in it being extremely difficult to maintain the time boundary, no matter how hard one tries. Some consistently arrive early despite knowing the time the session starts. Others will not leave and sit tight or tarry in the counselling room or on the doorstep; or ask to go to the lavatory after the end of the session; or do not pay until after the session time is over (it can take ages to write a cheque). Any of these actions could compromise the therapist with the arrival of the next client. There will be many ways in which arriving early or leaving late could be understood; such as never having enough; hunger; greed; envy of the next client; curiosity about one's family or personal life, the previous or the next client; needing to invade, etc. There will be no right way to deal with such problems but it is important to discuss them with one's supervisor. If the approach is psychodynamic the 'right' interpretation will ease if not solve the problem. However, one needs to be realistic that it will happen and allow for it, particularly if there is no receptionist to forestall the next client. It is best therefore to ensure that there is a reasonable gap between clients to allow for the possibility of the early arrival or a late departure and also to allow for one's own need to have a breathing space between clients. I think a quarter of an hour is the bare minimum and half an hour between clients is better. It is important not to overwork, which is a temptation when earnings are low. If I have only a quarter of an hour between clients I timetable myself at least an hour's break at some point during the working day.

With some clients, but not with others, I feel a sense of invasion when they ask to go to the lavatory. At times it seems as if it is a way to find out more about the house and the family and some clients have agreed that indeed they were curious and were trying to look into rooms and find out more about my life. This may be a case for the lavatory to be close to the counselling room where possible. It is important not to presume that it is curiosity but it is worth exploring a client's feelings in going into another part of the house. What actually surprises me is how few clients do ask to use the lavatory. I do not believe that everyone has such amazing bladder control, and can only presume that for many people it is, in fact, embarrassing to ask to go to the lavatory in someone else's house; or is it rigid potty training from long ago which insisted that the last thing to be done before leaving home is to go to the lavatory? This perhaps makes it all the more significant for the few that do ask.

Another boundary that needs to be discussed is the possibility of a chance meeting outside the counselling room. The smaller the town the more difficult it is to avoid. Some codes of ethics forbid any social contact, but it can happen quite accidentally. For instance, both counsellor and client could find themselves invited to an exhibition of someone's work without having realised earlier that they had an acquaintance in common. The possibility of meeting by chance should be discussed at the first meeting and an agreement reached. I normally suggest that I will not acknowledge a client in any way unless they make some acknowledgement of me first. I stress that this is to maintain their confidentiality. I warn that if talking is unavoidable I will be as brief as possible. I do the same with a counsellor who is in therapy with me, where being at the same meeting may be unavoidable. Other therapists insist that their clients do not attend meetings they attend or place a rule of abstinence on themselves and do not attend these meetings.

The third boundary that needs to be maintained is not accepting referrals from within one's own group of colleagues, friends, neighbours or children of such people. It is always wise to refer them on and some codes of ethics specifically forbid such dual relationships. I also would never knowingly start work with someone who was a friend, neighbour, colleague or member of the family of someone who I am currently or have recently counselled and in the latter case I would discuss it with my supervisor before making a decision.

### Letters and telephone calls

For some clients who become dependent, a week between sessions may be too long. Where possible and in discussion with one's supervisor the right decision might be to have two sessions per week. Some clients start sending letters or ringing up when they are having difficulty in managing the gaps between sessions. This can become a burden but need not be so if plans are made for such an eventuality. Indeed the letters and phone calls could provide a useful adjunct to the therapy and help manage the gaps between sessions. Obviously both phone calls and letters could occur regardless of the setting in which a counsellor works. However, I received neither when I worked in a student counselling service or with a voluntary counselling agency. It is thus likely that it is the knowledge of where the counsellor lives that stimulates both letters and phone calls. The first decision is whether letters and phone calls are acceptable or not. For some counsellors phone calls outside session times are breaking the 'frame' of the relationship (Gray, 1994) and so are kept to a minimum and brief, with the explicit aim of bringing any concerns back to the face-to-face meeting. Of course business calls are acceptable to cancel sessions or forewarn of a late arrival. If phone calls are acceptable then clients need clear guidelines about them. I think it helps if these guidelines are written down and in the contract (Syme, 1994). The main reason for this is that clients are often very anxious in the assessment and the early sessions and therefore may not take in all that is said. (How many of us can recall all the details given to one as a patient in a medical consultation?) Later when they feel less stressed they still have the contract leaflet with which to check their memory. I suggest to clients that if they feel the desire to ring me they first see if they can work through the difficulty on their own and also consider their likely feelings if I am not able to respond as or when they expect. If it is still a good idea and necessary to ring then we will both know that managing without a phone call is too difficult or there is an emergency. I also ask that they respect my need for free time. My experience is that clients are actually very respectful of this and generally very apologetic that they have had to ring. From the client's point of view, particularly if they leave a message on an answerphone, they need to know when they might reasonably expect a response, particularly because an answerphone message is likely to leave them with no idea of whether their counsellor is even at home to respond to their message and has probably taken more 'courage' to leave in any case. To counter this I tell clients that if I have not rung back by 2200 hours on the day they have rung they can assume I cannot respond that day. Clients also need to know how long their counsellor is prepared to spend on the phone and the financial consequences of ringing. In my initial contract I state that I charge for phone calls that are part of the therapy on a pro rata basis and I usually preface a phone call with how much time I have. I have found that accepting phone calls has helped very dependent and regressed clients last from one session to the next; metaphorically the phone call could be seen as a gentle 'cradle rock'.

Letters can also be useful to contain clients between sessions; again it has to be clear whether they are acceptable, what their function might be and the terms upon which they will be handled. For some clients the feelings after a session are so intense that it is unbearable to hang on to them and they want to tell the person they believe caused them; this might even be to punish the person who 'caused' the feelings. Alternatively they may retrieve a repressed memory between sessions and want to tell the person they believe to be most interested. Sometimes sending a letter telling of the memory may be a way of dumping something that is unbearable with the therapist. I have certainly had clients dealing with sexual abuse who have found it useful to leave the memory with me until the next session. If containing the 'frame' is important then every effort should be made to keep them in the session.

The client needs to know whether you will read the letters and charge on a pro rata basis for the time taken if reading them, or keep the letters safe and read them together during subsequent sessions, and whether you will reply, again charging for the time or not. As with telephone calls I think it is helpful if all this information is in the initial written contract. Any letters written or postcards sent to clients can become an important talisman and comforter between sessions, particularly where there are long gaps, so it is important to think carefully about the wording and to remember that words can be given unintended significance.

Some counsellors deliberately send a letter or card to help clients manage breaks if they are in a very dependent and child-like phase and may also have experienced loss or abandonment as an infant or small child (Syme, 1994). I have found this useful with a very vulnerable client who may have just retrieved a traumatic memory. Of course it is significant that this has happened just before a break, and how I handled it so no further acting out happens is important. At times a postcard has been a 'good' way of reminding a client that he or she is not forgotten. No one should send a card if there could be resentment in doing this while on holiday, nor should it be done without discussion with the client and their express agreement. Some clients want the postcard but also feel ashamed or secretive about their need; also an open card invades the confidentiality of the relationship, so the card may need to be in an envelope.

### Managing breaks

Obviously all counsellors take holidays, are ill, have sudden family emergencies, retire and die (sometimes suddenly), so there are planned breaks in the counselling as well as unexpected ones. I mention this specifically in the context of private practice and working from home because, whatever happens, the private practitioner and her or his family do not have institutional support and colleagues to help, and are unlikely to have a secretary or receptionist. It is important to make contingency plans so that if one is ill or there is an emergency one's family is not burdened with having to phone clients and cancel appointments at a time when they are already under stress. It is wise to have a fallback plan which might involve one's supervisor (Syme, 1994) or a network of therapist colleagues and written instructions for one's family detailing whom they should contact and where such instructions are kept. This is a good example of collaboration between therapists. One ought also to have instructions in one's will on what to do if one dies while still working and who will act as a therapist executor to manage one's private practice (Traynor and Clarkson, 1992).

Regardless of setting one may move house, but this probably only impinges on clients if one is in private practice. Obviously the situation is different if one is moving away and the practice has to be closed, but one may move house within the same area and be 'taking' one's clients along too. I think it important that clients know of the intended move before the 'for sale' board goes up. It will be a time of uncertainty and may well resonate with past experiences. Children frequently are not consulted before a move is inevitable and cannot prevent it happening, which is happening again to them as an adult when their therapist moves. All of this will be a rich seam for the therapy (Syme, 1994) but it may give added stress for the counsellor, who is likely to be personally stressed by the move, so increased supervision may be essential.

A house move is one of a number of times when, if one has a young family, the clients may be envious of the children and the children of the clients. The children may be envious that the client is getting your time (considerably more than they get) and given a peaceful uncluttered environment compared to the rest of the house. The clients may be envious that the children are really involved and being treated considerately, which may well be a fantasy! This is another clear reason to make sure more supervision is available (see Chapter 5).

## Difficulties

There are many reasons why I enjoy working from home but it is important to look at the difficulties. If one has a family or other people living with you they will inevitably be affected because they are sharing their house with outsiders they cannot know. What is more, the outsiders are taking your time and are likely to be getting it in bigger private chunks. This can result in the family feeling envious and resentful, which will need to be expected, understood and managed.

A second difficulty is that working from home means that one is isolated, without any therapist colleagues, and any of the colleagues in the locality where one works are competitors as well. I believe it can be dangerous to become too isolated and lead to someone working unethically without the challenge of other practitioners with whom to discuss work; a supervisor alone may be not enough to counteract this. Other ways of counteracting the aloneness is to meet with other colleagues regularly, perhaps attending meetings of a local counselling association or meeting a group of therapists to read papers in journals. Of course each of these activities reduces the time when one is earning money.

A final difficulty which all home-workers have is the tendency, particularly if one tends to be a workaholic, to overwork. Clients in the private sector often expect to be able to come for sessions out of their normal working hours, and if you decide to work very early in the morning or into the evening it will impinge on your family or your personal social space. If after consideration one decides to do this then it is sensible to take time off during the day to compensate. It is all too easy to overwork when working from home; a trait not confined to therapists! All the letters that need dealing with, the reports to be written, references to be written for supervisees (if one is a supervisor and is prepared to write references), and accreditation forms to be completed for supervisees, have to be done on top of the client work. I would advise being very strict with oneself about reasonable working hours. If I am honest that is something that is easy to say and hard to do for I enjoy working as a counsellor from my own home but am not always so expert at the juggling necessary to do this. There is no doubt in my mind that it is rewarding but demanding and should not be done by inexperienced counsellors.

## References

Gray, A. (1994) *An Introduction to the Therapeutic Frame*. London: Routledge.

Syme, G. B. (1994) *Counselling in Independent Practice*. Buckingham: Open University Press.

Thistle, R. (1998) *Counselling and Psychotherapy in Private Practice*. London: Sage.

Traynor, B. and Clarkson, P. (1992) What happens if a psychotherapist dies? *Counselling*, 3(1): 23–24.

# Postscript

*Jean Clark*

Writing about their experiences of working freelance, contributors speak of insecurity, isolation, risk, competition, emotional and financial costs, yet words like freedom, choice, collaboration, integrity, trust and self-acceptance appear too. I am aware that what enables me to hold these tensions, as well as the emotional stresses and satisfactions of my work with clients, are the significant relationships I have with many colleagues—locally, nationally and internationally.

My postscript is a poem about this relationship which I wrote for Armin, a colleague in the USA, who also writes poetry about therapy.

*A particular way of being*

Recently I have been reflecting upon
   colleagueship between therapists
And have come to recognise that there is
   a particular way of being in this relationship
   of peers and equals in ways
Which are uniquely different from my ways of being
   with family or friends.

There is a boundaried focus in our relating
which can go deep, sometimes ocean deep
There may be communion heart to heart
unspoken felt sense of profound
acceptance
Respecting difference and rejoicing
in that difference.

There are times
when only my colleague can understand
the impact of my client's world upon
my vulnerability.
We can create that space of safety

in which we share our struggles and our pain—
knowing we shall not be judged as the world may judge—
(expecting perfection from those who seek to heal).

Times we spin ideas
creatively and joyfully in that world
we inhabit as therapists who are colleagues.
Colleagues can be challenging, but not destructive.
We challenge from a place of real concern
(not a place of labels or assumptions).

We can acknowledge too it is a place
where we may hold in conscious balance
the tension of our collaboration and the competition
within our working relationships.

Colleagueship may be built
over time, steadily,
or sparked by meeting
at a particular moment
in our working lives.
Both are gift.

Jean Clark

# Recommended reading

Carroll, M. (1996) *Workplace Counselling*. London: Sage.
Carroll, M. and Walton, M. (eds) (1997) *Handbook of Counselling in Organisations*. London: Sage.
Coltart, N. (1993) *How to Survive as a Psychotherapist*. London: Sheldon.
Feltham, C. (1997) *Time-Limited Counselling*. London: Sage.
Feltham, C. and Horton, I. (eds) (2000) *Handbook of Counselling and Psychotherapy*. London: Sage.
Furnham, A. and Argyle, M. (1998) *The Psychology of Money*. London: Routledge.
Horton, I. with Varma, V. (eds) (1997) *The Needs of Counsellors and Psychotherapists*. London: Sage.
House, R. and Totton, N. (eds) (1997) *Implausible Professions*. Ross-on-Wye: PCCS Books.
Hudson-Allez, G. (1997) *Time Limited Therapy in a General Practice Setting: How to Help Within Six Sessions*. London: Sage.
McMahon, G. (1994) *Setting up your own Private Practice in Counselling and Psychotherapy*. Cambridge: NEC.
Page, S. (1999) *The Shadow and the Counsellor*. London: Routledge.
Syme, G. (1994) *Counselling in Independent Practice*. Buckingham: Open University Press.
Thistle, R. (1998) *Counselling and Psychotherapy in Private Practice*. London: Sage.
Wheeler, S. and King, D. (2001) *Supervising Counsellors: Issues of Responsibility*. London: Sage.
Whyte, D. (1997) *The Heart Aroused: Poetry and the Preservation of the Soul at Work*. London: The Industrial Society.
Wiener, J. and Sher, M. (1998) *Counselling and Psychotherapy in Primary Care*. London: Macmillan.
Wilkins, P. (1997) *Personal and Professional Development for Counsellors*. London: Sage.

# Index

abuse, of client 43, 186; false accusations of 188; in supervision 78
academic qualifications, relevance of 60, 141
acceptability, of therapy 17
accidents, in home 186
accountability 49, 50, 56, 118–119, see also accreditation; registration
accreditation 14–16, 53–55, see also registration; regulation
Addington-Hall, J. 18
advertising 68, 136–138
affiliate counsellors see EAPs
answerphones 138, 185–186
Anthony Smith inquiry 70
Argyle, M. 82
Arthur, A. 166
assessment, meeting 188, 191; of risk 1, 74–75, 177–178
attitudes, from other counsellors 135; towards counselling 17, 109–110; towards money 82–83, 138
autonomy 43, 45
availability, of work 13, 17–18
awareness, of difference 96–97, 122–123; organisational 171–173

BAC (British Association for Counselling), directories of 12–13, 15, 69; on financial agreements 88; renaming of 28, 50; survey of members 10, see also BACP
BACP (British Association for Counselling and Psychotherapy), on awareness of difference 122–123; and CPD 55, 115, 121, 122–123, 124, 126; formation of 11; and personal development 125; on private practice

while training 14, 86; and registration 53–55, 61, 75, 122; and supervision 64, 66, 67–68, 73, see also BAC
Barlow, N. 56
Bell, D. 57
Binner, P. R. 46
Bond, T. 10, 54
Borneman, E. 83
boundaries, setting 106–107, 174, 189–190
Bozarth, J. 83, 148
Brady, J. L. 27–28, 33
breaks, in counselling 192–193, see also holidays; overwork; scheduling work
Brennerman, D. 18
brief therapy 122, 154, 168–170
British Association for Counselling see BAC
British Association for Counselling and Psychotherapy see BACP
British Psychoanalytic Society, formation of 9
Browne, S. 57
Burley, P. 51, 52, 55, 56
Burton, M. 72
business skills 40–42, 69, 139, see also entrepreneurial personality
businesses, offering services to 137, see also EAPs

capitalism 81, 85, 87
Carroll, M. 167
case management 176–177
change 31–34, 94, 97, see also transition
charging clients 41, 42, 138
Chessick, R. D. 112
children, care of 106–107; perspective of 107–110, 193; time with 113

choice, in early stages 116–117; of
  supervisor 31, 69–72
Clark, J. 145
Clarkson, P. 193
Clement, P. W. 45
clients, charging 41, 42, 138; corporate
  137; dangerous 44–45, 187–188;
  finding 136–138, 140–141, 143; long-
  term see long-term clients; short-term
  122, 154, 168–170
closed shop, therapists as 86
co-operation see collaboration
Code of Ethics and Practice for
  Supervisors of Counsellors (BAC) 67,
  73
codes of practice 32–33
collaboration, and competition
  28–29; contingency plans and
  192–193; in EAPs 178; and financial
  relationship 87–88; within family 109,
  110, see also group practice;
  partnership
collusion 2, 3, 28–30, 77, 86–87
Combs, A. 100
committee work 125
competition, attitudes to 20–21, 28, 142;
  and collaboration 28–29; and
  financial relationship 85–87, 138;
  increase in 13
Competition – A Feminist Taboo?
  (Miner and Longine) 29
complaints 50, 186
conditionality, and money 83
Confederation of Scottish Counsellors
  Associations 53
conferences, and CPD 124
confidentiality 40, 172–173, 175–176,
  185
conflict of interests, and EAPs 172–173;
  and regulation 58–59
consumer protection 50, 68–69 see also
  regulation
Consumer Protection Act 1987 68
contingency plans 106–107, 192–193
Continuing Professional Development
  see CPD
contracts, with EAPs 174–176; and
  financial agreement 88; with long-
  term clients 191, 192; supervision
  71–72, 76
Cooper, C. L. 165
corporate clients 137, see also EAPs

COSCA (Confederation of Scottish
  Counsellors Associations) 53
Costello, J. 85
costs, of training 16–17, 147, see also
  finance
Counselling People partnership
  135–139
counselling skills 14
courses, post-qualification 121–124,
  146–148, see also training
CPD (Continuing Professional
  Development), BACP and 55, 115,
  121, 122–123, 124, 126; conference
  attendance 124; expense of 116, 117,
  147; IPN and 115; meetings 24–25,
  125, 160; post-qualification courses
  121–124, 146–148; supervision as part
  of 78; UKCP and 55, 115; as unique
  journey 129
Cray, C. 108, 109
Cray, M. 108, 109
creative development 102, 119–121, 123,
  126, 129
cross-cultural counselling 96–97
cultural differences 96–97, 122–123
culture, medical vs. counselling
  150–151, 153–154
Curtins Jenkins, G. 72

dangerous clients 44–45, 187–188
Dansey, R. 24, 26
d'Ardenne, P. 97
Data Protection Act 1998 68
death, acknowledgement of 101; of
  therapist 40, 193
Department of Health 18, see also
  NHS
dependency, on supervisor 76; on
  therapist 43, 189
development, committee work 125;
  creative 102, 119–121, 123, 126, 129;
  models of 119–121; of others
  124–125; training and 116, 124,
  146–148, see also CPD; personal
  development
difference, awareness of 96–97,
  122–123
directories, BAC 12–13, 15, 69
doctors see GPs
domestic arrangements see family
  dynamics; home, working from;
  premises

EAPs, business contract 174–176; case management 176–177; confidentiality 172–173, 175–176; finding work with 144, 178–179; nature of counselling in 168–170; organisational awareness 171–173; premises 144, 174; private practice and 175; qualifications 170; services provided 165–166; training 170, *see also* organisations; workplace counselling
earnings 140
economics *see* charging clients; costs; earnings; finance
Edwards, M. 32, 33
emotional intelligence 120
emotional withdrawal 109
Employee Assistance Programmes *see* EAPs
entrepreneurial personality 44
Erickson, Milton 46–47
evidence-informed practice 50
exhaustion 109, *see also* overworking
expectations, in supervisory relationship 75–76
experience, for EAPs 170; necessity of 16, 38, 65; and standard of care 68; and supervision 70–71; therapists' personal 135–149

family dynamics, boundary setting 106–107, 174, 189–190; children's perspective 107–110, 193; emotional withdrawal 109; partner 110–112; priority setting 106–107, 112; privacy 106, 183–184; stress within 108–109, 110–111, 112, 193
Farrell, P. 145
fear, of change 97; of failure 142
fees *see* charging clients; earnings; finance
Feltham, C. 37, 40, 43, 45, 169
female counsellors, and male clients 44, 188
feminist therapists 42
finance, attitudes to money 82–83, 138; collaboration and 87–88; competition and 85–87, 138; CPD 116, 117, 147; and family dynamics 111; registration 58; starting private practice 40–42, *see also* costs; earnings
finding, clients 136–138, 140–141, 143; supervisor 31, 69–72

first aid 186
flagging, in EAPs 177–178
flexibility 107, 110
freedom 97, 99, 107, 135
freelance work, challenges of 31–34; development of in the UK 10–12; dynamics of 27–30; insecurity and 22, 30–31, 146; mentoring and 25–27; within NHS 150, *see also* private practice; starting private practice
Freeling, P. 18
Freud, Sigmund 9–10
Freudenberger, H. J. 112
friends, referrals from 190; relationship with 109, 112
Furnham, A. 82

general practice *see* primary care; GPs
Gilchrist, A. 21, 33
Goleman, D. 24, 120
Goss, S. 18, 50, 75
GPs, advertising with 137; communicating with 156, 162; reference from 187; sessional work 18, 143, 144, *see also* NHS; primary care
Gray, A. 191
group practice 44, 66, *see also* collaboration; partnership
group supervision 73–75
group work, and CPD 123–124
growth, of private practice 12–14; transition and 102, *see also* development
Guy, J. D. 27–28, 33, 108, 109, 110, 112

Healy, F. C. 27–28, 33
Henderson, P. 72
Hewson, J. 76
Highley-Marchington, J. C. 165
holidays 45, 106–107, 120, 192
home, working from 106–107, 136, 174, 193, *see also* family dynamics; long-term clients
Horton, I. 40
House, R. 50, 86

identity 96, 97, 109
illness 106–107, 192
*In Midlife* (Stein) 101
income *see* charging clients; earnings; scheduling work

Independent Practitioners Network (IPN) 60, 115
individual supervision 31, 72–73
inequality 85, 87
information technology 123, *see also* Internet counselling; Internet supervision
Iniss, S. 57
insecurity 22, 30–31, 146, *see also* risk
Inskipp, F. 72, 76
insurance 174, 186
International Employee Assistance Providers Association (EAPA) 166
Internet counselling 46, 75
Internet supervision 75
IPN (Independent Practitioners Network) 60, 115
isolation 27–28, 43, 102, 156, 162, 193
IT *see* information technology

Jacobs, M. 169
jealousy, within family 108
Jenkins, P. 40, 68, 166
Johns, H. 26, 118–119, 120
Jones, Ernest 9
Jones, G. 73, 78
journeys 95–98, 129, 139–142
Jung, Carl 97

Kaberry, S. 78
Kell, C. 72
Kierkegaard, Soren 146
King, D. 70
King, M. 160
Krueger, K. 83

Laurence, J. 58
lavatory, clients using 189–190; bathroom 45
lecturing 124–125, 144
legal issues 68–69, *see also* regulation
letters, from clients 190–192
liminality 98–104, 149
Linsley, J. 46
litigation *see* legal issues; regulation
living arrangements *see* family dynamics; home, working from; premises
location 38–39, 144, 182–183
loneliness 27–28, 43, 102, 156, 162, 193

long-term clients, accommodation for 182–185; boundary setting 106–107, 189–190; breaks in counselling 192–193; difficulties with 193–194; income from 43; letters 190–192; safety 186–188; telephone 185–186, 190–191
Longine, H. 29

Mace, David 10–11
McGauley, G. 44
McLellan, B. 42
McLeod, J. 149
McMahon, G. 16, 45
Mahtani, A. 97
managers, as supervisors 73
Mann, D. 43
market research 137
marketing 136–138
*Marriage Counselling: The First Full Account of the Remedial Work of the MGC* (Mace) 10
marriage guidance counselling 11
Matsumoto, D. A. 29
Matthews, A. 82
Mearns, D. 80
medical knowledge 163
medical model 150–151, 153–154
meeting clients, by chance 190
meetings, assessment 188, 191; support 24–25, 125, 160, 193
Member Organisations, and registration 53
mental health, short courses on 122
mentoring 25–27
midlife transition 101
mind-body split 154
Miner, V. 29
money, attitudes to 82–83, 138, *see also* charging clients; earnings; finance
monitoring *see* regulation
motivations, to become counsellor 23, 46, 109, 110, 141
moving house 193
Mowbray, R. 49, 58, 59–60, 86
*Multi-Cultural Journal* 122–123
Munion, W. M. 46

Natiello, P. 88, 89
National Register of Psychotherapists 53

National Vocational Qualification (NVQ) in counselling 17
needs, balancing in EAP counselling 172–173, *see also* motivations
negotiation, with clients 138; in primary care 156; with supervisor 75–76, *see also* business skills; contracts
networking 29, 139, 140, *see also* conferences; meetings; seminars
NHS, counselling within 150, 158–160; on regulation 61, *see also* primary care
Norcross, J. C. 27–28, 33
Norton, K. 44
NVQ (National Vocational Qualification) in counselling 17

offices 38–40, 46–47, 106, 136, 174, 182–185
O'Leary, C. J. 147, 148
organisations, freedom from 141; supervision within 74, *see also* EAPs; workplace counselling
overworking 45, 120, 189, 194

Palmer Barnes, F. 58
parenting role 106–110, 113
partner 110–112; importance of time with 113; support from 140
partnership, entering existing 40; setting up new 135–139, *see also* collaboration; group practice
Pearl, K. 25
person-centred approach 143, 147
personal development 102–104, 125–126, 142, 146–148
personal experience, therapists' 135–149
personal life 112, 126, 149, *see also* relationships
personal therapy 16, 125–126
personality traits 27, 43, 44, 45, 156, 170
Pilgrim, D. 18
Poelstra, P. 114
politics, and counselling 31–33, *see also* NHS
Pollecoff, P. 166
POPAN (Prevention of Professional Abuse Network) 186
portfolio working 1, 17–18, 41, 116–117

Postle, D. 59
Powell, G. N. 109
power, abuse of 43; hierarchies and 30–31; and medical profession 151; and professional bodies 59; in supervision 75–76
prejudice 28, 96, 122–123, 144
premises 38–40, 46–47, 106, 136, 174, 182–185
primary care, brief therapy 154, 168–170; communication with colleagues 156, 157, 162; counselling appropriate to 151; loneliness 156, 162; medical approach 150–151, 153–154; medical knowledge 163; NHS counselling 150, 158–160; racism 144; resource sharing 154; role of counsellor 154–155; support groups 160; voluntary work 163
priorities, setting 106–107, 112
privacy 106, 183–184
private practice, and EAPs 175; growth of 12–14; starting *see* starting private practice; suitability for 27, 43, 44, 45; while training 14, 16, 38, 86, *see also* freelance work
Proctor, B. 72, 76
profession, counselling as 57–58, 59–60, 160
professional development *see* CPD
protection *see* regulation
psychiatry, psychotherapy and 57
psychology, counselling and 159; psychotherapy and 57
*Psychology of Money* (Furnham and Argyle) 82
psychotherapy, different views of 28, 57–58
publicity 68, 136–138
Pyne, R. 55–56, 57

qualification, feelings after 25–27; relevance of 60, 141, *see also* training
quality assurance 50, 56, *see also* accreditation; registration; regulation

racism 96, 122, 144
recognition *see* accreditation; registration

'Recognition of Counsellor Training Courses' 54
recording sessions 188
records storage 40, 68
reference, from supervisor 174
reflective practice 127
Register of Independent Counsellors 53
registration, BACP and 53–55, 61; financial issues 58; UKCP and 53–55, 60, *see also* accreditation; regulation
regulation, case against 59–60; case for 56–57; conflict of interests 58–59; development and 118–119; features of 55–56; need for 49–51; problems with 57–59; statutory 51–53, 57, 60–61; voluntary 52, *see also* accreditation; registration
Reid, M. 150
relationships, between counsellor and NHS 158–160; collaboration within 88; with colleagues 31, 195–196; with friends 109, 112; sexual 183; with supervisor 31, 72, 75–76; within family 108–113
religion, and counselling 10, 143
renting premises 39–40, 136, 182
resentment, family 108, 193
responsibility, in supervision 67–68, 70, 76–77
RIC (Register of Independent Counsellors) 53
risk 96, 97, 100, 146
risk assessment 1, 74–75, 177–178
rites of passage 98–99
rivalry *see* competition; sibling rivalry
Robbins, A. 112
Rogers, Carl 10, 80, 146
roles, switching 107
Rowland, N. 18, 50
Roy, B. 85, 87

safety 44–45, 186–188
Samuels, A. 81, 87
Sands, A. 43
scheduling work 41–42, 120, 126, 149, 189, 190
Schon, D. A. 127
SDHA (South Derbyshire Health Authority) 70
security *see* insecurity; risk

self-belief 44, 141, 148
self-development *see* CPD; development; personal development
self-employed status 174
self-esteem 78
self-regulation 52, 55–56
seminars 124
Sen, G. 32, 33
sexual relationships 183
short-term counselling 122, 154, 168–170
Shorter, B. 97
Sibbald, B. 18
sibling rivalry 31, *see also* competition
Sills, C. 76
skills, business 40–42, 69, 139; counselling 14
social learning 120
social life *see* personal life; relationships
society, and counselling 31–33
specific issues, courses on 121–123, 146–147
spiritual development 123
standards, establishing professional 55, *see also* regulation
Standing Conference for the Advancement of Counselling (SCAC) 11
Stark, M. 110
starting private practice, financial issues 40–42; premises 38–40, 46–47, 106, 136, 174, 182–185; psychological issues 23–25, 42–45; storage of records 40, 68, *see also* freelance work; long-term clients
status, letting go of 100; and regulation 49, 56
statutory regulation 51–52, 57, 60–61
Stein, M. 101
Steiner, C. 85, 87, 88
Stevens, B. 146
storage of records 40, 68
Storr, A. 112
stress, and family dynamics 108–109, 110–111, 112, 193; personal development and 125–126
'stroke economy' 88
suitability, for freelance work 27, 43, 44, 45, 156, 170; of supervisee 70
*Summer of the Red Wolf* (West) 96

supervision, BACP and 64, 66; business issues 69; contract 71–72, 76; ending 77; experience and 70–71; group 31, 72–73; imposed 73–75; individual 31, 72–73; invisible 75; legal issues 68–69; of others 78; and professional development 119; requirements of 66–68; responsibility within 67–68, 70, 76–77; and risk assessment 74–75; and self-esteem 78; UKCP and 64; within organisations 74, see also supervisor

supervisor, assessing supervisee suitability 70; becoming 78; choice of 31, 69–72; manager as 73; more than one 66–68; reference from 174; relationship with 31, 72, 75–76; responsibilities of 67–68, 70; training of 72, 78, see also supervision

support, from case manager 177–178; from partner 140; local groups 24–25, 125, 160, 193, see also group work; mentoring; supervision

Syme, G. 12, 14, 16, 18, 40, 57, 58, 112, 185, 191, 192, 193

Tantum, D. 57
tape recording sessions 188
teaching counselling 124–125, 144
team-working 141, see also collaboration; group practice; partnership
telephone, answering 138, 185–186, 190–191; counselling 75, 166, 190–191; marketing 137; supervision 75
Thistle, R. 16, 40, 112, 182, 185, 186, 187
Thorne, B. 10, 57, 145
time, setting boundaries 189, see also scheduling work
time management see overworking; scheduling work
timing, of starting private practice 16, 38
Totton, N. 50, 86, 115
training, and accreditation 14–16, 54–55; costs of 16–17, 147; further for CPD 121–124, 146–148; and development 116, 124, 146–148; motivations to begin 23, 46, 109, 110, 141; as preparation for private practice 136; private practice while 14,

16, 38, 86; and registration 53; of supervisor 72, 78, see also courses; qualification
traits 27, 43, 44, 45, 156, 170
transition 94–96, 97, 100–104, see also change; liminality
travelling, for work 140
Traynor, B. 193
Tudor, K. 80, 88
Turner, V. 99
Tyndall, N. 11

UK, availability of work in 13, 17–18; development of freelance counselling in 10–12
UKCP (United Kingdom Council for Psychotherapy), and CPD 55, 115; and registration 53–55, 60; and supervision 64, 69
UKRC (United Kingdom Register of Counsellors) 13–14, 53
uncertainty 31–34, 96, 98, 193
unconditionality, and money 83
understanding, between partners 111
United Kingdom Council for Psychotherapy see UKCP
United Kingdom Register of Counsellors 13–14, 53
unpaid work 29–30, 139–140, 147, 163
USA, development of freelance counselling in 9–10

violent clients 187–188
voluntary regulation 52
voluntary work 29–30, 139–140, 147, 163

waiting area 106, 183, 184
Waller, D. 52
Webb, A. 31, 73, 75, 77
West, M. 96
Wheeler, S. 31, 57, 70
Whyte, D. 24, 31, 32, 126
Wilkins, P. 126
withdrawal, emotional 109
work, availability of 13, 17–18; combining with family 107; hours of 45, 188; maintaining regular 140; non-counselling day job 145, 148; scheduling 41–42, 120, 126, 149, 189, 190; voluntary 29–30, 139–140, 147, 163, see also freelance work

workplace counselling 167–168, *see also* EAPs

Worrall, M. 80, 88

Wosket, V. 45

writing on counselling 124–125, *see also* reflective practice

Zeig, J. K. 46